Clojure for Machine Learning

Successfully leverage advanced machine learning
techniques using the Clojure ecosystem

Akhil Wali

[PACKT] open source ✳
PUBLISHING
community experience distilled

BIRMINGHAM - MUMBAI

Clojure for Machine Learning

First published: April 2014

Production Reference: 1180414

Published by Packt Publishing Ltd.
Livery Place
35 Livery Street
Birmingham B3 2PB, UK.

ISBN 978-1-78328-435-1

www.packtpub.com

Cover Image by Jarek Blaminsky (milak6@wp.pl)

Credits

Author

Akhil Wali

Reviewers

Jan Borgelin

Thomas A. Faulhaber, Jr.

Shantanu Kumar

Dr. Uday Wali

Commissioning Editor

Rubal Kaur

Acquisition Editor

Llewellyn Rozario

Content Development Editor

Akshay Nair

Technical Editors

Humera Shaikh

Ritika Singh

Copy Editors

Roshni Banerjee

Karuna Narayanan

Laxmi Subramanian

Project Coordinator

Mary Alex

Proofreaders

Simran Bhogal

Maria Gould

Ameesha Green

Paul Hindle

Indexer

Mehreen Deshmukh

Graphics

Ronak Dhruv

Yuvraj Mannari

Abhinash Sahu

Production Coordinator

Nitesh Thakur

Cover Work

Nitesh Thakur

About the Author

Akhil Wali is a software developer, and has been writing code since 1997. Currently, his areas of work are ERP and business intelligence systems. He has also worked in several other areas of computer engineering, such as search engines, document collaboration, and network protocol design. He mostly works with C# and Clojure. He is also well versed in several other popular programming languages such as Ruby, Python, Scheme, and C. He currently works with Computer Generated Solutions, Inc. This is his first book.

I would like to thank my family and friends for their constant encouragement and support. I want to thank my father in particular for his technical guidance and help, which helped me complete this book and also my education. Thank you to my close friends, Kiranmai, Nalin, and Avinash, for supporting me throughout the course of writing this book.

About the Reviewers

Jan Borgelin is the co-founder and CTO of BA Group Ltd., a Finnish IT consultancy that provides services to global enterprise clients. With over 10 years of professional software development experience, he has had a chance to work with multiple programming languages and different technologies in international projects, where the performance requirements have always been critical to the success of the project.

Thomas A. Faulhaber, Jr. is the Principal of Infolace (www.infolace.com), a San Francisco-based consultancy. Infolace helps clients from start-ups and global brands turn raw data into information and information into action. Throughout his career, he has developed systems for high-performance networking, large-scale scientific visualization, energy trading, and many more.

He has been a contributor to, and user of, Clojure and Incanter since their earliest days. The power of Clojure and its ecosystem (for both code and people) is an important "magic bullet" in his practice. He was also a technical reviewer for *Clojure Data Analysis Cookbook*, *Packt Publishing*.

Shantanu Kumar is a software developer living in Bangalore, India, with his wife. He started programming using QBasic on MS-DOS when he was at school (1991). There, he developed a keen interest in the x86 hardware and assembly language, and dabbled in it for a good while after. Later, he programmed professionally in several business domains and technologies while working with IT companies and the Indian Air Force.

Having used Java for a long time, he discovered Clojure in early 2009 and has been a fan ever since. Clojure's pragmatism and fine-grained orthogonality continues to amaze him, and he believes that this is the reason he became a better developer. He is the author of *Clojure High Performance Programming*, *Packt Publishing*, is an active participant in the Bangalore Clojure users group, and develops several open source Clojure projects on GitHub.

Dr. Uday Wali has a bachelor's degree in Electrical Engineering from Karnatak University, Dharwad. He obtained a PhD from IIT Kharagpur in 1986 for his work on the simulation of switched capacitor networks.

He has worked in various areas related to computer-aided design, such as solid modeling, FEM, and analog and digital circuit analysis.

He worked extensively with Intergraph's CAD software for over 10 years since 1986. He then founded C-Quad in 1996, a software development company located in Belgaum, Karnataka. C-Quad develops custom ERP software solutions for local industries and educational institutions. He is also a professor of Electronics and Communication at KLE Engineering College, Belgaum. He guides several research scholars who are affiliated to Visvesvaraya Technological University, Belgaum.

www.PacktPub.com

Support files, eBooks, discount offers and more

You might want to visit www.PacktPub.com for support files and downloads related to your book.

Did you know that Packt offers eBook versions of every book published, with PDF and ePub files available? You can upgrade to the eBook version at www.PacktPub.com and as a print book customer, you are entitled to a discount on the eBook copy. Get in touch with us at service@packtpub.com for more details.

At www.PacktPub.com, you can also read a collection of free technical articles, sign up for a range of free newsletters and receive exclusive discounts and offers on Packt books and eBooks.

http://PacktLib.PacktPub.com

Do you need instant solutions to your IT questions? PacktLib is Packt's online digital book library. Here, you can access, read and search across Packt's entire library of books.

Why Subscribe?

- Fully searchable across every book published by Packt
- Copy and paste, print and bookmark content
- On demand and accessible via web browser

Free Access for Packt account holders

If you have an account with Packt at www.PacktPub.com, you can use this to access PacktLib today and view nine entirely free books. Simply use your login credentials for immediate access.

Table of Contents

Preface

Machine learning has a vast variety of applications in computing. Software systems that use machine learning techniques tend to provide their users with a better user experience. With cloud data becoming more relevant these days, developers will eventually build more intelligent systems that simplify and optimize any routine task for their users.

This book will introduce several machine learning techniques and also describe how we can leverage these techniques in the Clojure programming language.

Clojure is a dynamic and functional programming language built on the Java Virtual Machine (JVM). It's important to note that Clojure is a member of the Lisp family of languages. Lisp played a key role in the artificial intelligence revolution that took place during the 70s and 80s. Unfortunately, artificial intelligence lost its spark in the late 80s. Lisp, however, continued to evolve, and several dialects of Lisp have been concocted throughout the ages. Clojure is a simple and powerful dialect of Lisp that was first released in 2007. At the time of writing this book, Clojure is one of the most rapidly growing programming languages for the JVM. It currently supports some of the most advanced language features and programming methodologies out there, such as optional typing, software transactional memory, asynchronous programming, and logic programming. The Clojure community is known to mesmerize developers with their elegant and powerful libraries, which is yet another compelling reason to use Clojure.

Machine learning techniques are based on statistics and logic-based reasoning. In this book, we will focus on the statistical side of machine learning. Most of these techniques are based on principles from the artificial intelligence revolution. Machine learning is still an active area of research and development. Large players from the software world, such as Google and Microsoft, have also made significant contributions to machine learning. More software companies are now realizing that applications that use machine learning techniques provide a much better experience to their users.

Although there is a lot of mathematics involved in machine learning, we will focus more on the ideas and practical usage of these techniques, rather than concentrating on the theory and mathematical notations used by these techniques. This book seeks to provide a gentle introduction to machine learning techniques and how they can be used in Clojure.

What this book covers

Chapter 1, Working with Matrices, explains matrices and the basic operations on matrices that are useful for implementing the machine learning algorithms.

Chapter 2, Understanding Linear Regression, introduces linear regression as a form of supervised learning. We will also discuss the gradient descent algorithm and the ordinary least-squares (OLS) method for fitting the linear regression models.

Chapter 3, Categorizing Data, covers classification, which is another form of supervised learning. We will study the Bayesian method of classification, decision trees, and the k-nearest neighbors algorithm.

Chapter 4, Building Neural Networks, explains artificial neural networks (ANNs) that are useful in the classification of nonlinear data, and describes a few ANN models. We will also study and implement the backpropagation algorithm that is used to train an ANN and describe self-organizing maps (SOMs).

Chapter 5, Selecting and Evaluating Data, covers evaluation of machine learning models. In this chapter, we will discuss several methods that can be used to improve the effectiveness of a given machine learning model. We will also implement a working spam classifier as an example of how to build machine learning systems that incorporate evaluation.

Chapter 6, Building Support Vector Machines, covers support vector machines (SVMs). We will also describe how SVMs can be used to classify both linear and nonlinear sample data.

Chapter 7, Clustering Data, explains clustering techniques as a form of unsupervised learning and how we can use them to find patterns in unlabeled sample data. In this chapter, we will discuss the K-means and expectation maximization (EM) algorithms. We will also explore dimensionality reduction.

Chapter 8, Anomaly Detection and Recommendation, explains anomaly detection, which is another useful form of unsupervised learning. We will also discuss recommendation systems and several recommendation algorithms.

Chapter 9, Large-scale Machine Learning, covers techniques that are used to handle a large amount of data. Here, we explain the concept of MapReduce, which is a parallel data-processing technique. We will also demonstrate how we can store data in MongoDB and how we can use the BigML cloud service to build machine learning models.

Appendix, References, lists all the bibliographic references used throughout the chapters of this book.

What you need for this book

One of the pieces of software required for this book is the Java Development Kit (JDK), which you can get from `http://www.oracle.com/technetwork/java/javase/downloads/`. JDK is necessary to run and develop applications on the Java platform.

The other major software that you'll need is Leiningen, which you can download and install from `http://github.com/technomancy/leiningen`. Leiningen is a tool for managing Clojure projects and their dependencies. We will explain how to work with Leiningen in *Chapter 1, Working with Matrices*.

Throughout this book, we'll use a number of other Clojure and Java libraries, including Clojure itself. Leiningen will take care of the downloading of these libraries for us as required. You'll also need a text editor or an integrated development environment (IDE). If you already have a text editor that you like, you can probably use it. Navigate to `http://dev.clojure.org/display/doc/Getting+Started` to check the tips and plugins required for using your particular favorite environment. If you don't have a preference, I suggest that you look at using Eclipse with Counterclockwise. There are instructions for getting this set up at `http://dev.clojure.org/display/doc/Getting+Started+with+Eclipse+and+Counterclockwise`.

In *Chapter 9, Large-scale Machine Learning*, we also use MongoDB, which can be downloaded and installed from `http://www.mongodb.org/`.

Who this book is for

This book is for programmers or software architects who are familiar with Clojure and want to use it to build machine learning systems. This book does not introduce the syntax and features of the Clojure language (you are expected to be familiar with the language, but you need not be a Clojure expert).

Similarly, although you don't need to be an expert in statistics and coordinate geometry, you should be familiar with these concepts to understand the theory behind the several machine learning techniques that we will discuss. When in doubt, don't hesitate to look up and learn more about the mathematical concepts used in this book.

Conventions

In this book, you will find a number of styles of text that distinguish between different kinds of information. Here are some examples of these styles, and an explanation of their meaning.

Code words in text are shown as follows: "The previously defined `probability` function requires a single argument to represent the attribute or condition whose probability of occurrence we wish to calculate."

A block of code is set as follows:

```
(defn predict [coefs X]
  {:pre [(= (count coefs)
            (+ 1 (count X)))]}
  (let [X-with-1 (conj X 1)
        products (map * coefs X-with-1)]
    (reduce + products)))
```

When we wish to draw your attention to a particular part of a code block, the relevant lines or items are set in bold:

```
:dependencies [[org.clojure/clojure "1.5.1"]
               [incanter "1.5.2"]
               [clatrix "0.3.0"]
               [net.mikera/core.matrix "0.10.0"]]
```

Any command-line input or output is written as follows:

```
$ lein deps
```

Another simple convention that we use is to always show the Clojure code that's entered in the REPL (read-eval-print-loop) starting with the `user>` prompt. In practice, this prompt will change depending on the Clojure namespace that we are currently using. However, for simplicity, REPL code starts with the `user>` prompt, as follows:

```
user> (every? #(< % 0.0001)
              (map - ols-linear-model-coefs
              (:coefs iris-linear-model))
true
```

New terms and important words are shown in bold. Words that you see on the screen, in menus or dialog boxes for example, appear in the text like this: "clicking the **Next** button moves you to the next screen".

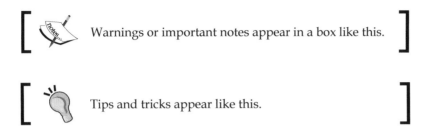

Warnings or important notes appear in a box like this.

Tips and tricks appear like this.

Reader feedback

Feedback from our readers is always welcome. Let us know what you think about this book—what you liked or may have disliked. Reader feedback is important for us to develop titles that you really get the most out of.

To send us general feedback, simply send an e-mail to feedback@packtpub.com, and mention the book title via the subject of your message.

If there is a topic that you have expertise in and you are interested in either writing or contributing to a book, see our author guide on www.packtpub.com/authors.

Customer support

Now that you are the proud owner of a Packt book, we have a number of things to help you to get the most from your purchase.

Downloading the example code

You can download the example code files for all Packt books you have purchased from your account at http://www.packtpub.com. If you purchased this book elsewhere, you can visit http://www.packtpub.com/support and register to have the files e-mailed directly to you.

Downloading the color images of this book

We also provide you a PDF file that has color images of the screenshots/diagrams used in this book. The color images will help you better understand the changes in he output. You can download this file from `https://www.packtpub.com/sites/default/files/downloads/4351OS_Graphics.pdf`.

Errata

Although we have taken every care to ensure the accuracy of our content, mistakes do happen. If you find a mistake in one of our books—maybe a mistake in the text or the code—we would be grateful if you would report this to us. By doing so, you can save other readers from frustration and help us improve subsequent versions of this book. If you find any errata, please report them by visiting `http://www.packtpub.com/submit-errata`, selecting your book, clicking on the **errata submission form** link, and entering the details of your errata. Once your errata are verified, your submission will be accepted and the errata will be uploaded on our website, or added to any list of existing errata, under the Errata section of that title. Any existing errata can be viewed by selecting your title from `http://www.packtpub.com/support`.

Piracy

Piracy of copyright material on the Internet is an ongoing problem across all media. At Packt, we take the protection of our copyright and licenses very seriously. If you come across any illegal copies of our works, in any form, on the Internet, please provide us with the location address or website name immediately so that we can pursue a remedy.

Please contact us at `copyright@packtpub.com` with a link to the suspected pirated material.

We appreciate your help in protecting our authors, and our ability to bring you valuable content.

Questions

You can contact us at `questions@packtpub.com` if you are having a problem with any aspect of the book, and we will do our best to address it.

1
Working with Matrices

In this chapter, we will explore an elementary yet elegant mathematical data structure—the **matrix**. Most computer science and mathematics graduates would already be familiar with matrices and their applications. In the context of machine learning, matrices are used to implement several types of machine-learning techniques, such as linear regression and classification. We will study more about these techniques in the later chapters.

Although this chapter may seem mostly theoretical at first, we will soon see that matrices are a very useful abstraction for quickly organizing and indexing data with multiple dimensions. The data used by machine-learning techniques contains a large number of sample values in several dimensions. Thus, matrices can be used to store and manipulate this sample data.

An interesting application that uses matrices is Google Search, which is built on the **PageRank** algorithm. Although a detailed explanation of this algorithm is beyond the scope of this book, it's worth knowing that Google Search essentially finds the *eigen-vector* of an extremely massive matrix of data (for more information, refer to *The Anatomy of a Large-Scale Hypertextual Web Search Engine*). Matrices are used for a variety of applications in computing. Although we do not discuss the eigen-vector matrix operation used by Google Search in this book, we will encounter a variety of matrix operations while implementing machine-learning algorithms. In this chapter, we will describe the useful operations that we can perform on matrices.

Introducing Leiningen

Over the course of this book, we will use Leiningen (`http://leiningen.org/`) to manage third-party libraries and dependencies. Leiningen, or `lein`, is the standard Clojure package management and automation tool, and has several powerful features used to manage Clojure projects.

To get instructions on how to install Leiningen, visit the project site at http://leiningen.org/. The first run of the lein program could take a while, as it downloads and installs the Leiningen binaries when it's run for the first time. We can create a new Leiningen project using the new subcommand of lein, as follows:

```
$ lein new default my-project
```

The preceding command creates a new directory, my-project, which will contain all source and configuration files for a Clojure project. This folder contains the source files in the src subdirectory and a single project.clj file. In this command, default is the type of project template to be used for the new project. All the examples in this book use the preceding default project template.

The project.clj file contains all the configuration associated with the project and will have the following structure:

```
(defproject my-project "0.1.0-SNAPSHOT"
  :description "FIXME: write description"
  :url "http://example.com/FIXME"
  :license
  {:name "Eclipse Public License"
   :url "http://www.eclipse.org/legal/epl-v10.html"}
  :dependencies [[org.clojure/clojure "1.5.1"]])
```

Downloading the example code

You can download the example code files for all Packt books you have purchased from your account at http://www.packtpub.com. If you purchased this book elsewhere, you can visit http://www.packtpub.com/support and register to have the files e-mailed directly to you.

Third-party Clojure libraries can be included in a project by adding the declarations to the vector with the :dependencies key. For example, the core.matrix Clojure library package on Clojars (https://clojars.org/net.mikera/core.matrix) gives us the package declaration [net.mikera/core.matrix "0.20.0"]. We simply paste this declaration into the :dependencies vector to add the core.matrix library package as a dependency for our Clojure project, as shown in the following code:

```
:dependencies [[org.clojure/clojure "1.5.1"]
               [net.mikera/core.matrix "0.20.0"]])
```

To download all the dependencies declared in the project.clj file, simply run the following deps subcommand:

```
$ lein deps
```

Leiningen also provides an **REPL (read-evaluate-print-loop)**, which is simply an interactive interpreter that contains all the dependencies declared in the project.clj file. This REPL will also reference all the Clojure namespaces that we have defined in our project. We can start the REPL using the following repl subcommand of lein. This will start a new REPL session:

```
$ lein repl
```

Representing matrices

A matrix is simply a rectangular array of data arranged in rows and columns. Most programming languages, such as C# and Java, have direct support for rectangular arrays, while others, such as Clojure, use the heterogeneous array-of-arrays representation for rectangular arrays. Keep in mind that Clojure has no direct support for handling arrays, and an idiomatic Clojure code uses *vectors* to store and index an array of elements. As we will see later, a matrix is represented as a vector whose elements are the other vectors in Clojure.

Matrices also support several arithmetic operations, such as addition and multiplication, which constitute an important field of mathematics known as **Linear Algebra**. Almost every popular programming language has at least one linear algebra library. Clojure takes this a step ahead by letting us choose from several such libraries, all of which have a single standardized API interface that works with matrices.

The *core.matrix* library is a versatile Clojure library used to work with matrices. Core. matrix also contains a specification to handle matrices. An interesting fact about core. matrix is that while it provides a default implementation of this specification, it also supports multiple implementations. The core.matrix library is hosted and developed on GitHub at http://github.com/mikera/core.matrix.

The core.matrix library can be added to a Leiningen project by adding the following dependency to the project.clj file:

```
[net.mikera/core.matrix "0.20.0"]
```

For the upcoming example, the namespace declaration should look similar to the following declaration:

```
(ns my-namespace
   (:use clojure.core.matrix))
```

Note that the use of :import to include library namespaces in Clojure is generally discouraged. Instead, aliased namespaces with the :require form are preferred. However, for the examples in the following section, we will use the preceding namespace declaration.

In Clojure, a matrix is simply a vector of vectors. This means that a matrix is represented as a vector whose elements are other vectors. A vector is an array of elements that takes near-constant time to retrieve an element, unlike a list that has linear lookup time. However, in the mathematical context of matrices, vectors are simply matrices with a single row or column.

To create a matrix from a vector of vectors, we use the following `matrix` function and pass a vector of vectors or a quoted list to it. Note that all the elements of the matrix are internally represented as a `double` data type (`java.lang.Double`) for added precision.

```
user> (matrix [[0 1 2] [3 4 5]])      ;; using a vector
[[0 1 2] [3 4 5]]
user> (matrix '((0 1 2) (3 4 5)))     ;; using a quoted list
[[0 1 2] [3 4 5]]
```

In the preceding example, the matrix has two rows and three columns, or is a 2 x 3 matrix to be more concise. It should be noted that when a matrix is represented by a vector of vectors, all the vectors that represent the individual rows of the matrix should have the same length.

The matrix that is created is printed as a vector, which is not the best way to visually represent it. We can use the pm function to print the matrix as follows:

```
user> (def A (matrix [[0 1 2] [3 4 5]]))
#'user/A
user> (pm A)
[[0.000 1.000 2.000]
 [3.000 4.000 5.000]]
```

Here, we define a matrix *A*, which is mathematically represented as follows. Note that the use of uppercase variable names is for illustration only, as all the Clojure variables are conventionally written in lowercase.

$$A_{2\times3} = \begin{bmatrix} 0 & 1 & 2 \\ 3 & 4 & 5 \end{bmatrix}$$

The matrix *A* is composed of elements $a_{i,j}$ where *i* is the row index and *j* is the column index of the matrix. We can mathematically represent a matrix *A* using brackets as follows:

$$A_{m\times n} = \begin{bmatrix} a_{i,j} \end{bmatrix}$$

We can use the `matrix?` function to check whether a symbol or variable is, in fact, a matrix. The `matrix?` function will return `true` for all the matrices that implement the core.matrix specification. Interestingly, the `matrix?` function will also return `true` for an ordinary vector of vectors.

The default implementation of core.matrix is written in pure Clojure, which does affect performance when handling large matrices. The core.matrix specification has two popular contrib implementations, namely **vectorz-clj** (`http://github.com/mikera/vectorz-clj`) that is implemented using pure Java and **clatrix** (`http://github.com/tel/clatrix`) that is implemented through native libraries. While there are several other libraries that implement the core.matrix specification, these two libraries are seen as the most mature ones.

Clojure has three kinds of libraries, namely core, contrib, and third-party libraries. Core and contrib libraries are part of the standard Clojure library. The documentation for both the core and contrib libraries can be found at `http://clojure.github.io/`. The only difference between the core and contrib libraries is that the contrib libraries are not shipped with the Clojure language and have to be downloaded separately.

Third-party libraries can be developed by anyone and are made available via Clojars (`https://clojars.org/`). Leiningen supports all of the previous libraries and doesn't make much of a distinction between them.

The contrib libraries are often originally developed as third-party libraries. Interestingly, core.matrix was first developed as a third-party library and was later promoted to a contrib library.

The clatrix library uses the **Basic Linear Algebra Subprograms (BLAS)** specification to interface the native libraries that it uses. BLAS is also a stable specification of the linear algebra operations on matrices and vectors that are mostly used by native languages. In practice, clatrix performs significantly better than other implementations of core.matrix, and defines several utility functions used to work with matrices as well. You should note that matrices are treated as mutable objects by the clatrix library, as opposed to other implementations of the core.matrix specification that idiomatically treat a matrix as an immutable type.

For most of this chapter, we will use clatrix to represent and manipulate matrices. However, we can effectively reuse functions from core.matrix that perform matrix operations (such as addition and multiplication) on the matrices created through clatrix. The only difference is that instead of using the `matrix` function from the `core.matrix` namespace to create matrices, we should use the one defined in the clatrix library.

The clatrix library can be added to a Leiningen project by adding the following dependency to the `project.clj` file:

```
[clatrix "0.3.0"]
```

For the upcoming example, the namespace declaration should look similar to the following declaration:

```
(ns my-namespace
  (:use clojure.core.matrix)
  (:require [clatrix.core :as cl]))
```

Keep in mind that we can use both the `clatrix.core` and `clojure.core.matrix` namespaces in the same source file, but a good practice would be to import both these namespaces into aliased namespaces to prevent naming conflicts.

We can create a matrix from the clatrix library using the following `cl/matrix` function. Note that clatrix produces a slightly different, yet more informative representation of the matrix than core.matrix. As mentioned earlier, the pm function can be used to print the matrix as a vector of vectors:

```
user> (def A (cl/matrix [[0 1 2] [3 4 5]]))
#'user/A
user> A
 A 2x3 matrix
 -------------
 0.00e+00  1.00e+00  2.00e+00
 3.00e+00  4.00e+00  5.00e+00
user> (pm A)
[[0.000 1.000 2.000]
 [3.000 4.000 5.000]]
nil
```

We can also use an overloaded version of the matrix function, which takes a matrix implementation name as the first parameter, and is followed by the usual definition of the matrix as a vector, to create a matrix. The implementation name is specified as a keyword. For example, the default persistent vector implementation is specified as :persistent-vector and the clatrix implementation is specified as :clatrix. We can call the matrix function by specifying this keyword argument to create matrices of different implementations, as shown in the following code. In the first call, we call the matrix function with the :persistent-vector keyword to specify the default persistent vector implementation. Similarly, we call the matrix function with the :clatrix keyword to create a clatrix implementation.

```
user> (matrix :persistent-vector [[1 2] [2 1]])
[[1 2] [2 1]]
user> (matrix :clatrix [[1 2] [2 1]])
```

```
A 2x2 matrix
-------------
1.00e+00   2.00e+00
2.00e+00   1.00e+00
```

An interesting point is that the vectors of both vectors and numbers are treated as valid parameters for the matrix function by clatrix, which is different from how core.matrix handles it. For example, [0 1] produces a 2 x 1 matrix, while [[0 1]] produces a 1 x 2 matrix. The matrix function from core.matrix does not have this functionality and always expects a vector of vectors to be passed to it. However, calling the cl/matrix function with either [0 1] or [[0 1]] will create the following matrices without any error:

```
user> (cl/matrix [0 1])
  A 2x1 matrix
  -------------
  0.00e+00
  1.00e+00
user> (cl/matrix [[0 1]])
  A 1x2 matrix
  -------------
  0.00e+00   1.00e+00
```

Analogous to the matrix? function, we can use the cl/clatrix? function to check whether a symbol or variable is a matrix from the clatrix library. While matrix? actually checks for an implementation of the core.matrix specification or protocol, the cl/clatrix? function checks for a specific type. If the cl/clatrix? function returns true for a particular variable, matrix? should return true as well; however, the converse of this axiom isn't true. If we call cl/clatrix? on a matrix created using the matrix function and not the cl/matrix function, it will return false; this is shown in the following code:

```
user> (def A (cl/matrix [[0 1]]))
#'user/A
user> (matrix? A)
true
user> (cl/clatrix? A)
true
user> (def B (matrix [[0 1]]))
#'user/B
user> (matrix? B)
true
user> (cl/clatrix? B)
false
```

Size is an important attribute of a matrix, and it often needs to be calculated. We can find the number of rows in a matrix using the `row-count` function. It's actually just the length of the vector composing a matrix, and thus, we can also use the standard `count` function to determine the row count of a matrix. Similarly, the `column-count` function returns the number of columns in a matrix. Considering the fact that a matrix comprises equally long vectors, the number of columns should be the length of any inner vector, or rather any row, of a matrix. We can check the return value of the `count`, `row-count`, and `column-count` functions on the following sample matrix in the REPL:

```
user> (count (cl/matrix [0 1 2]))
3
user> (row-count (cl/matrix [0 1 2]))
3
user> (column-count (cl/matrix [0 1 2]))
1
```

To retrieve an element from a matrix using its row and column indexes, use the following `cl/get` function. Apart from the matrix to perform the operation on, this function accepts two parameters as indexes to the matrix. Note that all elements are indexed relative to *0* in Clojure code, as opposed to the mathematical notation of treating *1* as the position of the first element in a matrix.

```
user> (def A (cl/matrix [[0 1 2] [3 4 5]]))
#'user/A
user> (cl/get A 1 1)
4.0
user> (cl/get A 3)
4.0
```

As shown in the preceding example, the `cl/get` function also has an alternate form where only a single index value is accepted as a function parameter. In this case, the elements are indexed through a row-first traversal. For example, `(cl/get A 1)` returns `3.0` and `(cl/get A 3)` returns `4.0`. We can use the following `cl/set` function to change an element of a matrix. This function takes parameters similar to `cl/get`—a matrix, a row index, a column index, and lastly, the new element to be set in the specified position in the matrix. The `cl/set` function actually mutates or modifies the matrix it is supplied.

```
user> (pm A)
[[0.000 1.0002.000]
 [3.000 4.0005.000]]
nil
```

```
user> (cl/set A 1 2 0)
#<DoubleMatrix [0.000000, 1.000000, … , 0.000000]>
user> (pm A)
[[0.000 1.000 2.000]
 [3.000 4.000 0.000]]
nil
```

The clatrix library also provides two handy functions for functional composition: cl/map and cl/map-indexed. Both these functions accept a function and matrix as arguments and apply the passed function to each element in the matrix, in a manner that is similar to the standard map function. Also, both these functions return new matrices and do not mutate the matrix that they are supplied as parameters. Note that the function passed to cl/map-indexed should accept three arguments—the row index, the column index, and the element itself:

```
user> (cl/map-indexed
        (fn [i j m] (* m 2)) A)
 A 2x3 matrix
 -------------
 0.00e+00   2.00e+00   4.00e+00
 6.00e+00   8.00e+00   1.00e+01
user> (pm (cl/map-indexed (fn [i j m] i) A))
[[0.000 0.000 0.000]
 [1.000 1.000 1.000]]
nil
user> (pm (cl/map-indexed (fn [i j m] j) A))
[[0.000 1.000 2.000]
 [0.000 1.000 2.000]]
nil
```

Generating matrices

If the number of rows and columns in a matrix are equal, then we term the matrix as a *square matrix*. We can easily generate a simple square matrix of $n \times n$ size by using the repeat function to repeat a single element as follows:

```
(defn square-mat
  "Creates a square matrix of size n x n
  whose elements are all e"
  [n e]
  (let [repeater #(repeat n %)]
    (matrix (-> e repeater repeater)))))
```

In the preceding example, we define a closure to repeat a value *n* times, which is shown as the `repeater`. We then use the *thread* macro (`->`) to pass the element `e` through the closure twice, and finally apply the `matrix` function to the result of the thread macro. We can extend this definition to allow us to specify the matrix implementation to be used for the generated matrix; this is done as follows:

```
(defn square-mat
  "Creates a square matrix of size n x n whose
  elements are all e. Accepts an option argument
  for the matrix implementation."
  [n e & {:keys [implementation]
          :or {implementation :persistent-vector}}]
  (let [repeater #(repeat n %)]
    (matrix implementation (-> e repeater repeater))))
```

The `square-mat` function is defined as one that accepts optional keyword arguments, which specify the matrix implementation of the generated matrix. We specify the default `:persistent-vector` implementation of core.matrix as the default value for the `:implementation` keyword.

Now, we can use this function to create square matrices and optionally specify the matrix implementation when required:

```
user> (square-mat 2 1)
[[1 1] [1 1]]
user> (square-mat 2 1 :implementation :clatrix)
 A 2x2 matrix
 -------------
 1.00e+00  1.00e+00
 1.00e+00  1.00e+00
```

A special type of matrix that's used frequently is the identity matrix. An **identity matrix** is a square matrix whose diagonal elements are *1* and all the other elements are *0*. We formally define an identity matrix I_n as follows:

$$I_n = \left[a_{i,j}\right] \forall i,j$$

$$where\ a_{i,j} = 1\ if\ i = j$$

$$and\ a_{i,j} = 0\ if\ i \neq j$$

$$I_1 = \left[1\right], I_2 = \begin{bmatrix} 1 & 0 \\ 0 & 1 \end{bmatrix}, \dots$$

$$I_n = \begin{bmatrix} 1 & 0 & \cdots & 0 \\ 0 & 1 & \cdots & 0 \\ \vdots & \vdots & \ddots & \vdots \\ 0 & 0 & \cdots & 1 \end{bmatrix}$$

We can implement a function to create an identity matrix using the `cl/map-indexed` function that we previously mentioned, as shown in the following code snippet. We first create a square matrix init of $n \times n$ size by using the previously defined square-mat function, and then map all the diagonal elements to 1 using `cl/map-indexed`:

```
(defn id-mat
  "Creates an identity matrix of n x n size"
  [n]
  (let [init (square-mat :clatrix n 0)
        identity-f (fn [i j n]
                     (if (= i j) 1 n))]
    (cl/map-indexed identity-f init)))
```

The core.matrix library also has its own version of this function, named `identity-matrix`:

```
user> (id-mat 5)
 A 5x5 matrix
 -------------
 1.00e+00   0.00e+00 0.00e+00 0.00e+00 0.00e+00
 0.00e+00   1.00e+00 0.00e+00 0.00e+00 0.00e+00
 0.00e+00   0.00e+00 1.00e+00 0.00e+00 0.00e+00
 0.00e+00   0.00e+00 0.00e+00 1.00e+00 0.00e+00
 0.00e+00   0.00e+00 0.00e+00 0.00e+00 1.00e+00
user> (pm (identity-matrix 5))
[[1.000 0.000 0.000 0.000 0.000]
 [0.000 1.000 0.000 0.000 0.000]
 [0.000 0.000 1.000 0.000 0.000]
 [0.000 0.000 0.000 1.000 0.000]
 [0.000 0.000 0.000 0.000 1.000]]
nil
```

Another common scenario that we will encounter is the need to generate a matrix with random data. Let's implement the following function to generate a random matrix, just like the previously defined `square-mat` function, using the `rand-int` function. Note that the `rand-int` function accepts a single argument n, and returns a random integer between 0 and n:

```
(defn rand-square-mat
  "Generates a random matrix of size n x n"
  [n]
  ;; this won't work
  (matrix (repeat n (repeat n (rand-int 100)))))
```

But this function produces a matrix whose elements are all single random numbers, which is not very useful. For example, if we call the rand-square-mat function with any integer as its parameter, then it returns a matrix with a single distinct random number, as shown in the following code snippet:

```
user> (rand-square-mat 4)
[[94 94] [94 94] [94 94] [94 94]]
```

Instead, we should map each element of the square matrix generated by the square-mat function using the rand-int function, to generate a random number for each element. Unfortunately, cl/map only works with matrices created by the clatrix library, but we can easily replicate this behavior in Clojure using a lazy sequence, as returned by the repeatedly function. Note that the repeatedly function accepts the length of a lazily generated sequence and a function to be used as a generator for this sequence as arguments. Thus, we can implement functions to generate random matrices using the clatrix and core.matrix libraries as follows:

```
(defn rand-square-clmat
  "Generates a random clatrix matrix of size n x n"
  [n]
  (cl/map rand-int (square-mat :clatrix n 100)))

(defn rand-square-mat
  "Generates a random matrix of size n x n"
  [n]
  (matrix
    (repeatedly n #(map rand-int (repeat n 100))))))
```

This implementation works as expected, and each element of the new matrix is now an independently generated random number. We can verify this in the REPL by calling the following modified rand-square-mat function:

```
user> (pm (rand-square-mat 4))
[[97.000 35.000 69.000 69.000]
 [50.000 93.000 26.000  4.000]
 [27.000 14.000 69.000 30.000]
 [68.000 73.000 0.0007 3.000]]
nil
user> (rand-square-clmat 4)
 A 4x4 matrix
 -------------
 5.30e+01  5.00e+00  3.00e+00  6.40e+01
 6.20e+01  1.10e+01  4.10e+01  4.20e+01
 4.30e+01  1.00e+00  3.80e+01  4.70e+01
 3.00e+00  8.10e+01  1.00e+01  2.00e+01
```

We can also generate a matrix of random elements using the `cl/rnorm` function from the clatrix library. This function generates a matrix of normally distributed random elements with optionally specified mean and standard deviations. The matrix is normally distributed in the sense that all the elements are distributed evenly around the specified mean value with a spread specified by the standard deviation. Thus, a low standard deviation produces a set of values that are almost equal to the mean.

The `cl/rnorm` function has several overloads. Let's examine a couple of them in the REPL:

```
user> (cl/rnorm 10 25 10 10)
A 10x10 matrix
---------------
-1.25e-01  5.02e+01 -5.20e+01  .  5.07e+01  2.92e+01  2.18e+01
-2.13e+01  3.13e+01 -2.05e+01  . -8.84e+00  2.58e+01  8.61e+00
 4.32e+01  3.35e+00  2.78e+01  . -8.48e+00  4.18e+01  3.94e+01
 ...
 1.43e+01 -6.74e+00  2.62e+01  . -2.06e+01  8.14e+00 -2.69e+01
user> (cl/rnorm 5)
A 5x1 matrix
--------------
 1.18e+00
 3.46e-01
-1.32e-01
 3.13e-01
-8.26e-02
user> (cl/rnorm 3 4)
A 3x4 matrix
-------------
-4.61e-01 -1.81e+00 -6.68e-01  7.46e-01
 1.87e+00 -7.76e-01 -1.33e+00  5.85e-01
 1.06e+00 -3.54e-01  3.73e-01 -2.72e-02
```

In the preceding example, the first call specifies the mean, the standard deviation, and the number of rows and columns. The second call specifies a single argument n and produces a matrix of size $n \times 1$. Lastly, the third call specifies the number of rows and columns of the matrix.

The core.matrix library also provides a `compute-matrix` function to generate matrices, and will feel idiomatic to Clojure programmers. This function requires a vector that represents the size of the matrix, and a function that takes a number of arguments that is equal to the number of dimensions of the matrix. In fact, `compute-matrix` is versatile enough to implement the generation of an identity matrix, as well as a matrix of randomly generated elements.

We can implement the following functions to create an identity matrix, as well as a matrix of random elements using the `compute-matrix` function:

```
(defn id-computed-mat
  "Creates an identity matrix of size n x n
  using compute-matrix"
  [n]
  (compute-matrix [n n] #(if (= %1 %2) 1 0)))

(defn rand-computed-mat
  "Creates an n x m matrix of random elements
  using compute-matrix"
  [n m]
  (compute-matrix [n m]
   (fn [i j] (rand-int 100))))
```

Adding matrices

Operations on matrices are not directly supported by the Clojure language but are implemented through the core.matrix specification. Trying to add two matrices in the REPL, as shown in the following code snippet, simply throws an error stating that a vector was found where an integer was expected:

```
user> (+ (matrix [[0 1]]) (matrix [[0 1]]))
ClassCastException clojure.lang.PersistentVector cannot be cast to
java.lang.Number  clojure.lang.Numbers.add (Numbers.java:126)
```

This is because the + function operates on numbers rather than matrices. To add matrices, we should use functions from the `core.matrix.operators` namespace. The namespace declaration should look like the following code snippet after we have included `core.matrix.operators`:

```
(ns my-namespace
  (:use clojure.core.matrix)
  (:require [clojure.core.matrix.operators :as M]))
```

Note that the functions are actually imported into an aliased namespace, as function names such as + and * conflict with those in the default Clojure namespace. In practice, we should always try to use aliased namespaces via the `:require` and `:as` filters and avoid the `:use` filter. Alternatively, we could simply not refer to conflicting function names by using the `:refer-clojure` filter in the namespace declaration, which is shown in the following code. However, this should be used sparingly and only as a last resort.

For the code examples in this section, we will use the previous declaration for clarity:

```
(ns my-namespace
  (:use clojure.core.matrix)
  (:require clojure.core.matrix.operators)
  (:refer-clojure :exclude [+ - *]))
```

We can use the M/+ function to perform the matrix addition of two or more matrices. To check the equality of any number of matrices, we use the M/== function:

```
user> (def A (matrix [[0 1 2] [3 4 5]]))
#'user/A
user> (def B (matrix [[0 0 0] [0 0 0]]))
#'user/B
user> (M/== B A)
false
user> (def C (M/+ A B))
#'user/C
user> C
[[0 1 2] [3 4 5]]
user> (M/== C A)
true
```

Two matrices *A* and *B* are said to be equal if the following equality holds true:

$$Let \ A_{m \times n} = \begin{bmatrix} a_{i,j} \end{bmatrix} and \ B_{p \times q} = \begin{bmatrix} b_{i,j} \end{bmatrix}$$

$$A = B, if \ and \ only \ if \ m = p, n = q \ and \ a_{i,j} = b_{i,j} \ \forall \ i \ and \ j$$

Hence, the preceding equation explains that two or more matrices are equal if and only if the following conditions are satisfied:

- Each matrix has the same number of rows and columns
- All elements with the same row and column indices are equal

The following is a simple, yet elegant implementation of matrix equality. It's basically comparing vector equality using the standard reduce and map functions:

```
(defn mat-eq
  "Checks if two matrices are equal"
  [A B]
  (and (= (count A) (count B))
       (reduce #(and %1 %2) (map = A B))))
```

We first compare the row lengths of the two matrices using the count and = functions, and then use the reduce function to compare the inner vector elements. Essentially, the reduce function repeatedly applies a function that accepts two arguments to consecutive elements in a sequence and returns the final result when all the elements in the sequence have been *reduced* by the applied function.

Alternatively, we could use a similar composition using the every? and true? Clojure functions. Using the expression (every? true? (map = A B)), we can check the equality of two matrices. Keep in mind that the true? function returns true if it is passed true (and false otherwise), and the every? function returns true if a given predicate function returns true for all the values in a given sequence.

To add two matrices, they must have an equal number of rows and columns, and the sum is essentially a matrix composed of the sum of elements with the same row and column indices. The sum of two matrices *A* and *B* has been formally defined as follows:

$$Let\ A_{m \times n} = \left[a_{i,j} \right] and\ B_{m \times n} = \left[b_{i,j} \right]$$
$$C_{i,j} = \left[a_{i,j} + b_{i,j} \right]$$

It's almost trivial to implement matrix addition using the standard mapv function, which is simply a variant of the map function that returns a vector. We apply mapv to each row of the matrix as well as to the entire matrix. Note that this implementation is intended for a vector of vectors, although it can be easily used with the matrix and as-vec functions from core.matrix to operate on matrices. We can implement the following function to perform matrix addition using the standard mapv function:

```
(defn mat-add
  "Add two matrices"
  [A B]
  (mapv #(mapv + %1 %2) A B))
```

We can just as easily generalize the mat-add function for any number of matrices by using the reduce function. As shown in the following code, we can extend the previous definition of mat-add to apply it to any number of matrices using the reduce function:

```
(defn mat-add
  "Add two or more matrices"
  ([A B]
     (mapv #(mapv + %1 %2) A B))
  ([A B & more]
     (let [M (concat [A B] more)]
       (reduce mat-add M))))
```

An interesting unary operation on a $n \times n$ matrix A is the trace of a matrix, represented as $tr(A)$. The trace of a matrix is essentially the sum of its diagonal elements:

$$tr(A) = a_{1,1} + a_{2,2} + \dots a_{n,n} = \sum_{i=1}^{n} a_{i,i}$$

It's fairly simple enough to implement the trace function of a matrix using the `cl/map-indexed` and `repeatedly` functions as described earlier. We have skipped it here to serve as an exercise for you.

Multiplying matrices

Multiplication is another important binary operation on matrices. In the broader sense, the term **matrix multiplication** refers to several techniques that multiply matrices to produce a new matrix.

Let's define three matrices, A, B, and C, and a single value N, in the REPL. The matrices have the following values:

$$A = \begin{bmatrix} 1 & 2 & 3 \\ 4 & 5 & 6 \end{bmatrix}, B = \begin{bmatrix} 10 & 20 \\ 20 & 30 \\ 30 & 40 \end{bmatrix}, C = \begin{bmatrix} 11 & 12 \\ 13 & 14 \end{bmatrix}, N = 10$$

We can multiply the matrices by using the `M/*` function from the core.matrix library. Apart from being used to multiply two matrices, this function can also be used to multiply any number of matrices, and scalar values as well. We can try out the following `M/*` function to multiply two given matrices in the REPL:

```
user> (pm (M/* A B))
[[140.000 200.000]
 [320.000 470.000]]
nil
user> (pm (M/* A C))
RuntimeException Mismatched vector sizes  clojure.core.matrix.impl.
persistent-vector/...
user> (def N 10)
#'user/N
user> (pm (M/* A N))
[[10.000 20.000 30.000]
 [40.000 50.000 60.000]]
nil
```

First, we calculated the product of two matrices. This operation is termed as **matrix-matrix multiplication**. However, multiplying matrices A and C doesn't work, as the matrices have incompatible sizes. This brings us to the first rule of multiplying matrices: to multiply two matrices A and B, the number of columns in A have to be equal to the number of rows in B. The resultant matrix has the same number of rows as A and columns as B. That's the reason the REPL didn't agree to multiply A and C, but simply threw an exception.

For matrix A of size $m \times n$, and B of size $p \times q$, the product of the two matrices only exists if $n = p$, and the product of A and B is a new matrix of size $n \times q$.

The product of matrices A and B is calculated by multiplying the elements of rows in A with the corresponding columns in B, and then adding the resulting values to produce a single value for each row in A and each column in B. Hence, the resulting product has the same number of rows as A and columns as B.

We can define the product of two matrices with compatible sizes as follows:

$$If \ A = \begin{bmatrix} A_{1,1} & \cdots & A_{1,m} \\ \vdots & \ddots & \vdots \\ A_{n,1} & \cdots & A_{n,m} \end{bmatrix} and \ B = \begin{bmatrix} B_{1,1} & \cdots & B_{1,q} \\ \vdots & \ddots & \vdots \\ B_{m,1} & \cdots & B_{m,q} \end{bmatrix}$$

$$A \times B = \begin{bmatrix} AB_{1,1} & \cdots & AB_{1,q} \\ \vdots & \ddots & \vdots \\ AB_{n,1} & \cdots & AB_{n,q} \end{bmatrix}, where \ AB_{i,j} = \sum_{i=1}^{m} A_{i,k} \times B_{k,j}$$

The following is an illustration of how the elements from A and B are used to calculate the product of the two matrices:

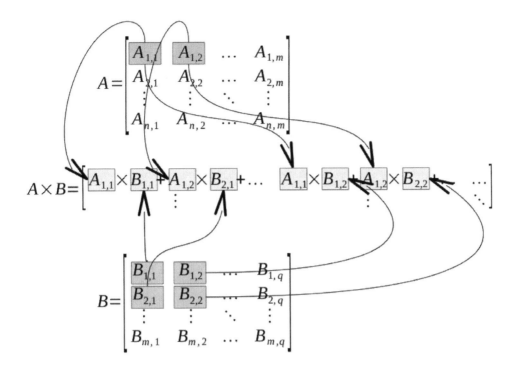

This does look slightly complicated, so let's demonstrate the preceding definition with an example, using the matrices A and B as we had previously defined. The following calculation does, in fact, agree to the value produced in the REPL:

$$A = \begin{bmatrix} 1 & 2 & 3 \\ 4 & 5 & 6 \end{bmatrix}, B = \begin{bmatrix} 10 & 20 \\ 20 & 30 \\ 30 & 40 \end{bmatrix}$$

$$A \times B = \begin{bmatrix} 1 \times 10 + 2 \times 20 + 3 \times 30 & 1 \times 20 + 2 \times 30 + 3 \times 40 \\ 4 \times 10 + 5 \times 20 + 6 \times 30 & 4 \times 20 + 5 \times 30 + 6 \times 40 \end{bmatrix} = \begin{bmatrix} 140 & 200 \\ 320 & 470 \end{bmatrix}$$

Note that multiplying matrices is not a commutative operation. However, the operation does exhibit the associative property of functions. For matrices A, B, and C of product-compatible sizes, the following properties are always true, with one exception that we will uncover later:

$$A \times B \neq B \times A$$
$$A \times (B \times C) = (A \times B) \times C$$

An obvious corollary is that a square matrix when multiplied with another square matrix of the same size produces a resultant matrix that has the same size as the two original matrices. Also, the square, cube, and other powers of a square matrix results in matrices of the same size.

Another interesting property of square matrices is that they have an identity element for multiplication, that is, an identity matrix of product-compatible size. But, an identity matrix is itself a square matrix, which brings us to the conclusion that *the multiplication of a square matrix with an identity matrix is a commutative operation*. Hence, the commutative rule for matrices, which states that matrix multiplication is not commutative, is actually not true when one of the matrices is an identity matrix and the other one is a square matrix. This can be formally summarized by the following equality:

If A is a square matrix of size $n \times n$, and I is an identity matrix of size $n \times n$,
$A \times I = I \times A = A$

A naïve implementation of matrix multiplication would have a time complexity of $O(n^3)$, and requires eight multiplication operations for a 2×2 matrix. By time complexity, we mean the time taken by a particular algorithm to run till completion. Hence, linear algebra libraries use more efficient algorithms, such as *Strassen's algorithm*, to implement matrix multiplication, which needs only seven multiplication operations and reduces the complexity to $O\left(n^{\log_2 7}\right) \approx O\left(n^{2.807}\right)$.

The clatrix library implementation for matrix multiplication performs significantly better than the default persistent vector implementation, since it interfaces with native libraries. In practice, we can use a benchmarking library such as criterium for Clojure (http://github.com/hugoduncan/criterium) to perform this comparison. Alternatively, we can also compare the performance of these two implementations in brief by defining a simple function to multiply two matrices and then passing large matrices of different implementations to it using our previously defined `rand-square-mat` and `rand-square-clmat` functions. We can define a function to measure the time taken to multiply two matrices.

Also, we can define two functions to multiply the matrices that were created using the `rand-square-mat` and `rand-square-clmat` functions that we previously defined, as follows:

```
(defn time-mat-mul
  "Measures the time for multiplication of two matrices A and B"
  [A B]
  (time (M/* A B)))

(defn core-matrix-mul-time []
  (let [A (rand-square-mat 100)
        B (rand-square-mat 100)]
    (time-mat-mul A B)))

(defn clatrix-mul-time []
  (let [A (rand-square-clmat 100)
        B (rand-square-clmat 100)]
    (time-mat-mul A B)))
```

We can see that the core.matrix implementation takes a second on average to compute the product of two randomly generated matrices. The clatrix implementation, however, takes less than a millisecond on average, although the first call that's made usually takes 35 to 40 ms to load the native BLAS library. Of course, this value could be slightly different depending on the hardware it's calculated on. Nevertheless, clatrix is preferred when dealing with large matrices unless there's a valid reason, such as hardware incompatibilities or the avoidance of an additional dependency, to avoid its usage.

Next, let's look at *scalar multiplication*, which invloves simply multiplying a single value N or a scalar with a matrix. The resultant matrix has the same size as the original matrix. For a 2 x 2 matrix, we can define scalar multiplication as follows:

$$Let \ A = \begin{bmatrix} a_{1,1} & a_{1,2} \\ a_{2,1} & a_{2,2} \end{bmatrix}$$

$$N \times A = A \times N = N \times \begin{bmatrix} a_{1,1} & a_{1,2} \\ a_{2,1} & a_{2,2} \end{bmatrix} = \begin{bmatrix} N \times a_{1,1} & N \times a_{1,2} \\ N \times a_{2,1} & N \times a_{2,2} \end{bmatrix}$$

For matrices $A = \begin{bmatrix} 1 & 2 \\ 3 & 4 \end{bmatrix}$ and $N = 10$, the following is the product:

$$N \times A = \begin{bmatrix} 1 \times 10 & 2 \times 10 \\ 3 \times 10 & 4 \times 10 \end{bmatrix} = \begin{bmatrix} 10 & 20 \\ 30 & 40 \end{bmatrix}$$

Note that we can also use the `scale` function from the core.matrix library to perform scalar multiplication:

```
user> (pm (scale A 10))
[[10.000 20.000 30.000]
 [40.000 50.000 60.000]]
nil
user> (M/== (scale A 10) (M/* A 10))
true
```

Finally, we will briefly take a look at a special form of matrix multiplication, termed as **matrix-vector multiplication**. A vector is simply a matrix with a single row, which on multiplication with a square matrix of product-compatible size produces a new vector with the same size as the original vector. After multiplying a matrix *A* of size $M \times N$ and the transpose *V'* of a vector *V*, of size $N \times 1$, a new vector *V"* of size $M \times 1$ is produced. If *A* is a square matrix, then *V"* has an identical size as that of the transpose *V'*.

$$A_{M \times N} \times V'_{N \times 1} = V''_{M \times 1}$$

$$A_{N \times N} \times V'_{N \times 1} = V''_{N \times 1}$$

Transposing and inverting matrices

Another frequently used elementary matrix operation is the *transpose* of a matrix. The transpose of a matrix *A* is represented as A^T or *A'*. A simple way to define the transpose of a matrix is by reflecting the matrix over its *prime diagonal*. By prime diagonal, we mean the diagonal comprising elements whose row and column indices are equal. We can also describe the transpose of a matrix by swapping of the rows and columns of a matrix. We can use the following `transpose` function from core. matrix to perform this operation:

```
user> (def A (matrix [[1 2 3] [4 5 6]]))
#'user/A
user> (pm (transpose A))
[[1.000 4.000]
 [2.000 5.000]
 [3.000 6.000]]
nil
```

We can define the following three possible ways to obtain the transpose of a matrix:

- The original matrix is reflected over its main diagonal
- The rows of the matrix become the columns of its transpose
- The columns of the matrix become the rows of its transpose

Hence, every element in a matrix has its row and column swapped in its transpose, and vice versa. This can be formally represented using the following equation:

$$\left[A^T \right]_{i,j} = \left[A \right]_{j,i}$$

This brings us to the notion of an invertible matrix. A square matrix is said to be invertible if there exists another square matrix that is the inverse of a matrix, and which produces an identity matrix when multiplied with the original matrix. A matrix A of size $n \times n$, is said to have an inverse matrix B if the following equality is true:

$$A \times B = B \times A = I_n$$

Let's test this equality using the inverse function from core.matrix. Note that the default persistent implementation of the core.matrix library does not implement the inverse operation, so we use a matrix from the clatrix library instead. In the following example, we create a matrix from the clatrix library using the cl/matrix function, determine its inverse using the inverse function, and multiply these two matrices using the M/* function:

```
user> (def A (cl/matrix [[2 0] [0 2]]))
#'user/A
user> (M/* (inverse A) A)
 A 2x2 matrix
 -------------
 1.00e+00  0.00e+00
 0.00e+00  1.00e+00
```

In the preceding example, we first define a matrix A and then multiply it with its inverse to produce the corresponding identity matrix. An interesting observation when we use double precision numeric types for the elements in a matrix is that not all matrices produce an identity matrix on multiplication with their inverse.

A small amount of error can be observed for some matrices, and this happens due to the limitations of using a 32-bit representation for floating-point numbers; this is shown as follows:

```
user> (def A (cl/matrix [[1 2] [3 4]]))
#'user/A
user> (inverse A)
 A 2x2 matrix
 ------------
-2.00e+00  1.00e+00
 1.50e+00 -5.00e-01
```

In order to find the inverse of a matrix, we must first define the *determinant* of that matrix, which is simply another value determined from a given matrix. First off, determinants only exist for square matrices, and thus, inverses only exist for matrices with an equal number of rows and columns. The determinant of a matrix is represented as $det(A)$ or $|A|$. A matrix whose determinant is zero is termed as a *singular matrix*. For a matrix A, we define its determinant as follows:

$$\text{For } A = \begin{bmatrix} a & b \\ c & d \end{bmatrix},$$

$$det(A) = \begin{vmatrix} a & b \\ c & d \end{vmatrix} = ad - bc$$

$$\text{For } A = \begin{bmatrix} a & b & c \\ d & e & f \\ g & h & i \end{bmatrix},$$

$$det(A) = \begin{vmatrix} a & b & c \\ d & e & f \\ g & h & i \end{vmatrix}$$

$$= a \begin{vmatrix} e & f \\ h & i \end{vmatrix} - b \begin{vmatrix} d & f \\ g & i \end{vmatrix} + c \begin{vmatrix} d & e \\ g & h \end{vmatrix}$$

$$= aei + bfg + cdh - ceg - bdi - afh$$

We can use the preceding definitions to express the determinant of a matrix of any size. An interesting observation is that the determinant of an identity matrix is always 1. As an example, we will find the determinant of a given matrix as follows:

$$\text{Let } A = \begin{bmatrix} -2 & 2 & 3 \\ -1 & 1 & 3 \\ 2 & 0 & -1 \end{bmatrix}$$

$$det(A) = -2 \times \begin{vmatrix} 1 & 3 \\ 0 & -1 \end{vmatrix} - 2 \times \begin{vmatrix} -1 & 3 \\ 2 & -1 \end{vmatrix} + 3 \times \begin{vmatrix} -1 & 1 \\ 2 & 0 \end{vmatrix}$$

$$= -2 \times (-1-0) - 2 \times (1-6) + 3 \times (0-2)$$

$$= 2 + 10 - 6$$

$$= 6$$

For a 3×3 matrix, we can use *Sarrus' rule* as an alternative means to calculate the determinant of a matrix. To find the determinant of a matrix using this scheme, we first write out the first two columns of the matrix to the right of the third column, so that there are five columns in a row. Next, we add the products of the diagonals going from top to bottom, and subtract the products of diagonals from bottom. This process can be illustrated using the following diagram:

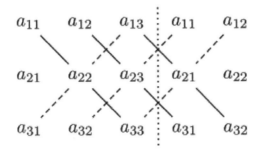

By using Sarrus' rule, we formally express the determinant of a matrix A as follows:

$$det(A) = \begin{vmatrix} a_{11} & a_{12} & a_{13} \\ a_{21} & a_{22} & a_{23} \\ a_{31} & a_{32} & a_{33} \end{vmatrix}$$

$$= a_{11}a_{22}a_{33} + a_{12}a_{23}a_{31} + a_{13}a_{21}a_{32} - a_{31}a_{22}a_{13} - a_{32}a_{23}a_{11} - a_{33}a_{21}a_{12}$$

We can calculate the determinant of a matrix in the REPL using the following det function from core.matrix. Note that this operation is not implemented by the default persistent vector implementation of core.matrix.

```
user> (def A (cl/matrix [[-2 2 3] [-1 1 3] [2 0 -1]]))
#'user/A
user> (det A)
6.0
```

Now that we've defined the determinant of a matrix, let's use it to define the inverse of a matrix. We've already discussed the notion of an invertible matrix; finding the inverse of a matrix is simply determining a matrix such that it produces an identity matrix when multiplied with the original matrix.

For the inverse of a matrix to exist, its determinant must be nonzero. Next, for each element in the original matrix, we find the determinant of the matrix without the row and column of the selected element. This produces a matrix of an identical size as that of the original matrix (termed as the *cofactor matrix* of the original matrix). The transpose of the cofactor matrix is called the *adjoint* of the original matrix. The adjoint produces the inverse on dividing it by the determinant of the original matrix. Now, let's formally define the inverse of a 2×2 matrix A. We denote the inverse of a matrix A as A^{-1}, and it can be formally expressed as follows:

$$\text{For } A = \begin{bmatrix} a & b \\ c & d \end{bmatrix},$$

$$A^{-1} = \frac{1}{det(A)} \begin{bmatrix} d & -b \\ -c & a \end{bmatrix}^T$$

$$= \frac{1}{det(A)} \begin{bmatrix} d & -c \\ -b & a \end{bmatrix}$$

$$= \frac{1}{ad - bc} \begin{bmatrix} d & -c \\ -b & a \end{bmatrix}$$

As an example, let's find the inverse of a sample 2×2 matrix. We can actually verify that the inverse produces an identity matrix when multiplied with the original matrix, as shown in the following example:

$$\text{Let } A = \begin{bmatrix} 1 & 2 \\ 3 & 4 \end{bmatrix}$$

$$det(A) = 4 \times 1 - 2 \times 3 = -2$$

$$A^{-1} = \frac{1}{det(A)} \begin{bmatrix} 4 & -3 \\ -2 & 1 \end{bmatrix} = \frac{1}{-2} \begin{bmatrix} 4 & -3 \\ -2 & 1 \end{bmatrix}$$

$$= \begin{bmatrix} -2 & 1 \\ 3/2 & -1/2 \end{bmatrix}$$

Similarly, we define the inverse of a 3×3 matrix as follows:

$$\text{For } A = \begin{bmatrix} a_{11} & a_{12} & a_{13} \\ a_{21} & a_{22} & a_{23} \\ a_{31} & a_{32} & a_{33} \end{bmatrix}$$

$$A^{-1} = \frac{1}{det(A)} \begin{bmatrix} \begin{vmatrix} a_{22} & a_{23} \\ a_{32} & a_{33} \end{vmatrix} & \begin{vmatrix} a_{21} & a_{23} \\ a_{31} & a_{33} \end{vmatrix} & \begin{vmatrix} a_{21} & a_{22} \\ a_{31} & a_{32} \end{vmatrix} \\ \begin{vmatrix} a_{12} & a_{13} \\ a_{32} & a_{33} \end{vmatrix} & \begin{vmatrix} a_{11} & a_{13} \\ a_{31} & a_{33} \end{vmatrix} & \begin{vmatrix} a_{11} & a_{12} \\ a_{31} & a_{32} \end{vmatrix} \\ \begin{vmatrix} a_{12} & a_{13} \\ a_{22} & a_{23} \end{vmatrix} & \begin{vmatrix} a_{12} & a_{13} \\ a_{21} & a_{23} \end{vmatrix} & \begin{vmatrix} a_{12} & a_{12} \\ a_{21} & a_{22} \end{vmatrix} \end{bmatrix}^T$$

Now, let's calculate the inverse of a 3×3 matrix:

$$\text{Let } A = \begin{bmatrix} 1 & 2 & 3 \\ 0 & 4 & 5 \\ 1 & 0 & 6 \end{bmatrix}$$

$$det(A) = 22$$

$$A^{-1} = \frac{1}{det(A)} \begin{bmatrix} \begin{vmatrix} 4 & 5 \\ 0 & 6 \end{vmatrix} & \begin{vmatrix} 0 & 5 \\ 1 & 6 \end{vmatrix} & \begin{vmatrix} 0 & 4 \\ 1 & 0 \end{vmatrix} \\ \begin{vmatrix} 2 & 3 \\ 0 & 6 \end{vmatrix} & \begin{vmatrix} 1 & 3 \\ 1 & 6 \end{vmatrix} & \begin{vmatrix} 1 & 2 \\ 1 & 0 \end{vmatrix} \\ \begin{vmatrix} 2 & 3 \\ 4 & 5 \end{vmatrix} & \begin{vmatrix} 1 & 3 \\ 0 & 5 \end{vmatrix} & \begin{vmatrix} 1 & 2 \\ 0 & 4 \end{vmatrix} \end{bmatrix}^{T}$$

$$= \frac{1}{22} \begin{bmatrix} 23 & 5 & -4 \\ -12 & 3 & 2 \\ -2 & -5 & 4 \end{bmatrix}^{T} = \begin{bmatrix} 23 & -12 & -2 \\ 5 & 3 & -5 \\ -4 & 2 & 4 \end{bmatrix}$$

$$= \begin{bmatrix} 12/11 & -6/11 & -1/11 \\ 5/22 & 3/22 & -5/22 \\ -2/11 & 1/11 & 2/11 \end{bmatrix}$$

We've mentioned that singular and nonsquare matrices don't have inverses, and we can see that the `inverse` function throws an error when supplied with such a matrix. As shown in the following REPL output, the `inverse` function will throw an error if the given matrix is not a square matrix, or if the given matrix is singular:

```
user> (def A (cl/matrix [[1 2 3] [4 5 6]]))
#'user/A
user> (inverse A)
ExceptionInfo throw+: {:exception "Cannot invert a non-square
matrix."} clatrix.core/i (core.clj:1033)
user> (def A (cl/matrix [[2 0] [2 0]]))
#'user/A
user> (M/* (inverse A) A)
LapackException LAPACK DGESV: Linear equation cannot be solved
because the matrix was singular.  org.jblas.SimpleBlas.gesv
(SimpleBlas.java:274)
```

Interpolating using matrices

Let's try out an example to demonstrate how we use matrices. This example uses matrices to interpolate a curve between a given set of points. Suppose we have a given set of points representing some data. The objective is to trace a smooth line between the points in order to produce a curve that estimates the shape of the data. Although the mathematical formulae in this example may seem difficult, we should know that this technique is actually just a form of regularization for a linear regression model, and is termed as **Tichonov regularization**. For now, we'll focus on how to use matrices in this technique, and we shall revisit regularization in depth in *Chapter 2, Understanding Linear Regression*.

We will first define an interpolation matrix *L* that can be used to determine an estimated curve of the given data points. It's essentially the vector *[-1, 2, -1]* moving diagonally across the columns of the matrix. This kind of a matrix is called a **band matrix**:

$$L = \begin{bmatrix} -1 & 2 & -1 & 0 & \cdots & 0 \\ 0 & -1 & 2 & -1 & \cdots & 0 \\ & & \ddots & & & \\ 0 & \cdots & 0 & -1 & 2 & -1 \end{bmatrix}$$

We can concisely define the matrix *L* using the following `compute-matrix` function. Note that for a given size *n*, we generate a matrix of size $n \times (n+2)$:

```
(defn lmatrix [n]
  (compute-matrix :clatrix [n (+ n 2)]
                  (fn [i j] ({0 -1, 1 2, 2 -1} (- j i) 0))))
```

The anonymous closure in the preceding example uses a map to decide the value of an element at a specified row and column index. For example, the element at row index 2 and column index 3 is 2, since `(- j i)` is *1* and the key *1* in the map has *2* as its value. We can verify that the generated matrix has a similar structure as that of the matrix `lmatrix` through the REPL as follows:

```
user> (pm (lmatrix 4))
[[-1.000 2.000 -1.000  0.000  0.000  0.000]
 [ 0.000 -1.000  2.000 -1.000  0.000  0.000]
 [ 0.000  0.000 -1.000  2.000 -1.000  0.000]
 [ 0.000  0.000  0.000 -1.000  2.000 -1.000]]
nil
```

Next, we define how to represent the data points that we intend to interpolate over. Each point has an observed value *x* that is passed to some function to produce another observed value *y*. For this example, we simply choose a random value for *x* and another random value for *y*. We perform this repeatedly to produce the data points.

In order to represent the data points along with an *L* matrix of compatible size, we define the following simple function named `problem` that returns a map of the problem definition. This comprises the *L* matrix, the observed values for *x*, the hidden values of *x* for which we have to estimate values of *y* to create a curve, and the observed values for *y*.

```
(defn problem
  "Return a map of the problem setup for a
  given matrix size, number of observed values
  and regularization parameter"
  [n n-observed lambda]
  (let [i (shuffle (range n))]
    {:L (M/* (lmatrix n) lambda)
     :observed (take n-observed i)
     :hidden (drop n-observed i)
     :observed-values (matrix :clatrix
                              (repeatedly n-observed rand))}))
```

The first two parameters of the function are the number of rows n in the *L* matrix, and the number of observed *x* values n-observed. The function takes a third argument lambda, which is actually the regularization parameter for our model. This parameter determines how accurate the estimated curve is, and we shall study more about how it's relevant to this model in the later chapters. In the map returned by the preceding function, the observed values for *x* and *y* have keys :observed and :observed-values, and the hidden values for *x* have the key :hidden. Similarly, the key :L is mapped to an *L* matrix of compatible size.

Now that we've defined our problem (or model), we can plot a smooth curve over the given points. By *smooth*, we mean that each point in the curve is the average of its immediate neighbors, along with some Gaussian noise. Thus, all the points on the curve of this noise have a Gaussian distribution, in which all the values are scattered about some mean value along with a spread specified by some standard deviation.

If we partition matrix *L* into L_1 and L_2 over the observed and hidden points respectively, we can define a formula to determine the curve as follows. The following equation may seem a bit daunting, but as mentioned earlier, we shall study the reasoning behind this equation in the following chapters. The curve can be represented by a matrix that can be calculated as follows, using the matrix *L*:

$$[\mu] = -\Lambda_{11}^{-1}\Lambda_{12}[y_{\text{obs}}], \quad \text{where } \Lambda_{11} = L_1^T L_1 \text{ and } \Lambda_{12} = L_1^T L_2$$

We estimate the observed values for the hidden values of x as $[\mu]$, using the originally observed values of y, that is, $[y_{obs}]$ and the two matrices that are calculated from the interpolation matrix L. These two matrices are calculated using only the transpose and inverse functions of a matrix. As all the values on the right-hand side of this equation are either matrices or vectors, we use matrix multiplication to find the product of these values.

The previous equation can be implemented using the functions that we've explored earlier. In fact, the code comprises just this equation written as a prefix expression for the map returned by the `problem` function that we defined previously. We now define the following function to solve the problem returned by the `problem` function:

```
(defn solve
  "Return a map containing the approximated value
y of each hidden point x"
  [{:keys [L observed hidden observed-values] :as problem}]
  (let [nc  (column-count L)
        nr  (row-count L)
        L1  (cl/get L (range nr) hidden)
        L2  (cl/get L (range nr) observed)
        l11 (M/* (transpose L1) L1)
        l12 (M/* (transpose L1) L2)]
    (assoc problem :hidden-values
      (M/* -1 (inverse l11) l12 observed-values)))))
```

The preceding function calculates the estimated values for y and simply adds them to the original map with the key `:hidden-values` using the `assoc` function.

It's rather difficult to mentally visualize the calculated values of the curve, so we will now use the *Incanter* library (`http://github.com/liebke/incanter`) to plot the estimated curve and the original points. This library essentially provides a simple and idiomatic API to create and view various types of plots and charts.

The Incanter library can be added to a Leiningen project by adding the following dependency to the `project.clj` file:

```
[incanter "1.5.4"]
```

For the upcoming example, the namespace declaration should look similar to the following:

```
(ns my-namespace
  (:use [incanter.charts :only [xy-plot add-points]]
        [incanter.core   :only [view]])
  (:require [clojure.core.matrix.operators :as M]
            [clatrix.core :as cl]))
```

We now define a simple function that will plot a graph of the given data using functions, such as xy-plot and view, from the Incanter library:

```
(defn plot-points
  "Plots sample points of a solution s"
  [s]
  (let [X (concat (:hidden s) (:observed s))
        Y (concat (:hidden-values s) (:observed-values s))]
    (view
      (add-points
        (xy-plot X Y) (:observed s) (:observed-values s)))))
```

As this is our first encounter with the Incanter library, let's discuss some of the functions that are used to implement plot-points. We first bind all the values on the *x* axis to X, and all values on the *y* axis to Y. Then, we plot the points as a curve using the xy-plot function, which takes two sets of values to plot on the *x* and *y* axes as arguments and returns a chart or plot. Next, we add the originally observed points to the plot using the add-points function. The add-points function requires three arguments: the original plot, a vector of all the values of the *x* axis component, and a vector of all the values of the *y* axis component. This function also returns a plot such as the xy-plot function, and we can view this plot using the view function. Note that we could have equivalently used the thread macro (->) to compose the xy-plot, add-points, and view functions.

Now, we can intuitively visualize the estimated curve using the plot-points function on some random data as shown in the following function:

```
(defn plot-rand-sample []
  (plot-points (solve (problem 150 10 30))))
```

When we execute the plot-rand-sample function, the following plot of the values is displayed:

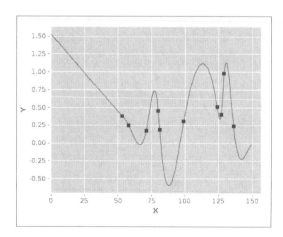

Summary

In this chapter, we introduced matrices through the core.matrix and clatrix libraries. The following are the points that we covered:

- We've discussed how to represent, print, and fetch information from matrices through core.matrix and clatrix. We've also discussed how we can generate matrices with some random data.

- We've talked about some of the rudimentary operations on matrices, such as equality, addition, multiplication, transpose, and inverse.

- We've also introduced the versatile Incanter library that is used to visualize plots and charts of data, through an example on using matrices.

Next, we will study some basic techniques for prediction using linear regression. As we will see, some of these techniques, in fact, are based on simple matrix operations. Linear regression is actually a type of supervised learning, which we will discuss in the next chapter.

2
Understanding Linear Regression

In this chapter, we begin our exploration of machine learning models and techniques. The ultimate objective of machine learning is to *generalize* the facts from some empirical sample data. This is called **generalization**, and is essentially the ability to use these inferred facts to accurately perform at an accurate rate on new, unseen data. The two broad categories of machine learning are **supervised** learning and **unsupervised** learning. The term **supervised learning** is used to describe the task of machine learning in which an understanding or a model is formulated from some labeled data. By labeled, we mean that the sample data is associated with some observed value. In a basic sense, the model is a statistical description of the data and how the data varies over different parameters. The initial data used by supervised machine learning techniques to create the model is called the **training data** of the model. On the other hand, unsupervised learning techniques estimate models by finding patterns in unlabeled data. As the data used by unsupervised learning techniques is unlabeled, there is often no definite yes-or-no-based reward system to determine if an estimated model is accurate and correct.

We will now examine *linear regression*, which is an interesting model that can be used for prediction. As a type of supervised learning, regression models are created from some data in which a number of parameters are somehow combined to produce several target values. The model actually describes the relation between the target value and the model's parameters, and can be used to predict a target value when supplied with the values for the parameters of the model.

We will first study linear regression with single as well as multiple variables, and then describe the algorithms that can be used to formulate machine learning models from some given data. We will study the reasoning behind these models and simultaneously demonstrate how we can implement the algorithms to create these models in Clojure.

Understanding single-variable linear regression

We often come across situations where we would need to create an approximate model from some sample data. This model can then be used to predict more such data when its required parameters are supplied. For example, we might want to study the frequency of rainfall on a given day in a particular city, which we will assume varies depending on the humidity on that day. A formulated model could be useful in predicting the possibility of rainfall on a given day if we know the humidity on that day. We start formulating a model from some data by first fitting a straight line (that is, an equation) with some parameters and coefficients over this data. This type of model is called a **linear regression** model. We can think of linear regression as a way of fitting a straight line, $y = mx + c$, over the sample data, if we assume that the sample data has only a single dimension.

The linear regression model is simply described as a linear equation that represents the **regressand** or **dependent variable** of the model. The formulated regression model can have one to several parameters depending on the available data, and these parameters of the model are also termed as **regressors, features,** or **independent variables** of the model. We will first explore linear regression models with a single independent variable.

An example problem for using linear regression with a single variable would be to predict the probability of rainfall on a particular day, which depends on the humidity on that day. This training data can be represented in the following tabular form:

Amount of Rainfall	Humidity
y_1	x_1
y_2	x_2
$\vdots$	$\vdots$
y_N	x_N

For a single-variable linear model, the dependent variable must vary with respect to a single parameter. Thus, our sample data essentially consists of two vectors, that is, one for the values of the dependent parameter Y and the other for the values of the independent variable X. Both vectors have the same length. This data can be formally represented as two vectors, or single column matrices, as follows:

$$Y = \begin{bmatrix} y_1 \\ y_2 \\ \vdots \\ y_N \end{bmatrix}, X = \begin{bmatrix} x_1 \\ x_2 \\ \vdots \\ x_N \end{bmatrix}$$

Let's quickly define the following two matrices in Clojure, X and Y, to represent some sample data:

```
(def X (cl/matrix [8.401 14.475 13.396 12.127 5.044
                   8.339 15.692 17.108 9.253 12.029]))

(def Y (cl/matrix [-1.57 2.32  0.424  0.814 -2.3
          0.01 1.954 2.296 -0.635 0.328]))
```

Here, we define 10 points of data; these points can be easily plotted on a scatter graph using the following Incanter `scatter-plot` function:

```
(def linear-samp-scatter
  (scatter-plot X Y))

(defn plot-scatter []
  (view linear-samp-scatter))

(plot-scatter)
```

The preceding code displays the following scatter plot of our data:

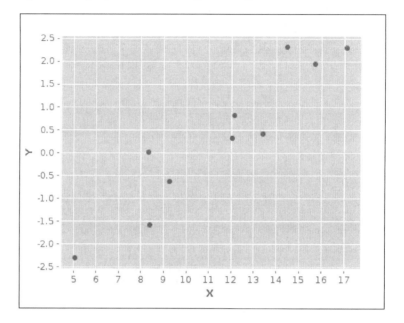

The previous scatter plot is a simple representation of the 10 data points that we defined in X and Y.

 The `scatter-plot` function can be found in the `charts` namespace of the Incanter library. The namespace declaration of a file using this function should look similar to the following declaration:

```
(ns my-namespace
    (:use [incanter.charts :only [scatter-plot]]))
```

Now that we have a visualization of our data, let's estimate a linear model over the given data points. We can generate a linear model of any data using the `linear-model` function from the Incanter library. This function returns a map that describes the formulated model and also a lot of useful data about this model. For starters, we can plot the linear model over our previous scatter plot by using the `:fitted` key-value pair from this map. We first get the value of the `:fitted` key from the returned map and add it to the scatter plot using the `add-lines` function; this is shown in the following code:

```
(def samp-linear-model
    (linear-model Y X))
```

```
(defn plot-model []
  (view (add-lines samp-scatter-plot
          X (:fitted linear-samp-scatter)))))

(plot-model)
```

This code produces the following self-explanatory plot of the linear model over the scatter plot we defined previously:

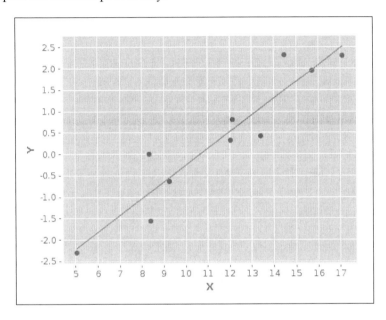

The previous plot depicts the linear model `samp-linear-model` as a straight line drawn over the 10 data points that we defined in X and Y.

> The `linear-model` function can be found in the `stats` namespace of the Incanter library. The namespace declaration of a file using `linear-model` should look similar to the following declaration:
>
> ```
> (ns my-namespace
>   (:use [incanter.stats :only [linear-model]]))
> ```

Well, it looks like Incanter's `linear-model` function did most of the work for us. Essentially, this function creates a linear model of our data by using the **ordinary-least squares (OLS)** curve-fitting algorithm. We will soon dive into the details of this algorithm, but let's first understand how exactly a curve is fit onto some given data.

Let's first define how a straight line can be represented. In coordinate geometry, a line is simply a function of an independent variable, *x*, which has a given slope, *m*, and an intercept, *c*. The function of the line *y* can be formally written as $y = mx + c$. The slope of the line represents how much the value of *y* changes when the value of *x* varies. The intercept of this equation is just where the line meets the *y* axis of the plot. Note that the equation *y* is not the same as *Y*, which actually represents the values of the equation that we have been provided with.

Analogous to this definition of a straight line from coordinate geometry, we formally define the linear regression model with a single variable using our definition of the matrices *X* and *Y*, as follows:

$$Y = \beta X + \varepsilon$$

This definition of the linear model with a single variable is actually quite versatile since we can use the same equation to define a linear model with multiple variables; we will see this later in the chapter. In the preceding definition, the term β is a coefficient that represents the linear scale of *y* with respect to *x*. In terms of geometry, it's simply the slope of a line that fits the given data in matrices *X* and *Y*. Since *X* is a matrix or vector, β can also be thought of as a scaling factor for the matrix *X*.

Also, the term ε is another coefficient that explains the value of *y* when *x* is zero. In other words, it's the *y* intercept of the equation. The coefficient β of the formulated model is termed as the **regression coefficient** or **effect** of the linear model, and the coefficient ε is termed as the **error term** or **bias** of the model. A model may even have several regression coefficients, as we will see later in this chapter. It turns out that the error ε is actually just another regression coefficient and can be conventionally mentioned along with the other effects of the model. Interestingly, this error determines the scatter or variance of the data in general.

Using the map returned by the `linear-model` function from our earlier example, we can easily inspect the coefficients of the generated model. The returned map has a `:coefs` key that maps to a vector containing the coefficients of the model. By convention, the error term is also included in this vector, simply as another coefficient:

```
user> (:coefs samp-linear-model)
[-4.1707801647266045 0.39139682427040384]
```

Now we've defined a linear model over our data. It's obvious that not all the points will be on a line that is plotted to represent the formulated model. Each data point has some deviation from the linear model's plot over the y axis, and this deviation can be either positive or negative. To represent the overall deviation of the model from the given data, we use the *residual sum of squares, mean-squared error*, and *root mean-squared error* functions. The values of these three functions represent a scalar measure of the amount of error in the formulated model.

The difference between the terms *error* and *residual* is that an error is a measure of the amount by which an observed value differs from its expected value, while a residual is an estimate of the unobservable statistical error, which is simply not modeled or understood by the statistical model that we are using. We can say that, in a set of observed values, the difference between an observed value and the mean of all values is a residual. The number of residuals in a formulated model must be equal to the number of observed values of the dependent variable in the sample data.

We can use the `:residuals` keyword to fetch the residuals from the linear model generated by the `linear-model` function, as shown in the following code:

```
user> (:residuals samp-linear-model)
[-0.6873445559690581 0.8253111334125092 -0.6483716931997257
0.2383108767994172 -0.10342541689331242 0.9169220471357067 -
0.01701880172457293 -0.22923670489146497 -0.08581465024744239 -
0.20933223442208365]
```

The **sum of squared errors of prediction** (**SSE**) is simply the sum of errors in a formulated model. Note that in the following equation, the sign of the error term $\hat{Y}_i - Y_i$ isn't significant since we square this difference value; thus, it will always produce a positive value. The SSE is also termed as the **residual sum of squares** (**RSS**).

$$SSE(\hat{Y}) = \sum_{i=1}^{N}\left(\hat{Y}_i - Y_i\right)^2$$

The `linear-model` function also calculates the SSE of the formulated model, and this value can be retrieved using the `:sse` keyword; this is illustrated in the following lines of code:

```
user> (:sse samp-linear-model)
2.5862250345284887
```

The **mean-squared error** (MSE) measures the average magnitude of errors in a formulated model without considering the direction of the errors. We can calculate this value by squaring the differences of all the given values of the dependent variable and their corresponding predicted values on the formulated linear model, and calculating the mean of these squared errors. The MSE is also termed as the **mean-squared prediction error** of a model. If the MSE of a formulated model is zero, then we can say that the model fits the given data perfectly. Of course, this is practically impossible for real data, although we could find a set of values that produce an MSE of zero in theory.

For a given set of N values of the dependent variable Y_i and an estimated set of values $\hat{Y}_i$ calculated from a formulated model, we can formally represent the MSE function of the formulated model $\hat{Y}$ as follows:

$$MSE(\hat{Y}) = \frac{1}{N} \sum_{i=1}^{N} \left(\hat{Y}_i - Y_i \right)^2$$

The **root mean-squared error** (RMSE) or **root-mean squared deviation** is simply the square root of the MSE and is often used to measure the deviation of a formulated linear model. The RMSE is partial to larger errors, and is hence scale-dependent. This means that the RMSE is particularly useful when large errors are undesirable.

We can formally define the RMSE of a formulated model as follows:

$$RMSE(\hat{Y}) = \sqrt{MSE(\hat{Y})} = \sqrt{\frac{1}{N} \sum_{i=1}^{N} \left(\hat{Y}_i - Y_i \right)^2}$$

Another measure of the accuracy of a formulated linear model is the **coefficient of determination**, which is written as R^2. The coefficient of determination indicates how well the formulated model fits the given sample data, and is defined as follows. This coefficient is defined in terms of the mean of observed values in the sample data $\hat{Y}$, the SSE, and the total sum of errors SS_{tot}.

$$R^2 = 1 - \frac{SS_{res}}{SS_{tot}},$$

$$\text{where } SS_{res} = SSE(\hat{Y}) = \sum_i (Y_i - \hat{Y}_i)^2$$

$$SS_{tot} = \sum_i (Y_i - \hat{Y}_i)^2$$

$$\hat{Y} = \frac{1}{N} \sum_{i=0}^{N} Y_i$$

We can retrieve the calculated value of R^2 from the model generated by the `linear-model` function by using the `:r-square` keyword as follows:

```
user> (:r-square samp-linear-model)
0.8837893226172282
```

In order to formulate a model that best fits the sample data, we should strive to minimize the previously described values. For some given data, we can formulate several models and calculate the total error for each model. This calculated error can then be used to determine which formulated model is the best fit for the data, thus selecting the optimal linear model for the given data.

Based on the MSE of a formulated model, the model is said to have a **cost function**. The problem of fitting a linear model over some data is equivalent to the problem of minimizing the cost function of a formulated linear model. The cost function, which is represented as $J(\beta, \varepsilon)$, can be simply thought of as a function of the parameters of a formulated model. Generally, this cost function translates to the MSE of a model. Since the RMSE varies with the formulated parameters of the model, the following cost function of the model is a function of these parameters:

$$J(\beta, \varepsilon) = \frac{1}{2N} \sum_{i=0}^{N} (\hat{Y}_i - Y_i)^2, \text{ where } \hat{Y}_i = \beta X_i + \varepsilon$$

This brings us to the following formal definition of the problem of fitting a linear regression model over some data for the estimated effects β and ε of a linear model:

To find the parameters β and $\in$ of an optimal linear regression model, where $J(\beta, \in)$ is the cost function of the model,

$$\left(\hat{\beta}, \hat{\in}\right) = \underset{\beta, \in}{\arg\min} \| J(\beta, \in) \|$$

This definition states that we can estimate a linear model, represented by the parameters β and ε, by determining the values of these parameters, for which the cost function $J(\beta, \varepsilon)$ takes on the least possible value, ideally zero.

In the preceding equation, the $\| \cdots \|$ expression represents the standard norm N-dimensional Euclidian space of the cost function. By the term *norm*, we mean a function that has only positive values in the N-dimensional space.

Let's visualize how the Euclidian space of the cost function of a formulated model varies with respect to the parameters of the model. For this, let's assume that the ε parameter that represents the constant error is zero. A plot of the cost function $J(\beta)$ of the linear model over the parameter β will ideally appear as a parabolic curve, similar to the following plot:

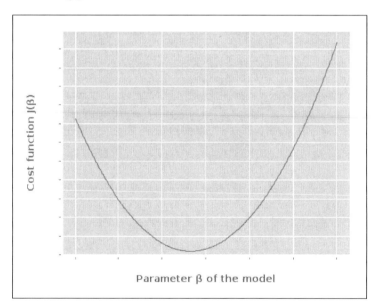

For a single parameter, β, we can plot the preceding chart, which has two dimensions. Similarly, for two parameters, β and ε, of the formulated model, a plot of three dimensions is produced. This plot appears bowl-shaped or having a convex surface, as illustrated in the following diagram. Also, we can generalize this for N parameters of the formulated model and produce a plot of $N+1$ dimensions.

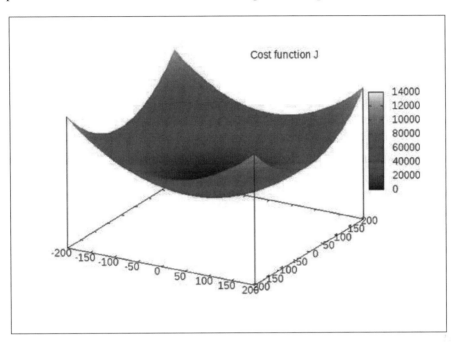

Understanding gradient descent

The gradient descent algorithm is one of the simplest, although not the most efficient techniques to formulate a linear model that has the least possible value for the cost function or error of the model. This algorithm essentially finds the local minimum of the cost function for a formulated linear model.

As we previously described, a three-dimensional plot of the cost function for a single-variable linear regression model would appear as a convex or bowl-shaped surface with a *global minimum*. By minimum, we mean that the cost function has the least possible value at this point on the surface of the plot. The gradient descent algorithm essentially starts from any point on the surface and performs a sequence of steps to approach the local minimum of the surface.

This process can be imagined as dropping a ball into a valley or between two adjacent hills, as a result of which the ball slowly rolls towards the point that has the least elevation above sea level. The algorithm is repeated until the value of the apparent cost function from the current point on the surface converges to zero, which figuratively means that the ball rolling down the hill comes to a stop, as we described earlier.

Of course, gradient descent may not really work if there are multiple local minimums on the surface of the plot. However, for an appropriately scaled single-variable linear regression model, the surface of the plot always has a single global minimum, as we illustrated earlier. Thus, we can still use the gradient descent algorithm in such situations to find the global minimum of the surface of the plot.

The gist of this algorithm is that we start from some point on the surface and then take several steps towards the lowest point. We can formally represent this with the following equality:

$$\text{Repeat } \beta_{n+1} = \beta_n - \gamma \, \nabla \, J \text{ until } \beta_{n+1} - \beta_n \approx 0,$$

$$\text{where } \nabla \, J = \frac{\partial}{\partial \beta_i} J, \text{and } \beta_i \in \{\text{the parameters of the model}\}$$

Here, we start from the point represented by β_n on the plot of the cost function J, and incrementally subtract the product of the first-order partial derivative of the cost function ∇J, which is derived with respect to the parameters of the formulated model. This means that we slowly step downwards on the surface towards the local minimum, until we cannot find a lower point on the surface. The term γ determines how large our steps towards the local minimum are, and is called the *step* of the gradient descent algorithm. We repeat this iteration until the difference between β_{n+1} and β_n converges to zero, or at least reduces to a threshold value close to zero.

The process of stepping down towards the local minimum of the surface of the cost functions plot is illustrated in the following diagram:

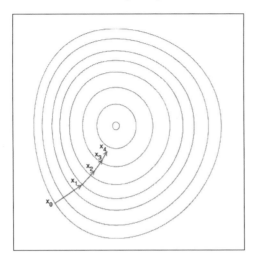

The preceding illustration is a contour diagram of the surface of the plot, in which the circular lines connect the points with an equal height. We start from the point x_0 and perform a single iteration of the gradient descent algorithm to step down the surface to point x_1. We repeat this process until we reach the local minimum of the surface with respect to the initial starting point x_0. Note that, through each iteration, the size of the step reduces since the slope of a tangent to this surface also tends to zero as we approach the local minimum.

For a single-variable linear regression model with an error constant ε that is equal to zero, we can simplify the partial derivative component ∇J of the gradient descent algorithm. When there is only one parameter of the model, β, the first order partial derivate is simply the slope of a tangent at that point on the surface of the plot. Thus, we calculate the slope of this tangent and take a step in the direction of this slope such that we arrive at a point of elevation above the y axis. This is shown in the following formula:

$$\text{When } \varepsilon \text{ is } 0, \ \nabla J = \frac{\partial}{\partial \beta} J(\beta)$$

We can implement this simplified version of the gradient descent algorithm as follows:

```
(def gradient-descent-precision 0.001)

(defn gradient-descent
  "Find the local minimum of the cost function's plot"
  [F' x-start step]
  (loop [x-old x-start]
    (let [x-new (- x-old
                   (* step (F' x-old)))
          dx (- x-new x-old)]
      (if (< dx gradient-descent-precision)
        x-new
        (recur x-new)))))
```

In the preceding function, we begin from the point x-start and recursively apply the gradient descent algorithm until the value x-new converges. Note that this process is implemented as a tail recursive function using the loop form.

Using partial differentiation, we can formally express how both the parameters β and ε can be calculated using the gradient descent algorithm as follows:

$$\text{Given } J(\beta, \in) = \frac{1}{2N} \sum_{i=0}^{N} (\hat{Y}_i - Y_i)^2 \text{ and } \hat{Y}_i = \beta X_i + \in,$$

$$\beta_{n+1} = \beta_n - Y \frac{\partial}{\partial \beta} J(\beta, \in)$$

$$= \beta_n - \frac{Y}{N} \sum_{i=0}^{N} (\hat{Y}_i - Y_i) X_i$$

$$\in_{n+1} = \in_n - Y \frac{\partial}{\partial \in} J(\beta, \in)$$

$$= \in_n - \frac{Y}{N} \sum_{i=0}^{N} (\hat{Y}_i - Y_i)$$

Repeat until $(\beta_{n+1} - \beta_n) \approx 0$ and $(\in_{n+1} - \in_n) \approx 0$

Understanding multivariable linear regression

A multivariable linear regression model can have multiple variables or features, as opposed to the linear regression model with a single variable that we previously studied. Interestingly, the definition of a linear model with a single variable can itself be extended via matrices to be applied to multiple variables.

We can extend our previous example for predicting the probability of rainfall on a particular day to a model with multiple variables by including more independent variables, such as the minimum and maximum temperatures, in the sample data. Thus, the training data for a multivariable linear regression model will look similar to the following illustration:

Amount of Rainfall	Humidity	Min. Temp	Max. Temp
y_1	$x_{1,1}$	$x_{1,2}$	$x_{1,3}$
y_2	$x_{2,1}$	$x_{2,2}$	$x_{2,3}$
$\vdots$	$\vdots$	$\vdots$	$\vdots$
y_N	$x_{N,1}$	$x_{N,2}$	$x_{N,3}$

For a multivariable linear regression model, the training data is defined by two matrices, X and Y. Here, X is an $N \times P$ matrix, where P is the number of independent variables in the model. The matrix Y is a vector of length N, just like in a linear model with a single variable. This model is illustrated as follows:

$$Y = \begin{bmatrix} y_1 \\ y_2 \\ \vdots \\ y_N \end{bmatrix}, X = \begin{bmatrix} x_{1,1} & x_{1,2} & \cdots & x_{1,P} \\ x_{2,1} & x_{2,2} & \cdots & x_{2,P} \\ \vdots & \vdots & \ddots & \vdots \\ x_{N,1} & x_{N,2} & \cdots & x_{N,P} \end{bmatrix}$$

For the following example of multivariable linear regression in Clojure, we will not generate the sample data through code but use the sample data from the Incanter library. We can fetch any dataset using the Incanter library's `get-dataset` function.

For the upcoming example, the `sel`, `to-matrix`, and `get-dataset` functions from the Incanter library can be imported into our namespace as follows:

```
(ns my-namespace
  (:use [incanter.datasets :only [get-dataset]]
        [incanter.core :only [sel to-matrix]]))
```

We can fetch the **Iris** dataset by calling the `get-dataset` function with the `:iris` keyword argument; this is shown as follows:

```
(def iris
  (to-matrix (get-dataset :iris)))

(def X (sel iris :cols (range 1 5)))
(def Y (sel iris :cols 0))
```

We first define the variable `iris` as a matrix using the `to-matrix` and `get-dataset` functions, and then define two matrices `X` and `Y`. Here, `Y` is actually a vector of 150 values, or a matrix of size 150×1, while `X` is a matrix of size 150×4. Hence, `X` can be used to represent the values of four independent variables, and `Y` represents the values of the dependent variable. Note that the `sel` function is used to select a set of columns from the `iris` matrix. In fact, we could select many more such columns from the `iris` data matrix, but we will use only four in the following example for the sake of simplicity.

The dataset that we used in the previous code example is the *Iris* dataset, which is available in the Incanter library. This dataset has quite a bit of historical significance, as it was used by Sir Ronald Fisher to first develop the **linear discriminant analysis** (**LDA**) method for classification (for more information, refer to "The Species Problem in Iris"). This dataset contains 50 samples of three distinct species of the Iris plant, namely *Setosa*, *Versicolor*, and *Virginica*. Four features of the flowers of these species are measured in each sample, namely the petal width, petal length, sepal width, and sepal length. Note that we will encounter this dataset several times over the course of this book.

Interestingly, the `linear-model` function accepts a matrix with multiple columns, so we can use this function to fit a linear regression model over both single variable and multivariable data as follows:

```
(def iris-linear-model
  (linear-model Y X))
```

```
(defn plot-iris-linear-model []
  (let [x (range -100 100)
        y (:fitted iris-linear-model)]
    (view (xy-plot x y :x-label "X" :y-label "Y"))))
```

```
(plot-iris-linear-model)
```

In the preceding code example, we plot the linear model using the xy-plot function while providing optional parameters to specify the labels of the axes in the defined plot. Also, we specify the range of the x axis by generating a vector using the range function. The plot-iris-linear-model function generates the following plot:

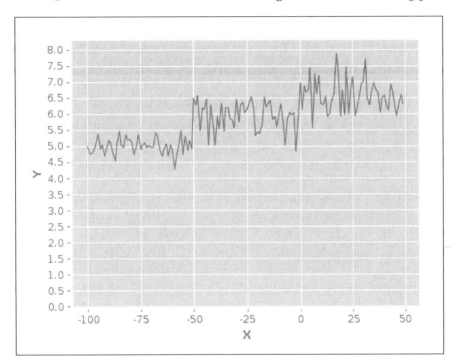

Although the curve in the plot produced from the previous example doesn't appear to have any definitive shape, we can still use this generated model to estimate or predict the value of the dependent variable by supplying values for the independent variables to the formulated model. In order to do this, we must first define the relationship between the dependent and independent variables of a linear regression model with multiple features.

A linear regression model of P independent variables produces $P+1$ regression coefficients, since we include the error constant along with the other coefficients of the model and also define an extra variable x_0, which is always 1.

The `linear-model` function agrees with the proposition that the number of coefficients P in the formulated model is always one more than the total number of independent variables in the sample data N; this is shown in the following code:

```
user> (= (count (:coefs iris-linear-model))
         (+ 1 (column-count X)))
true
```

We formally express the relationship between a multivariable regression model's dependent and independent variables as follows:

$$Y = \beta_0 x_0 + \beta_1 x_1 + \ldots + \beta_p x_p, \text{ where } x_0 = 1$$

Since the variable x_0 is always 1 in the preceding equation, the value β_0 is analogous to the error constant ε from the definition of a linear model with a single variable.

We can define a single vector to represent all the coefficients of the previous equation as β. This vector is termed as the **parameter vector** of the formulated regression model. Also, the independent variables of the model can be represented by a vector. Thus, we can define the regression variable Y as the product of the transpose of the parameter vector and the vector of independent variables of the model:

$$Y = X^T \beta,$$

$$\text{where } x_0 = 1, X = \begin{bmatrix} x_0 \\ x_1 \\ \vdots \\ x_p \end{bmatrix} \text{ and } \beta = \begin{bmatrix} \beta_0 \\ \beta_1 \\ \vdots \\ \beta_p \end{bmatrix}$$

Polynomial functions can also be reduced to the standard form by substituting a single variable for every higher-order variable in the polynomial equation. For example, consider the following polynomial equation:

$$y = \beta_0 + \beta_1 t + \beta_2 t^2$$

We can substitute the variables (X_1, X_2) for (t, t^2) to reduce the equation to the standard form of a multivariable linear regression model.

This brings us to the following formal definition of the cost function for a linear model with multiple variables, which is simply an extension of the definition of the cost function for a linear model with a single variable:

$$J(\beta_0, \beta_1, \cdots \beta_P) = \frac{1}{2N} \sum_{i=0}^{N} (\hat{Y_i} - Y_i)^2$$

$$\text{or } J(\beta) = \frac{1}{2N} \sum_{i=0}^{N} (\hat{Y_i} - Y_i)^2$$

Note that in the preceding definition, we can use the individual coefficients of the model interchangeably with the parameter vector β.

Analogous to our problem definition of fitting a model with a single variable over some given data, we can define the problem of formulating a multivariable linear model as the problem of minimizing the preceding cost function:

To find the parameter vector β of an optimal linear regression model,

where $J(\beta)$ is the *cost function* of the model,

$$\hat{\beta} = \arg \min_{\beta} \| J(\beta) \|$$

Gradient descent with multiple variables

We can apply the gradient descent algorithm to find the local minimum of a model with multiple variables. Of course, since we have multiple coefficients in the model, we have to apply the algorithm for all these coefficients as opposed to just two coefficients in a regression model with a single variable.

The gradient descent algorithm can thus be used to find the values of all the coefficients in the parameter vector β of a multivariable linear regression model, and is formally defined as follows:

Repeat $\beta_{n+1} = \beta_n - Y \nabla J$ until $\beta_{n+1} - \beta_n \approx 0$,

where $\nabla J = \frac{\partial}{\partial \beta_i} J$, and $\beta_i \in \{\text{the parameters of the model}\}$

$$\beta_{0,n+1} = \beta_{0,n} - \frac{Y}{N} \sum_{i=0}^{N} (\hat{Y_i} - Y_i) X_{i,0}$$

$$\beta_{1,n+1} = \beta_{1,n} - \frac{Y}{N} \sum_{i=0}^{N} (\hat{Y_i} - Y_i) X_{i,1}$$

$$\cdots$$

$$\beta_{k,n+1} = \beta_{k,n} - \frac{Y}{N} \sum_{i=0}^{N} (\hat{Y_i} - Y_i) X_{i,k}$$

In the preceding definition, the term $X_{i,j}$ simply refers to the sample values for the jth independent variable in the formulated model. Also, the variable $X_{i,0}$ is always *1*. Thus, this definition can be applied to just the two coefficients that correspond to our previous definition of the gradient descent algorithm for a linear regression model with a single variable.

As we've seen earlier, the gradient descent algorithm can be applied to a linear regression model with both single and multivariables. For some models, however, the gradient descent algorithm can actually take a lot of iterations, or rather time, to converge the estimated values of the model's coefficients. Sometimes, the algorithm can also diverge, and thus we will be unable to calculate the model's coefficients in such circumstances. Let's examine some of the factors that affect the behavior and performance of this algorithm:

- All the features of the sample data must be scaled with respect to each other. By scaling, we mean that all the values for the independent variables in the sample data take on a similar range of values. Ideally, all independent variables must have observed values between *-1* and *1*. This can be formally expressed as follows:

$$-1 \leq X_i \leq 1$$

- We can normalize the observed values for the independent variables about the mean of these values. We can further normalize this data by using the standard deviation of the observed values. In summary, we substitute the values with those produced by subtracting the mean of these values, $\hat{X}$, and dividing the resulting expression by the standard deviation σ_x. This is shown in the following formula:

$$X_i = \frac{X_i - \hat{X}}{\sigma_x}$$

- The stepping or learning rate, γ, is another important factor that determines how fast the algorithm converges towards the values of the parameters of the formulated model. Ideally, the stepping rate should be selected so that the differences between the old and new iterated values of the parameters of the model have an optimal amount of change in every iteration. On one hand, if this value is too large, the algorithm could even produce diverging values for the parameters of the model after each iteration. Thus, the algorithm will never find a global minimum in this case. On the other hand, a small value for this rate could result in slowing down the algorithm through an unnecessarily large number of iterations.

Understanding Ordinary Least Squares

Another technique to estimate the parameter vector of a linear regression model is the **Ordinary Least Squares (OLS)** method. The OLS method essentially works by minimizing the sum of squared errors in a linear regression model.

The sum of squared errors of prediction, or SSE, of a linear regression model can be defined in terms of the model's actual and expected values as follows:

$$SSE(\hat{Y}) = \sum_{i=1}^{N} \left(\hat{Y}_i - Y_i \right)^2 = \sum_{i=1}^{N} \left(Y_i - \hat{Y}_i \right)^2$$

where $\hat{Y} = X\hat{\beta}$

The preceding definition of the SSE can be factorized using matrix products as follows:

$$SSE(\hat{Y}) = \left(Y - X\beta \right)^2$$
$$= \left(Y - X\beta \right)^T \left(Y - X\beta \right)$$
$$= Y^T Y - \beta^T X^T Y - Y^T X\beta + \beta^T X^T X\beta$$

We can solve the preceding equation for the estimated parameter vector β by using the definition of a global minimum. Since this equation is a form of quadratic equation and the term $SSE(\hat{Y})$ is always greater than zero, the global minimum of the surface of the cost function can be defined as the point at which the rate of change of the slope of a tangent to the surface at that point is zero. Also, the plot is a function of the parameters of the linear model, and so the equation of the surface plot should be differentiated by the estimated parameter vector β. We can thus solve this equation for the optimal parameter vector β of the formulated model as follows:

At the global minimum, $\dfrac{\partial}{\partial \beta} \left(SSE(\hat{Y}) \right) = 0$

Solving for β where $\beta = \hat{\beta}$,

$$\frac{\partial}{\partial \beta} (Y^T Y - \beta^T X^T Y - Y^T X\beta + \beta^T X^T X\beta) = 0, \text{ at } \beta = \hat{\beta}$$

$$\Rightarrow -2X^T Y + 2X^T X\hat{\beta} = 0$$

$$\Rightarrow (X^T X)^{-1} X^T Y = \hat{\beta}$$

The last equation in the preceding derivation gives us the definition of the optimal parameter vector β, which is formally expressed as follows:

$$\hat{\beta} = (X^T X)^{-1} X^T Y$$

We can implement the preceding definition of the parameter vector through the OLS method using the core.matrix library's `transpose` and `inverse` functions and the Incanter library's `bind-columns` function:

```
(defn linear-model-ols
  "Estimates the coefficients of a multi-var linear
  regression model using Ordinary Least Squares (OLS) method"
  [MX MY]
  (let [X (bind-columns (repeat (row-count MX) 1) MX)
        Xt (cl/matrix (transpose X))
        Xt-X (cl/* Xt X)]
    (cl/* (inverse Xt-X) Xt MY)))

(def ols-linear-model
  (linear-model-ols X Y))

(def ols-linear-model-coefs
  (cl/as-vec ols-linear-model))
```

Here, we first add a column in which each element is 1, as the first column of the matrix MX uses the `bind-columns` function. The extra column that we add represents the independent variable x_0, whose value is always 1. We then use the `transpose` and `inverse` functions to calculate the estimated coefficients of the linear regression model for the data in matrices MX and MY.

For the current example, the `bind-columns` function from the Incanter library can be imported into our namespace as follows:

```
(ns my-namespace
  (:use [incanter.core :only [bind-columns]]))
```

The previously defined function can be applied to the matrices that we have previously defined (*X* and *Y*) as follows:

```
(def ols-linear-model
  (linear-model-ols X Y))

(def ols-linear-model-coefs
  (cl/as-vec ols-linear-model))
```

In the preceding code, `ols-linear-model-coefs` is simply the variable and `ols-linear-model` is a matrix with a single column, which is represented as a vector. We perform this conversion using the `as-vec` function from the clatrix library.

We can actually verify that the coefficients estimated by the `ols-linear-model` function are practically equal to the ones generated by the Incanter library's `linear-model` function, which is illustrated as follows:

```
user> (cl/as-vec (ols-linear-model X Y))
[1.851198344985435 0.6252788163253274 0.7429244752213087 -
0.4044785456588674 -0.22635635488532463]
user> (:coefs iris-linear-model)
[1.851198344985515 0.6252788163253129 0.7429244752213329 -
0.40447854565877606 -0.22635635488543926]
user> (every? #(< % 0.0001)
                    (map -
                        ols-linear-model-coefs
                        (:coefs iris-linear-model)))
true
```

In the last expression in the preceding code example, we find the difference between the coefficients produced by the `ols-linear-model` function, the difference produced by the `linear-model` function, and check whether each of these differences is less than `0.0001`.

Using linear regression for prediction

Once we've determined the coefficients of a linear regression model, we can use these coefficients to predict the value of the dependent variable of the model. The predicted value is defined by the linear regression model as the sum of the products of each coefficient and the value of its corresponding independent variable.

We can easily define the following generic function, which when supplied with the coefficients and values of independent variables, predicts the value of the dependent variable for a given formulated linear regression model:

```
(defn predict [coefs X]
  {:pre [(= (count coefs)
            (+ 1 (count X)))]}
  (let [X-with-1 (conj X 1)
        products (map * coefs X-with-1)]
    (reduce + products)))
```

In the preceding function, we use a precondition to assert the number of coefficients and the values of independent variables. This function expects that the number of values of the independent variables is one less than the number of coefficients of the model, as we add an extra parameter to represent an independent variable whose value is always 1. The function then calculates the product of the corresponding coefficients and the values of the independent variables using the map function, and then calculates the sum of these product terms using the reduce function.

Understanding regularization

Linear regression estimates some given training data using a linear equation; this solution may not always be the best fit for the given data. Of course, it depends largely on the problem that we are trying to model. **Regularization** is a commonly used technique to provide a better fit for the data. Generally, a given model is regularized by reducing the effect of some of the independent variables of the model. Alternatively, we could model it as a higher-order polynomial. Regularization isn't exclusive to linear regression, and most machine learning algorithms use some form of regularization in order to create a more accurate model from the given training data.

A model is said to be **underfit** or **high bias** when it doesn't estimate the dependent variable to a value that is close to the observed values of the dependent variable in the training data. On the other hand, a model can also be called **overfit**, or said to have **high variance**, when the estimated model fits the data perfectly, but isn't general enough to be useful for prediction. Overfit models often describe random errors or noise in the training data instead of the underlying relationship between the dependent and independent variables of the model. The best fit regression model generally lies in between the models created by underfitting and overfitting models and can be obtained through the process of regularization.

A commonly used method for the regularization of an underfit or overfit model is **Tikhnov regularization**. In statistics, this method is also called **ridge regression**. We can describe the general form of Tikhnov regularization as follows:

$$Ax = b$$

Suppose A represents a mapping from the vector of independent variables x to the dependent variable y. The value A is analogous to the parameter vector of a regression model. The relationship between the vector x and the observed values of the dependent variable, written as b, can be expressed as follows.

An underfit model has a significant error, or rather deviation, with respect to the actual data. We should strive to minimize this error. This can be formally expressed as follows and is based on the sum of residues of the estimated model:

$$\min \| Ax - b \|^2$$

Tikhnov regularization adds a penalized least squares term to the preceding equation to prevent overfitting and is formally defined as follows:

$$\min \left[\| Ax - b \|^2 + \| L_\mu x \|^2 \right]$$

The term L_μ in the preceding equation is called the regularization matrix. In the simplest form of Tikhnov regularization, this matrix takes the value $L_\mu = \mu \times I_N$, where μ is a constant. Although applying this equation to a regression model is beyond the scope of this book, we can use Tikhnov regularization to produce a linear regression model with the following cost function:

$$J(\beta) = \frac{1}{2N} \left[\sum_{i=0}^{N} \left(\hat{Y}_i - Y_i \right)^2 + \lambda \sum_{j=0}^{N} \beta_j^2 \right]$$

In the preceding equation, the term λ is called the regularization parameter of the model. This value must be chosen appropriately as larger values for this parameter could produce an underfit model.

Using the previously defined cost function, we can apply a gradient descent to determine the parameter vector as follows:

$$\beta_{j,n+1} = \beta_{j,n} - \frac{\gamma}{N} \left[\sum_{i=0}^{N} \left(\hat{Y}_i - Y_i \right) X_{i,j} + \lambda \beta_{j,n} \right]$$

We can also apply regularization to the OLS method of determining the parameter vector as follows:

$$\hat{\beta} = \left(X^T X + \lambda L \right)^{-1} X^T Y$$

In the preceding equation, L is called the smoothing matrix, and can take on the following forms. Note that we've used the latter form of the definition of L in *Chapter 1, Working with Matrices*.

$$L = \begin{bmatrix} 0 & 0 & 0 & \cdots & 0 \\ 0 & 1 & 0 & \cdots & 0 \\ & & \ddots & & \\ 0 & \cdots & 0 & 0 & 1 \end{bmatrix} \text{ or } \begin{bmatrix} -1 & 2 & -1 & 0 & \cdots & 0 & 0 \\ 0 & -1 & 2 & -1 & \cdots & 0 & 0 \\ & & & \ddots & & & \\ 0 & 0 & 0 & 0 & \cdots & 2 & -1 \end{bmatrix}$$

Interestingly, when the regularization parameter λ in the preceding equation is 0, the regularized solution reduces to the original solution using the OLS method.

Summary

In this chapter, we've studied linear regression and a couple of algorithms that can be used to formulate an optimal linear regression model from some sample data. The following are some of the other points that we covered:

- We discussed linear regression with single and multiple variables
- We implemented the gradient descent algorithm to formulate a linear regression model with one variable
- We implemented the **Ordinary Least Squares (OLS)** method to find the coefficients of an optimal linear regression model
- We introduced regularization and how it could be applied to linear regression

In the following chapter, we will study a different area of machine learning, that is, classification. Classification is also a form of regression and is used to categorize data into different classes or groups.

3
Categorizing Data

In this chapter, we will explore **classification**, which is yet another interesting problem in supervised learning. We will examine a handful of techniques for classifying data and also study how we can leverage these techniques in Clojure.

Classification can be defined as the problem of identifying the category or class of the observed data based on some empirical training data. The training data will have the values of the observable features or independent variables. It will also have a known category for these observed values. Classification is similar to regression in the sense that we predict a value based on another set of values. However, for classification, we are interested in the category of the observed values rather than predicting a value based on the given set of values. For example, if we train a linear regression model from a set of output values ranging from *0* to *5*, the trained classifier could predict the output value as *10* or *-1* for a set of input values. In classification, however, the predicted value of the output variable always belongs to a discrete set of values.

The independent variables of a classification model are also termed as the *explanatory variables* of the model, and the dependent variable is also called the *outcome*, *category*, or *class* of the observed values. The outcome of a classification model is always a discrete value, that is, a value from a predetermined set of values. This is one of the primary differences between classification and regression, as we predict a variable that can have a continuous range of values in regression modeling. Note that the terms "category" and "class" are used interchangeably in the context of classification.

Algorithms that implement classification techniques are called classifiers. A **classifier** can be formally defined as a function that maps a set of values to a category or class. Classification is still an active area of research in computer science, and there are several prominent classifier algorithms that are used in software today. There are several practical applications of classification, such as data mining, machine vision, speech and handwriting recognition, biological classification, and geostatistics.

Understanding the binary and multiclass classification

We will first study some theoretical aspects about data classification. As with other supervised machine learning techniques, the goal is to estimate a model or classifier from the sample data and use it to predict a given set of outcomes. Classification can be thought of as a way of determining a function that maps the features of the sample data to a specific class. The predicted class is selected from a given set of predetermined classes. Thus, similar to regression, the problem of classifying the observed values for the given independent variables is analogous to determining a best-fit function for the given training data.

In some cases, we might be interested in only a single class, that is, whether the observed values belong to a specific class. This form of classification is termed as **binary classification**, and the output variable of the model can have either the value *0* or *1*. Thus, we can say that $y \in \{0,1\}$, where y is the outcome or dependent variable of the classification model. The outcome is said to be negative when $y = 0$, and conversely, the outcome is termed positive when $y = 1$.

In this perspective, when some observed values for the independent variables of the model are provided, we must be able to determine the probability of a positive outcome. Thus, the estimated model of the given sample data has the probability $y = 1$, and can be expressed as follows:

$$\hat{Y} = P(y = 1 \mid \hat{\beta}, x_1, x_2, \dots x_n)$$

$$Thus, 0 \leq \hat{Y} \leq 1$$

In the preceding equation, the parameters $x_1, x_2, \dots x_n$ represent the independent variables of the estimated classification model $\hat{Y}$, and the term $\hat{\beta}$ represents the estimated parameter vector of this model.

An example of this kind of classification is deciding whether a new e-mail is spam or not, depending on the sender or the content within the e-mail. Another simple example of binary classification is determining the possibility of rainfall on a particular day depending on the observed humidity and the minimum and maximum temperatures on that day. The training data for this example might appear similar to the data in the following table:

Probability of Rainfall	Humidity	Min. Temp	Max. Temp
0	$X_{1,1}$	$X_{1,2}$	$X_{1,3}$
1	$X_{2,1}$	$X_{2,2}$	$X_{2,3}$
$\vdots$	$\vdots$	$\vdots$	$\vdots$
1	$X_{N,1}$	$X_{N,2}$	$X_{N,3}$

A mathematical function that we can use to model binary classification is the **sigmoid** or **logistic** function. If the outcome for the feature X has an estimated parameter vector β, we can define the estimated probability of the positive outcome Y (as a sigmoid function) as follows:

$$Y = \frac{1}{1 + e^{-\beta^T X}}$$

To visualize the preceding equation, we can simplify it by substituting Z as $Z = \beta^T X$ as follows:

$$Y = \frac{1}{1 + e^{-Z}}, \text{where } Z = \beta^T X$$

We could model the data using several other functions as well. However, the sample data for a binary classifier can be easily transformed such that it can be modeled using a sigmoid function. This modeling of a classification problem using the logistic function is called **logistic regression**. The simplified sigmoid function defined in the preceding equation produces the following plot:

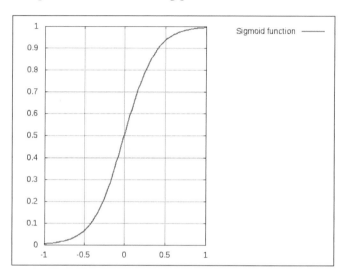

Note that if the term Z has a negative value, the plot appears reversed and is a mirror of the previous plot. We can visualize how the sigmoid function varies with respect to the term Z, through the following plot:

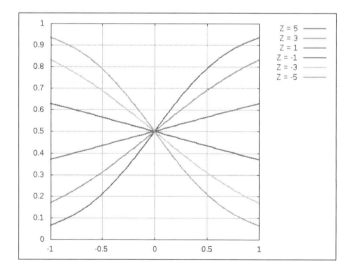

In the previous graph, the sigmoid function is shown for different values of the term Z; it ranges from -5 to 5. Note that for two dimensions, the term Z is a linear function of the independent variable x. Interestingly, for $Z = 1$ and $Z = -1$, the sigmoid function looks more or less like a straight line. This function reduces to a straight line when $Z = 0$ and can be represented by a constant y value (the equation $y = 0.5$ in this case).

We observe that the estimated outcome Y is always between 0 and 1, as it represents the probability of a positive outcome for the given observed values. Also, this range of the outcome Y is not affected by the sign of the term $\beta^T X$. Thus, in retrospect, the sigmoid function is an effective representation of binary classification.

To use the logistic function to estimate a classification model from the training data, we can define the cost function of a logistic regression model as follows:

$$J(\beta) = \frac{-1}{N} \sum_{i=0}^{N} \left[Y_i \log \hat{Y}_i + \left(1 - Y_i\right) \log \left(1 - \hat{Y}_i\right) \right]$$

The preceding equation essentially sums up the differences between the actual and predicted values of the output variables in our model, just like linear regression. However, as we are dealing with probability values between 0 and 1, we use the preceding log function to effectively measure the differences between the actual and predicted output values. Note that the term N denotes the number of samples in the training data. We can apply the gradient descent to this cost function to determine the local minimum or rather the predicted class of a set of observed values. This equation can be regularized to produce the following cost function:

$$J(\beta) = \frac{-1}{N} \sum_{i=0}^{N} \left[Y_i \log \hat{Y}_i + \left(1 - Y_i\right) \log \left(1 - \hat{Y}_i\right) \right] + \frac{\lambda}{2N} \sum_{j=0}^{N} \beta_j^2$$

Note that in this equation, the second summation term is added as a regularization term, like we discussed in *Chapter 2, Understanding Linear Regression*. This term basically prevents the *underfitting* and *overfitting* of the estimated model over the sample data. Note that the term λ is the regularization parameter and has to be appropriately selected depending on how accurate we want the model to be.

Multiclass classification, which is the other form of classification, predicts the outcome of the classification as a value from a specific set of predetermined values. Thus, the outcome is selected from k discrete values, that is, $y \in \{1, 2, ...k\}$. This model produces k probabilities for each possible class of the observed values. This brings us to the following formal definition of multiclass classification:

$$\hat{Y}_i = P\left(y = i \mid \hat{\beta}, x_1, x_2, ...x_n\right), \text{where } i \in \{1, 2, ...k\}$$

Thus, in multiclass classification, we predict k distinct values, in which each value indicates the probability of the input values belonging to a particular class. Interestingly, binary classification can be reasoned as a specialization of multiclass classification in which there are only two possible classes, that is, $k = 2$ and $y \in \{0,1\}$.

As a special case of multiclass classification, we can say that the class with the maximum probability is the outcome or simply, the predicted class of the given set of observed values. This specialization of multiclass classification is called **one-vs-all** classification. Here, a single class with the maximum (or minimum) probability of occurrence is determined from a given set of observed values instead of finding the probabilities of the occurrences of all the possible classes in our model. Thus, if we intend to predict a single class from a specific set of classes, we can define the outcome C as follows:

$$\text{Outcome } C = \arg\max_i \hat{Y}_i$$

$$\text{Outcome } C = \arg\max_i P(y = i \mid \hat{\beta}, x_1, x_2, ...x_n)$$

$$\text{where } i \in \{1, 2, ...k\}$$

For example, let's assume that we want to determine the classification model for a fish packing plant. In this scenario, the fish are separated into two distinct classes. Let's say that we can categorize the fish either as a sea bass or salmon. We can create some training data for our model by selecting a sufficiently large sample of fish and analyzing their distributions over some selected features. Let's say that we've identified two features to categorize the data, namely, the length of the fish and the lightness of its skin.

The distribution of the first feature, that is, the length of the fish, can be visualized as follows:

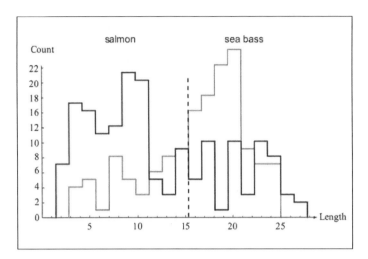

Similarly, the distribution of the lightness of the skin of the fish from the sample data can be visualized through the following plot:

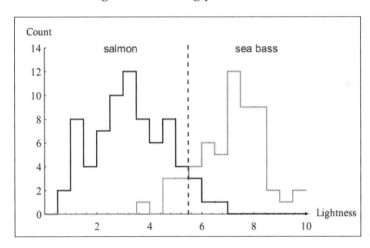

From the preceding graphs, we can say that only specifying the length of the fish is not enough information to determine its type. Thus, this feature has a smaller coefficient in the classification model. On the contrary, since the lightness of the skin of the fish plays a larger role in determining the type of the fish, this feature will have a larger coefficient in the parameter vector of the estimated classification model.

Once we have modeled a given classification problem, we can partition the training data into two (or more) sets. The surface in the vector space that partitions these two sets is called the **decision boundary** of the formulated classification model. All the points on one side of the decision boundary are part of one class, while the points on the other side of the decision boundary are part of the other class. An obvious corollary is that depending on the number of distinct classes, a given classification model can have several such decision boundaries.

We can now combine these two features to train our model, and this produces an estimated decision boundary between the two categories of fish. This boundary can be visualized over a scatter plot of the training data as follows:

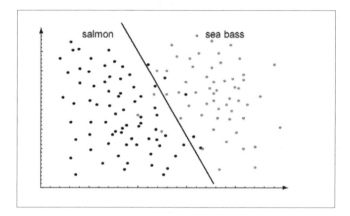

In the preceding plot, we approximate the classification model by using a straight line, and hence, we effectively model the classification as a linear function. We can alternatively model our data as a polynomial function, as it would produce a more accurate classification model. Such a model produces a decision boundary that can be visualized as follows:

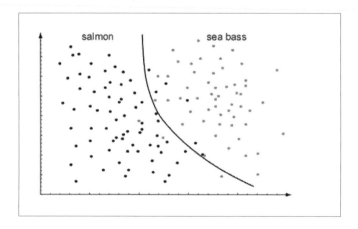

The decision boundary partitions the sample data into two dimensions as shown in the preceding graphs. The decision boundary will become more complex to visualize when the sample data has a higher number of features or dimensions. For example, for three features, the decision boundary will be a three-dimensional surface, as shown in the following plot. Note that the sample data points are not shown for the sake of clarity. Also, two of the plotted features are assumed to vary within the range [−10,10], and the third feature is assumed to vary within the range [−200, 200].

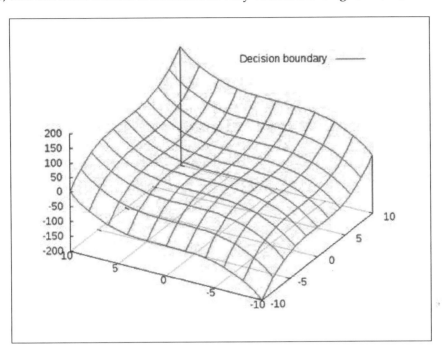

Understanding the Bayesian classification

We will now explore the Bayesian techniques that are used to classify data. A **Bayes** classifier is essentially a probabilistic classifier that is built using the Bayes' theorem of conditional probability. A model based on the Bayes classification assumes that the sample data has strongly independent features. By *independent*, we mean that every feature of the model can vary independent of the other features in the model. In other words, the features of the model are mutually exclusive. Thus, a Bayes classifier assumes that the presence or absence of a particular feature is completely independent of the presence or absence of the other features of the classification model.

The term $P(A)$ is used to represent the probability of occurrence of the condition or the feature A. Its value is always a fractional value within the range of *0* and *1*, both inclusive. It can also be represented as a percentage valve. For example, the probability *0.5* is also written as *50%* or *50 percent*. Let's assume that we want to find the probability of occurrence of a feature A or $P(A)$, from a given number of samples. Thus, a higher value of $P(A)$ indicates a higher chance of occurrence of the feature A. We can formally represent the probability $P(A)$ as follows:

$$P(A) = \frac{\text{number of samples with feature A}}{\text{total number of samples}}$$

If A and B are two conditions or features in our classification model, then we use the term $P(A \mid B)$ to represent the occurrence of A when B is known to have occurred. This value is called the **conditional probability** of A given B, and the term $P(A \mid B)$ is also read as the probability of A given B. In the term $P(A \mid B)$, B is also called the evidence of A. In conditional probability, the two events, A and B, may or may not be independent of each other. However, if A and B are indeed independent conditions, then the probability $P(A \mid B)$ is equal to the product of the probabilities of the separate occurrences of A and B. We can express this axiom as follows:

$$P(A \mid B) = P(A) \times P(B) \Rightarrow A \text{ and } B \text{ are mutually independent conditions}$$

Bayes' theorem describes a relation between the conditional probabilities, $P(A \mid B)$ and $P(B \mid A)$, and the probabilities, $P(A)$ and $P(B)$. It is formally expressed using the following equality:

$$P(A \mid B) = \frac{P(B \mid A) \times P(A)}{P(B)}$$

Of course, the probabilities, $P(A)$ and $P(B)$, must both be greater than *0* for the preceding relation to be true.

Let's revisit the classification example of the fish packaging plant that we described earlier. The problem is that we need to determine whether a fish is a sea bass or salmon depending on its physical features. We will now implement a solution to this problem using a Bayes classifier. Then, we will use Bayes' theorem to model our data.

Let's assume that each category of fish has three independent and distinct features, namely, the lightness of its skin and its length and width. Hence, our training data will look like that in the following table:

Class of fish	Length	Width	Lightness of skin
salmon	$X_{1,1}$	$X_{1,2}$	$X_{1,3}$
sea bass	$X_{2,1}$	$X_{2,2}$	$X_{2,3}$
$\vdots$	$\vdots$	$\vdots$	$\vdots$
salmon	$X_{N,1}$	$X_{N,2}$	$X_{N,3}$

For simplicity in implementation, let's use the Clojure symbols to represent these features. We need to first generate the following data:

```clojure
(defn make-sea-bass []
  ;; sea bass are mostly long and light in color
  #{:sea-bass
    (if (< (rand) 0.2) :fat :thin)
    (if (< (rand) 0.7) :long :short)
    (if (< (rand) 0.8) :light :dark)})

(defn make-salmon []
  ;; salmon are mostly fat and dark
  #{:salmon
    (if (< (rand) 0.8) :fat :thin)
    (if (< (rand) 0.5) :long :short)
    (if (< (rand) 0.3) :light :dark)})

(defn make-sample-fish []
  (if (< (rand) 0.3) (make-sea-bass) (make-salmon)))

(def fish-training-data
  (for [i (range 10000)] (make-sample-fish)))
```

Here, we define two functions, `make-sea-bass` and `make-salmon`, to create a set of symbols to represent the two categories of fish. We conveniently use the `:salmon` and `:sea-bass` keywords to represent these two categories. Similarly, we can also use Clojure keywords to enumerate the features of a fish. In this example, the lightness of skin is either `:light` or `:dark`, the length is either `:long` or `:short`, and the width is either `:fat` or `:thin`. Also, we define the `make-sample-fish` function to randomly create a fish that is represented by the set of features defined earlier.

Note that we define these two categories of fish such that the sea bass are mostly long and light in skin color, and the salmon are mostly fat and dark. Also, we generate more salmon than sea bass in the make-sample-fish function. We add this partiality in our data only to provide more illustrative results, and the reader is encouraged to experiment with a more realistic distribution of data. The *Iris* dataset, which is available in the Incanter library that we introduced in *Chapter 2, Understanding Linear Regression*, is an example of a real-world dataset that can be used to study classification.

Now, we will implement the following function to calculate the probability of a particular condition:

```
(defn probability
  "Calculates the probability of a specific category
   given some attributes, depending on the training data."
  [attribute & {:keys
                  [category prior-positive prior-negative data]
                :or {category nil
                     data fish-training-data}}]
  (let [by-category (if category
                        (filter category data)
                        data)
        positive (count (filter attribute by-category))
        negative (- (count by-category) positive)
        total (+ positive negative)]
    (/ positive negative)))
```

We essentially implement the basic definition of probability by the number of occurrences.

The probability function defined in the preceding code requires a single argument to represent the attribute or condition whose probability of occurrence we want to calculate. Also, the function accepts several optional arguments, such as the data to be used to calculate this value, which defaults to the fish-training-data sequence that we had defined earlier, and a category, which can be reasoned simply as another condition. The arguments, category and attribute, are in fact analogous to the conditions A and B in the $P(A \mid B)$ probability. The probability function determines the total positive occurrences of the condition by filtering the training data using the filter function. It then determines the number of negative occurrences by calculating the difference between the positive and total number of values represented by (count by-category), in the sample data. The function finally returns the ratio of the positive occurrences of the condition to the total number of occurrences in the given data.

Let's use the `probability` function to tell us a bit about our training data as follows:

```
user> (probability :dark :category :salmon)
1204/1733
user> (probability :dark :category :sea-bass)
621/3068
user> (probability :light :category :salmon)
529/1733
user> (probability :light :category :sea-bass)
2447/3068
```

As shown in the preceding code, the probability that a salmon is dark in appearance is high, or specifically, `1204/1733`. The probabilities of a sea bass being dark and a salmon being light are also low when compared to the probabilities of a sea bass being light and a salmon being dark.

Let's assume that our observed values for the features of a fish are that it is dark-skinned, long, and fat. Given these conditions, we need to classify the fish as either a sea bass or a salmon. In terms of probability, we need to determine the probability that a fish is a salmon or a sea bass given that the fish is dark, long, and fat. Formally, this probability is represented by the terms $P(\text{salmon} \mid \text{dark, long, fat})$ and $P(\text{sea-bass} \mid \text{dark, long, fat})$ for either category of fish. If we calculate these two probabilities, we can select the category with the highest of these two probabilities to determine the category of the fish.

Using Bayes' theorem, we define the terms, $P(\text{salmon} \mid \text{dark, long, fat})$ and $P(\text{sea-bass} \mid \text{dark, long, fat})$, as follows:

$$P(\text{salmon} \mid \text{dark, long, fat}) = \frac{P(\text{dark, long, fat} \mid \text{salmon}) \times P(\text{salmon})}{P(\text{dark, long, fat})}$$

$$P(\text{sea-bass} \mid \text{dark, long, fat}) = \frac{P(\text{dark, long, fat} \mid \text{sea-bass}) \times P(\text{sea-bass})}{P(\text{dark, long, fat})}$$

The terms, $P(\text{salmon} \mid \text{dark, long, fat})$ and $P(\text{dark, long, fat} \mid \text{salmon})$, might seem a bit confusing, but the difference between these two terms is the order of occurrence of the specified conditions. The term, $P(\text{salmon} \mid \text{dark, long, fat})$, represents the probability that a fish that is dark, long, and fat is a salmon, while the term, $P(\text{dark, long, fat} \mid \text{salmon})$, represents the probability that a salmon is a dark, long, and fat fish.

The $P(\text{dark, long, fat} \mid \text{salmon})$ probability can be calculated from the given training data as follows. As the three features of the fish are assumed to be mutually independent, the term, $P(\text{dark, long, fat} \mid \text{salmon})$, is simply the product of the probabilities of the occurrences of each individual feature. By mutually independent, we mean that the variance or distribution of these features does not depend on any of the other features of the classification model.

The term, $P(\text{dark, long, fat} \mid \text{salmon})$, is also called the **evidence** of the given category, which is the category "salmon" in this case. We can express the $P(\text{dark, long, fat} \mid \text{salmon})$ probability as the product of the probabilities of the independent features of the model; this is shown as follows:

$$P(\text{dark, long, fat} \mid \text{salmon}) =$$
$$P(\text{dark} \mid \text{salmon}) \times$$
$$P(\text{long} \mid \text{salmon}) \times$$
$$P(\text{fat} \mid \text{salmon})$$

Interestingly, the terms, $P(\text{dark} \mid \text{salmon})$, $P(\text{long} \mid \text{salmon})$, and $P(\text{fat} \mid \text{salmon})$, can be easily calculated from the training data and the `probability` function, which we had implemented earlier. Similarly, we can find the probability that a fish is a salmon or $P(\text{salmon})$. Thus, the only term that's not accounted for in the definition of $P(\text{salmon} \mid \text{dark, long, fat})$ is the term, $P(\text{dark, long, fat})$. We can actually avoid calculating this term altogether using a simple trick in probability.

Given that a fish is dark, long, and fat, it can either be a salmon or a sea bass. The two probabilities of occurrence of either category of fish are both complementary, that is, they both account for all the possible conditions that could occur in our model. In other words, these two probabilities both add up to a probability of *1*. Thus, we can formally express the term, $P(\text{dark, long, fat})$, as follows:

$$\text{Since } P(\text{salmon} \mid \text{dark, long, fat}) + P(\text{sea-bass} \mid \text{dark, long, fat}) = 1,$$
$$P(\text{dark, long, fat}) =$$
$$P(\text{dark, long, fat} \mid \text{salmon}) \times P(\text{salmon}) +$$
$$P(\text{dark, long, fat} \mid \text{sea-bass}) \times P(\text{sea-bass})$$

Both terms on the right-hand side of the preceding equality can be determined from the training data, which is similar to the terms, *P*(salmon), *P*(dark | salmon), and so on. Hence, we can calculate the *P*(salmon | dark, long, fat) probability directly from our training data. We express this probability through the following equality:

$$P(\text{salmon} \mid \text{dark, long, fat}) = \frac{P(\text{dark, long, fat} \mid \text{salmon}) \times P(\text{salmon})}{P(\text{dark, long, fat})}$$

$$\text{where } P(\text{dark, long, fat}) =$$

$$P(\text{dark, long, fat} \mid \text{salmon}) \times P(\text{salmon}) +$$

$$P(\text{dark, long, fat} \mid \text{sea-bass}) \times P(\text{sea-bass})$$

Now, let's implement the preceding equality using the training data and the `probability` function, which we defined earlier. Firstly, the evidence of a fish being a salmon, given that it's dark, long, and fat in appearance, can be expressed as follows:

```
(defn evidence-of-salmon [& attrs]
  (let [attr-probs (map #(probability % :category :salmon) attrs)
        class-and-attr-prob (conj attr-probs
                                  (probability :salmon))]
    (float (apply * class-and-attr-prob))))
```

To be explicit, we implement a function to calculate the probability of the term, *P*(dark, long, fat | salmon) × *P*(salmon), from the given training data. The equality of the terms, *P*(dark, long, fat | salmon), *P*(dark | salmon), *P*(long | salmon), and *P*(fat | salmon) will be used as a base for this implementation.

In the preceding code, we determine the terms, *P*(salmon) and *P*(i | salmon), for all the attributes or conditions of *i* by using the `probability` function. Then, we multiply all these terms using a composition of the `apply` and `*` functions. Since all the calculated probabilities are ratios returned by the `probability` function, we cast the final ratio to a floating-point value using the `float` function . We can try out this function in the REPL as follows:

```
user> (evidence-of-salmon :dark)
0.4816
user> (evidence-of-salmon :dark :long)
0.2396884
user> (evidence-of-salmon)
0.6932
```

As the REPL output indicates, 48.16 percent of all the fish in the training data are salmon with dark skin. Similarly, 23.96 percent of all the fish are dark and long salmon, and 69.32 percent of all the fish are salmon. The value returned by the `(evidence-of-salmon :dark :long)` call can be expressed as $P(dark, long \mid salmon)$, and similarly, $P(salmon)$ is returned by `(evidence-of-salmon)`.

Similarly, we can define the `evidence-of-sea-bass` function that determines the evidence of occurrence of a sea bass given some observed features of the fish. As we are dealing with only two categories, $P(salmon) + P(sea\text{-}bass) = 1$, we can easily verify this equality in the REPL. Interestingly, a small error is observed, but this error is not related to the training data. This small error is, in fact, a floating-point rounding error, which arises due to the limitations of floating-point numbers. In practice, we can avoid this using the decimal or `BigDecimal` (from `java.lang`) data types, instead of floating-point numbers. We can verify this using the `evidence-of-sea-bass` and `evidence-of-salmon` functions in the REPL as follows:

```
user> (+ (evidence-of-sea-bass) (evidence-of-salmon))
1.0000000298023224
```

We can generalize the `evidence-of-salmon` and `evidence-of-sea-bass` functions such that we are able to determine the probability of any category with some observed features; this is shown in the following code:

```
(defn evidence-of-category-with-attrs
  [category & attrs]
  (let [attr-probs (map #(probability % :category category) attrs)
        class-and-attr-prob (conj attr-probs
                                  (probability category))]
    (float (apply * class-and-attr-prob))))
```

The function defined in the preceding code returns values that agree with those returned by the following `evidence-of-salmon` and `evidence-of-sea-bass` functions:

```
user> (evidence-of-salmon :dark :fat)
0.38502988
user> (evidence-of-category-with-attrs :salmon :dark :fat)
0.38502988
```

Using the `evidence-of-salmon` and `evidence-of-sea-bass` functions, we can calculate the probability in terms of `probability-dark-long-fat-is-salmon` as follows:

```
(def probability-dark-long-fat-is-salmon
  (let [attrs [:dark :long :fat]
        sea-bass? (apply evidence-of-sea-bass attrs)
        salmon? (apply evidence-of-salmon attrs)]
    (/ salmon?
       (+ sea-bass? salmon?)))))
```

We can inspect the `probability-dark-long-fat-is-salmon` value in the REPL as follows:

```
user> probability-dark-long-fat-is-salmon
0.957091799207812
```

The `probability-dark-long-fat-is-salmon` value indicates that a fish that is dark, long, and fat and has a 95.7 percent probability of being a salmon.

Using the preceding definition of the `probability-dark-long-fat-is-salmon` function as a template, we can generalize the calculations that it performs. Let's first define a simple data structure that can be passed around. In the spirit of idiomatic Clojure, we conveniently use a map for this purpose. Using a map, we can represent a category in our model along with the evidence and probability of its occurrence. Also, given the evidences for several categories, we can calculate the total probability of occurrence of a particular category as shown in the following code:

```
(defn make-category-probability-pair
  [category attrs]
  (let [evidence-of-category (apply
  evidence-of-category-with-attrs
                              category attrs)]
    {:category category
     :evidence evidence-of-category}))

(defn calculate-probability-of-category
  [sum-of-evidences pair]
  (let [probability-of-category (/ (:evidence pair)
                                   sum-of-evidences)]
    (assoc pair :probability probability-of-category)))
```

The make-category-probability-pair function uses the evidence-category-with-attrs function we defined in the preceding code to calculate the evidence of a category and its conditions or attributes. Then, it returns this value, as a map, along with the category itself. Also, we define the calculate-probability-of-category function, which calculates the total probability of a category and its conditions using the sum-of-evidences parameter and a value returned by the make-category-probability-pair function.

We can compose the preceding two functions to determine the total probability of all the categories given some observed values and then select the category with the highest probability, as follows:

```
(defn classify-by-attrs
  "Performs Bayesian classification of the attributes,
   given some categories.
   Returns a map containing the predicted category and
   the category's
   probability of occurrence."
  [categories & attrs]
  (let [pairs (map #(make-category-probability-pair % attrs)
                   categories)
        sum-of-evidences (reduce + (map :evidence pairs))
        probabilities (map #(calculate-probability-of-category
                              sum-of-evidences %)
                           pairs)
        sorted-probabilities (sort-by :probability probabilities)
        predicted-category (last sorted-probabilities)]
    predicted-category))
```

The classify-by-attrs function defined in the preceding code maps all the possible categories over the make-category-probability-pair function, given some conditions or observed values for the features of our model. As we are dealing with a sequence of pairs returned by make-category-probability-pair, we can use a simple composition of the reduce, map, and + functions to calculate the sum of all the evidence in this sequence. We then map the calculate-probability-of-category function over the sequence of category-evidence pairs and select the category-evidence pair with the highest probability. We do this by sorting the sequence through ascending probabilities and selecting the last element in the sorted sequence.

Now, we can use the `classify-by-attrs` function to determine the probability that an observed fish, which is dark, long, and fat, is a salmon. It is also represented by the `probability-dark-long-fat-is-salmon` value, which we defined earlier. Both expressions produce the same probability of 95.7 percent of a fish being a salmon, given that it's dark, long, and fat in appearance. We will implement the `classify-by-attrs` function as shown in the following code:

```
user> (classify-by-attrs [:salmon :sea-bass] :dark :long :fat)
{:probability 0.957091799207812, :category :salmon, :evidence
0.1949689}
user> probability-dark-long-fat-is-salmon
0.957091799207812
```

The `classify-by-attrs` function also returns the predicted category (that is, `:salmon`) of the given observed conditions `:dark`, `:long`, and `:fat`. We can use this function to tell us more about the training data as follows:

```
user> (classify-by-attrs [:salmon :sea-bass] :dark)
{:probability 0.8857825967670728, :category :salmon, :evidence
0.4816}
user> (classify-by-attrs [:salmon :sea-bass] :light)
{:probability 0.5362699908806723, :category :sea-bass, :evidence
0.2447}
user> (classify-by-attrs [:salmon :sea-bass] :thin)
{:probability 0.6369809383442954, :category :sea-bass, :evidence
0.2439}
```

As shown in the preceding code, a fish that is dark in appearance is mostly a salmon, and the one that is light in appearance is mostly a sea bass. Also, a fish that's thin is most likely a sea bass. The following values do, in fact, agree with the training data that we defined earlier:

```
user> (classify-by-attrs [:salmon] :dark)
{:probability 1.0, :category :salmon, :evidence 0.4816}
user> (classify-by-attrs [:salmon])
{:probability 1.0, :category :salmon, :evidence 0.6932}
```

Note that calling the `classify-by-attrs` function with only `[:salmon]` as a parameter returns the probability that any given fish is a salmon. An obvious corollary is that given a single category, the `classify-by-attrs` function always predicts the supplied category with complete certainty, that is, a probability of *1.0*. However, the evidence returned by this function vary depending on the observed features passed to it as well as the sample data that we used to train our model.

In a nutshell, the preceding implementation describes a Bayes classifier that can be trained using some sample data. It also classifies some observed values for the features of our model.

We can describe a generic Bayes classifier by building upon the definition of the $P(\text{salmon} \mid \text{dark, long, fat})$ probability from our previous example. To quickly recap, the term $P(\text{salmon} \mid \text{dark, long, fat})$ can be formally expressed as follows:

$$P(\text{salmon} \mid \text{dark, long, fat}) = \frac{P(\text{dark, long, fat} \mid \text{salmon}) \times P(\text{salmon})}{P(\text{dark, long, fat})}$$

$$\text{where } P(\text{dark, long, fat}) =$$

$$P(\text{dark, long, fat} \mid \text{salmon}) \times P(\text{salmon}) +$$

$$P(\text{dark, long, fat} \mid \text{sea-bass}) \times P(\text{sea-bass})$$

In the preceding equality, we deal with a single class, namely salmon, and three mutually independent features, namely the length, width, and lightness of the skin of a fish. We can generalize this equality for N features as follows:

$$P\left(C \mid F_1, F_2, \ldots F_N\right) = \frac{P(C) \times P(F_1 \mid C) \times P(F_2 \mid C) \ldots \times P(F_N \mid C)}{Z}$$

$$\text{where, } Z = P(F_1 \mid C) \times P(C) + P(F_2 \mid C) \times P(C) + \ldots + P(F_N \mid C) \times P(C)$$

Here, the term Z is the evidence of the classification model, which we described in the preceding equation. We can use the sum and product notation to describe the preceding equality more concisely as follows:

$$P\left(C \mid F_1, F_2, \ldots F_N\right) = \frac{P(C) \prod_{i=1}^{N} P(F_i \mid C)}{\sum_{i=1}^{N} P(C) P(F_i \mid C)}$$

The preceding equality describes the probability of occurrence of a single class, C. If we are given a number of classes to choose from, we must select the class with the highest probability of occurrence. This brings us to the basic definition of a Bayes classifier, which is formally expressed as follows:

$$classify(f_1, f_2, \ldots f_N) = \arg\max_{c} \frac{P(C = c) \prod_{i=1}^{N} P(F_i \mid C = c)}{\sum_{i=1}^{N} P(C = c) P(F_i \mid C = c)}$$

In the preceding equation, the function $classify(f_1, f_2, \ldots f_N)$ describes a Bayes classifier that selects the class with the highest probability of occurrence. Note that the terms $F_1, F_2, \ldots F_N$ represent the various features of our classification model, whereas the terms $f_1, f_2, \ldots f_N$ represent the set of observed values of these features. Also, the variable c, on the right-hand side of the equation, can have values from within a set of all the distinct classes in the classification model.

We can further simplify the preceding equation of a Bayes classifier via the **Maximum a Posteriori (MAP)** estimation, which can be thought of as a regularization of the features in Bayesian statistics. A simplified Bayes classifier can be formally expressed as follows:

$$classify(f_1, f_2, \ldots f_N) = \arg\max_c P(C = c) \prod_{i=1}^{N} P(F_i \mid C = c)$$

This definition essentially means that the *classify* function determines the class with the maximum probability of occurrence for the given features. Thus, the preceding equation describes a Bayes classifier that can be trained using some sample data and then be used to predict the class of a given set of observed values. We will now focus on using an existing implementation of a Bayes classifier to model a given classification problem.

The clj-ml library (https://github.com/joshuaeckroth/clj-ml) contains several implemented algorithms that we can choose from to model a given classification problem. This library is actually just a Clojure wrapper for the popular **Weka** library (http://www.cs.waikato.ac.nz/ml/weka/), which is a Java library that contains implementations for several machine learning algorithms. It also has several methods for evaluating and validating a generated classification model. However, we will concentrate on the clj-ml library's implementations of classifiers within the context of this chapter.

The clj-ml library can be added to a Leiningen project by adding the following dependency to the project.clj file:

```
[cc.artifice/clj-ml "0.4.0"]
```

For the upcoming example, the namespace declaration should look similar to the following declaration:

```
(ns my-namespace
  (:use [clj-ml classifiers data]))
```

We'll now introduce the `clj-ml` library using an implementation of a Bayes classifier to model our previous problem involving the fish packaging plant. First, let's refine our training data to use numeric values rather than the keywords, which we described earlier, for the various features of our model. Of course, we will still maintain the partiality in our training data such that the salmon are mostly fat and dark-skinned, while the sea bass are mostly long and light-skinned. The following code implements this:

```
(defn rand-in-range
  "Generates a random integer within the given range"
  [min max]
  (let [len      (- max min)
        rand-len (rand-int len)]
    (+ min rand-len)))


;; sea bass are mostly long and light in color
(defn make-sea-bass []
  (vector :sea-bass
          (rand-in-range 6 10)          ; length
          (rand-in-range 0 5)           ; width
          (rand-in-range 4 10)))        ; lightness of skin


;; salmon are mostly fat and dark
(defn make-salmon []
  (vector :salmon
          (rand-in-range 0 7)           ; length
          (rand-in-range 4 10)          ; width
          (rand-in-range 0 6)))         ; lightness of skin
```

Here, we define the `rand-in-range` function, which simply generates random integers within a given range of values. We then redefine the `make-sea-bass` and `make-salmon` functions to use the `rand-in-range` function to generate values within the range of 0 and 10 for the three features of a fish, namely its length, width, and the darkness of its skin. A fish with a lighter skin color is indicated by a higher value for this feature. Note that we reuse the definitions of the `make-sample-fish` function and `fish-dataset` variable to generate our training data. Also, a fish is represented by a vector rather than a set, as described in the earlier definitions of the `make-sea-bass` and `make-salmon` functions.

We can create a classifier from the `clj-ml` library using the `make-classifier` function, which can be found in the `clj-ml.classifiers` namespace. We can specify the type of classifier to be used by passing two keywords as arguments to the functions. As we intend to use a Bayes classifier, we supply the keywords, `:bayes` and `:naive`, to the `make-classifier` function. In a nutshell, we can use the following declaration to create a Bayes classifier. Note that the keyword, `:naive`, used in the following code signifies a naïve Bayes classifier that assumes that the features in our model are independent:

```
(def bayes-classifier (make-classifier :bayes :naive))
```

The `clj-ml` library's classifier implementations use datasets that are defined or generated using functions from the `clj-ml.data` namespace. We can convert the `fish-dataset` sequence, which is a sequence of vectors, into such a dataset using the `make-dataset` function. This function requires an arbitrary string name for the dataset, a template for each item in the collection, and a collection of items to add to the dataset. The template supplied to the `make-dataset` function is easily represented by a map, which is shown as follows:

```
(def fish-template
  [{:category [:salmon :sea-bass]}
   :length :width :lightness])

(def fish-dataset
  (make-dataset "fish" fish-template fish-training-data))
```

The `fish-template` map defined in the preceding code simply says that a fish, as represented by a vector, comprises the fish's category, length, width, and lightness of its skin, in that specific order. Note that the category of the fish is described using either `:salmon` or `:sea-bass`. We can now use `fish-dataset` to train the classifier represented by the `bayes-classifier` variable.

Although the `fish-template` map defines all the attributes of a fish, it's still lacking one important detail. It doesn't specify which of these attributes represent the class or category of the fish. In order to specify a particular attribute in the vector to represent the category of an entire set of observed values, we use the `dataset-set-class` function. This function takes a single argument that specifies the index of an attribute and is used to represent the category of the set of observed values in the vector. Note that this function does actually mutate or modify the dataset it's supplied with. We can then train our classifier using the `classifier-train` function, which takes a classifier and a dataset as parameters; this is shown in the following code:

```
(defn train-bayes-classifier []
  (dataset-set-class fish-dataset 0)
  (classifier-train bayes-classifier fish-dataset))
```

The preceding `train-bayes-classifier` function simply calls the `dataset-set-class` and `classifier-train` functions to train our classifier. When we call the `train-bayes-classifier` function, the classifier is trained with the following supplied data and then printed to the REPL output:

```
user> (train-bayes-classifier)
#<NaiveBayes Naive Bayes Classifier
```

Attribute	Class salmon (0.7)	sea-bass (0.3)
==================================		
length		
mean	2.9791	7.5007
std. dev.	1.9897	1.1264
weight sum	7032	2968
precision	1	1
width		
mean	6.4822	1.9747
std. dev.	1.706	1.405
weight sum	7032	2968
precision	1	1
lightness		
mean	2.5146	6.4643
std. dev.	1.7047	1.7204
weight sum	7032	2968
precision	1	1

```
>
```

This output gives us some basic information about the training data, such as the mean and standard deviation of the various features that we model. We can now use this trained classifier to predict the category of a set of observed values for the features of our model.

Let's first define the observed values that we intend to classify. To do so, we use the following `make-instance` function, which requires a dataset and a vector of observed values that agree with the data template of the supplied dataset:

```
(def sample-fish
  (make-instance fish-dataset [:salmon 5.0 6.0 3.0]))
```

Here, we simply defined a sample fish using the `make-instance` function. We can now predict the class of the fish represented by `sample-fish` as follows:

```
user> (classifier-classify bayes-classifier sample-fish)
:salmon
```

As shown in the preceding code, the fish is classified as a `salmon`. Note that although we provide the class of the fish as `:salmon` while defining `sample-fish`, it's only for conformance with the data template defined by `fish-dataset`. In fact, we could specify the class of `sample-fish` as `:sea-bass` or a third value, say `:unknown`, to represent an undefined value, and the classifier would still classify `sample-fish` as a `salmon`.

When dealing with the continuous values for the various features of the given classification model, we can specify a Bayes classifier to use discretization of continuous features. By this, we mean that all the values for the various features of the model will be converted to discrete values by the probability density estimation. We can specify this option to the `make-classifier` function by simply passing an extra argument, `{:supervised-discretization true}`, to the function. This map actually describes all the possible options that can be provided to the specified classifier.

In conclusion, the `clj-ml` library provides a fully operational Bayes classifier that we can use to classify arbitrary data. Although we generated the training data ourselves in the previous example, this data can be fetched from the Web or a database as well.

Using the k-nearest neighbors algorithm

A simple technique that can be used to classify a set of observed values is the **k-nearest neighbors** (abbreviated as **k-NN**) algorithm. This algorithm is a form of **lazy learning** in which all the computation is deferred until classification. Also, in the classification phase, the k-NN algorithm approximates the class of the observed values using only a few values from the training data, and the reading of other values is deferred until they are actually needed.

While we now explore the k-NN algorithm in the context of classification, it can be applied to regression as well by simply selecting the predicted value as the average of the nearest values of the dependent variable for a set of observed feature values. Interestingly, this technique of modeling regression is, in fact, a generalization of **linear interpolation** (for more information, refer to *An introduction to kernel and nearest-neighbor nonparametric regression*).

The k-NN algorithm reads some training data and analyzes this data lazily, that is, only when needed. Apart from the training data, the algorithm requires a set of observed values and a constant k as parameters to classify the set of observed values. To classify these observed values, the algorithm predicts the class that is the most frequent among the k training samples nearest to the set of observed values. By nearest, we mean a point with the least Euclidean distance from the point that is represented by a set of observed values in the Euclidean space of the training data.

An obvious corollary is that when $k = 1$, the predicted class is the class of the single neighbor nearest to the set of observed values. This special case of the k-NN algorithm is called the **nearest neighbor** algorithm.

We can create a classifier that uses the k-NN algorithm using the `clj-ml` library's `make-classifier` function. Such a classifier is specified using the keywords `:lazy` and `:ibk` as arguments to the `make-classifier` function. We will now use such a classifier to model our previous example of a fish packaging plant, as follows:

```
(def K1-classifier (make-classifier :lazy :ibk))

(defn train-K1-classifier []
  (dataset-set-class fish-dataset 0)
  (classifier-train K1-classifier fish-dataset))
```

The preceding code defines a k-NN classifier as `K1-classifier` and a `train-K1-classifier` function to train the classifier with the training data using `fish-dataset`, which we defined in the preceding code.

Note that the `make-classifier` function defaults the constant k or rather the number of neighbors to 1, which implies a single nearest neighbor. We can optionally specify the constant k as a key-value pair with the `:num-neighbors` key to the `make-classifier` function as shown in the following code:

```
(def K10-classifier (make-classifier
                      :lazy :ibk {:num-neighbors 10}))
```

We can now call the `train-K1-classifier` function to train the classifier as follows:

```
user> (train-K1-classifier)
#<IBk IB1 instance-based classifier
using 1 nearest neighbour(s) for classification
>
```

We can now use the `classifier-classify` function to classify the fish represented by `sample-fish`, which we had defined earlier, using the classifier represented by the `K1-classifier` variable:

```
user> (classifier-classify K1-classifier sample-fish)
:salmon
```

As shown in the preceding code, the k-NN classifier predicts the fish class as salmon, thus agreeing with our earlier predictions that used a Bayes classifier. In conclusion, the `clj-ml` library provides a concise implementation of a classifier that uses the k-NN algorithm to predict the class of a set of observed values.

The k-NN classifier provided by the `clj-ml` library performs the normalization of the features of the classification model by default using the mean and standard deviation of the values of these features. We can specify an option to the `make-classifier` function to skip this normalization phase by passing a map entry with the `:no-normalization` key in the map of options passed to the `make-classifier` function.

Using decision trees

We can also use decision trees to model a given classification problem. A decision tree is, in fact, constructed from the given training data, and we can use this decision tree to predict the class of a given set of observed values. The process of constructing a decision tree is loosely based on the concepts of information entropy and information gain from information theory (for more information, refer to *Induction of Decision Trees*). It is also often termed as **decision tree learning**. Unfortunately, a detailed study of information theory is beyond the scope of this book. However, in this section, we will explore some concepts in information theory that will be used in the context of machine learning.

A decision tree is a tree or graph that describes a model of decisions and their possible consequences. An internal node in a decision tree represents a decision, or rather a condition of a particular feature in the context of classification. It has two possible outcomes that are represented by the left and right subtrees of the node. Of course, a node in the decision tree could also have more than two subtrees. Each leaf node in a decision tree represents a particular class, or a consequence, in our classification model.

For example, our previous classification problem involving the fish packaging plant could have the following decision tree:

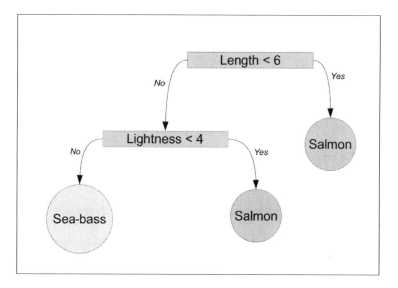

The previously illustrated decision tree uses two conditions to classify a fish as either a salmon or a sea bass. The internal nodes represent the two conditions based on the features of our classification model. Note that the decision tree uses only two of the three features of our classification model. We can thus say the tree is *pruned*. We shall briefly explore this technique as well in this section.

To classify a set of observed values using a decision tree, we traverse the tree starting from the root node until we reach a leaf node that represents the predicted class of the set of observed values. This technique of predicting the class of a set of observed values from a decision tree is always the same, irrespective of how the decision tree was constructed. For the decision tree described earlier, we can classify a fish by first comparing its length followed by the lightness of its skin. The second comparison is only needed if the length of the fish is greater than **6** as specified by the internal node with the expression **Length < 6** in the decision tree. If the length of the fish is indeed greater than **6**, we use the lightness of the skin of the fish to decide whether it's a salmon or a sea bass.

There are actually several algorithms that are used to construct a decision tree from some training data. Generally, the tree is constructed by splitting the set of sample values in the training data into smaller subsets based on an attribute value test. The process is repeated on each subset until splitting a given subset of sample values no longer adds internal nodes to the decision tree. As we mentioned earlier, it's possible for an internal node in a decision tree to have more than two subtrees.

We will now explore the **C4.5** algorithm to construct a decision tree (for more information, refer to *C4.5: Programs for Machine Learning*). This algorithm uses the concept of information entropy to decide the feature and the corresponding value on which the set of sample values must be partitioned. **Information entropy** is defined as the measure of uncertainty in a given feature or random variable (for more information, refer to "A Mathematical Theory of Communication").

For a given feature or attribute f, which has values within the range of 1 to m, we can define the information entropy of the $H(f)$ feature as follows:

$$\text{If } f \in [1, m],$$

$$H(f) = -\sum_{i=1}^{m} f_i \log_2 f_i$$

In the preceding equation, the term f_i represents the number of occurrences of the feature f with respect to the value i. Based on this definition of the information entropy of a feature, we define the normalized information gain $IG(T, f)$. In the following equality, the term T refers to the set of sample values or training data supplied to the algorithm:

$$IG(T, f) = H(T) - H(T \mid f)$$

In terms of information entropy, the preceding definition of the information gain of a given attribute is the change in information entropy of the total set of values when the attribute f is removed from the given set of features in the model.

The algorithm selects a feature A from the given set of features in the training data such that the feature A has the maximum possible information gain in the set of features. We can represent this with the help of the following equality:

$$\text{Feature } A = \arg \max_{a} IG(T, a)$$

$$\text{where } IG(T, a) = H(T) - \sum_{v \in vals(a)} \frac{|\{x \in T \mid x_a = v\}|}{|T|} \times H(\{x \in T \mid x_a = v\})$$

In the preceding equation, $vals(a)$ represents the set of all the possible values that a feature a is known to have. The $\{x \in T \mid x_a = v\}$ set represents the observed values in which the feature a has the value v and the term $H(\{x \in T \mid x_a = v\})$ represents the information entropy of this set of values.

Using the preceding equation to select a feature with the maximum information gain from the training data, we can describe the C4.5 algorithm through the following steps:

1. For each feature *a*, find the normalized information gain from partitioning the sample data on the feature *a*.

2. Select the feature *A* with the maximum normalized information gain.

3. Create an internal decision node based on the selected feature *A*. Both the subtrees created from this step are either leaf nodes or a new set of sample values to be partitioned further.

4. Repeat this process on each partitioned set of sample values produced from the previous step. We repeat the preceding steps until all the features in a subset of sample values have the same information entropy.

Once a decision tree has been created, we can optionally perform **pruning** on the tree. Pruning is simply the process of removing any extraneous decision nodes from the tree. This can be thought of as a form for the regularization of decision trees through which we prevent underfitting or overfitting of the estimated decision tree model.

J48 is an open source implementation of the C4.5 algorithm in Java, and the `clj-ml` library contains a working J48 decision tree classifier. We can create a decision tree classifier using the `make-classifier` function, and we supply the keywords `:decision-tree` and `:c45` as parameters to this function to create a J48 classifier as shown in the following code:

```
(def DT-classifier (make-classifier :decision-tree :c45))

(defn train-DT-classifier []
  (dataset-set-class fish-dataset 0)
  (classifier-train DT-classifier fish-dataset))
```

The `train-DT-classifier` function defined in the preceding code simply trains the classifier represented by `DT-classifier` with the training data from our previous example of the fish packaging plant. The `classifier-train` function also prints the following trained classifier:

```
user> (train-DT-classifier)
#<J48 J48 pruned tree
------------------
```

```
width <= 3: sea-bass (2320.0)
width > 3
|    length <= 6
|    |    lightness <= 5: salmon (7147.0/51.0)
|    |    lightness > 5: sea-bass (95.0)
|    length > 6: sea-bass (438.0)

Number of Leaves   : 4

Size of the tree : 7
>
```

The preceding output gives a good idea of what the decision tree of the trained classifier looks like as well as the size and number of leaf nodes in the decision tree. Apparently, the decision tree has three distinct internal nodes. The root node of the tree is based on the width of a fish, the subsequent node is based on the length of a fish, and the last decision node is based on the lightness of the skin of a fish.

We can now use the decision tree classifier to predict the class of a fish, and we use the following classifier-classify function to perform this classification:

```
user> (classifier-classify DT-classifier sample-fish)
:salmon
```

As shown in the preceding code, the classifier predicts the class of the fish represented by sample-fish as a :salmon keyword just like the other classifiers used in the earlier examples.

The J48 decision tree classifier implementation provided by the clj-ml library performs pruning as a final step while training the classifier. We can generate an unpruned tree by specifying the :unpruned key in the map of options passed to the make-classifier function as shown in the following code:

```
(def UDT-classifier (make-classifier
                        :decision-tree :c45 {:unpruned true}))
```

The previously defined classifier will not perform pruning on the decision tree generated from training the classifier with the given training data. We can inspect what an unpruned tree looks like by defining and calling the train-UDT-classifier function, which simply trains the classifier using the classifier-train function with the fish-dataset training data. This function can be defined as being analogous to the train-UDT-classifier function and produces the following output when it is called:

```
user> (train-UDT-classifier)
#<J48 J48 unpruned tree
------------------
```

```
width <= 3: sea-bass (2320.0)
width > 3
|   length <= 6
|   |   lightness <= 5
|   |   |   length <= 5: salmon (6073.0)
|   |   |   length > 5
|   |   |   |   width <= 4
|   |   |   |   |   lightness <= 3: salmon (121.0)
|   |   |   |   |   lightness > 3
|   |   |   |   |   |   lightness <= 4: salmon (52.0/25.0)
|   |   |   |   |   |   lightness > 4: sea-bass (50.0/24.0)
|   |   |   |   width > 4: salmon (851.0)
|   |   lightness > 5: sea-bass (95.0)
|   length > 6: sea-bass (438.0)

Number of Leaves  : 8

Size of the tree : 15
```

As shown in the preceding code, the unpruned decision tree has a lot more internal decision nodes as compared to the decision tree that is generated after pruning it. We can now use the following `classifier-classify` function to predict the class of a fish using the trained classifier:

```
user> (classifier-classify UDT-classifier sample-fish)
:salmon
```

Interestingly, the unpruned tree also predicts the class of the fish represented by `sample-fish` as `:salmon`, thus agreeing with the class predicted by the pruned decision tree, which we had described earlier. In summary, the `clj-ml` library provides us with a working implementation of a decision tree classifier based on the C4.5 algorithm.

The `make-classifier` function supports several interesting options for the J48 decision tree classifier. We've already explored the `:unpruned` option, which indicated that the decision tree is not pruned. We can specify the `:reduced-error-pruning` option to the `make-classifier` function to force the usage of reduced error pruning (for more information, refer to "Pessimistic decision tree pruning based on tree size"), which is a form of pruning based on reducing the overall error of the model. Another interesting option that we can specify to the `make-classifier` function is the maximum number of internal nodes or folds that can be removed by pruning the decision tree. We can specify this option using the `:pruning-number-of-folds` option, and by default, the `make-classifier` function imposes no such limit while pruning the decision tree. Also, we can specify that each internal decision node in the decision tree has only two subtrees by specifying the `:only-binary-splits` option to the `make-classifier` function.

Summary

In this chapter, we explored classification and the various algorithms that can be used to model a given classification problem. Although classification techniques are very useful, they do not perform too well when the sample data has a large number of dimensions. Also, the features may vary in a nonlinear manner, as we will describe in *Chapter 4*, *Building Neural Networks*. We will also explore more about these aspects and the alternate methods of supervised learning in the following chapters. The following are few of the points that we looked at in this chapter:

- We described two broad types of classifications, namely, binary and multiclass classification. We also briefly studied the logistic function and how it can be used to model classification problems through logistic regression.

- We studied and implemented a Bayes classifier, which used a probabilistic model used for modeling classification. We also described how we could use the `clj-ml` library's Bayes classifier implementation to model a given classification problem.

- We also explored the simple k-nearest neighbor algorithm and how we can leverage it using the `clj-ml` library.

- We studied decision trees and the C4.5 algorithm. The `clj-ml` library provides us with a configurable implementation of a classifier based on the C4.5 algorithm, and we described how this implementation could be used as well.

We will explore artificial neural networks in the following chapter. Interestingly, we can use artificial neural networks to model regression and classification problems, and we will study these aspects of neural networks as well.

4
Building Neural Networks

In this chapter, we will introduce **Artificial Neural Networks (ANNs)**. We will study the basic representation of ANNs and then discuss several ANN models that can be used in both supervised and unsupervised machine learning problems. We also introduce the **Enclog** Clojure library to build ANNs.

Neural networks are well suited for finding patterns in some given data and have several practical applications, such as handwriting recognition and machine vision, in computing. ANNs are often combined or interconnected to model a given problem. Interestingly, they can be applied to several machine learning problems, such as regression and classification. ANNs have applications in several areas in computing and are not restricted to the scope of machine learning.

Unsupervised learning is a form of machine learning in which the given training data doesn't contain any information about which class a given sample of input belongs to. As the training data is *unlabeled*, an unsupervised learning algorithm must determine the various categories in the given data completely on its own. Generally, this is done by seeking out similarities between different pieces of data and then grouping the data into several categories. This technique is called **cluster analysis,** and we shall study more about this methodology in the following chapters. ANNs are used in unsupervised machine learning techniques mostly due to their ability to quickly recognize patterns in some unlabeled data. This specialized form of unsupervised learning exhibited by ANNs is termed as **competitive learning**.

An interesting fact about ANNs is that they are modeled from the structure and behavior of the central nervous system of higher-order animals that demonstrate learning capabilities.

Understanding nonlinear regression

By this time, the reader must be aware of the fact that the gradient descent algorithm can be used to estimate both linear and logistic regression models for regression and classification problems. An obvious question would be: what is the need of neural networks when we can use gradient descent to estimate linear regression and logistic regression models from the training data? To understand the necessity of ANNs, we must first understand *nonlinear regression*.

Let's assume that we have a single feature variable X and a dependent variable Y that varies with X, as shown in the following plot:

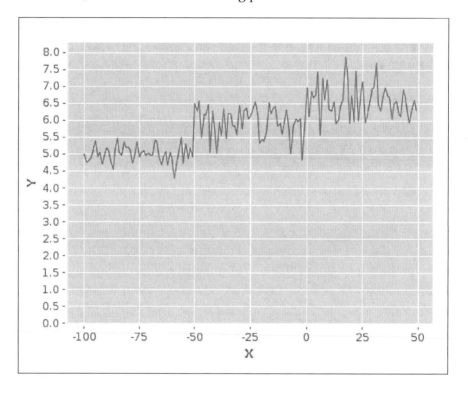

As illustrated in the preceding plot, it's hard, if not impossible, to model the dependent variable Y as a linear equation of the independent variable X. We could model the dependent variable Y to be a high-order polynomial equation of the dependent variable X, thus converting the problem into the standard form of linear regressions. Hence, the dependent variable Y is said to vary nonlinearly with the independent variable X. Of course, there is also a good chance that data cannot be modeled using a polynomial function either.

It can also be shown that calculating the weights or coefficients of all the terms in a polynomial function using gradient descent has a time complexity of $O(n^2)$, where n is the number of features in the training data. Similarly, the algorithmic complexity of calculating the coefficients of all the terms in a third-order polynomial equation is $O(n^3)$. It's apparent that the time complexity of gradient descent increases geometrically with the number of features of the model. Thus, gradient descent on its own is not efficient enough to model nonlinear regression models with a large number of features.

ANNs, on the other hand, are very efficient at modeling nonlinear regression models of data with a high number of features. We will now study the foundational ideas of ANNs and several ANN models that can be used in supervised and unsupervised learning problems.

Representing neural networks

ANNs are modeled from the behavior of the central nervous system of organisms, such as mammals and reptiles, that are capable of learning. The central nervous system of these organisms comprises the organism's brain, spinal cord, and a network of supporting neural tissues. The brain processes information and generates electric signals that are transported through the network of neural fibers to the various organs of the organism. Although the organism's brain performs a lot of complex processing and control, it is actually a collection of neurons. The actual processing of sensory signals, however, is performed by several complex combinations of these neurons. Of course, each neuron is capable of processing an extremely small portion of the information processed by the brain. The brain actually functions by routing electrical signals from the various sensory organs of the body to its motor organs through this complex network of neurons. An individual neuron has a cellular structure as illustrated in the following diagram:

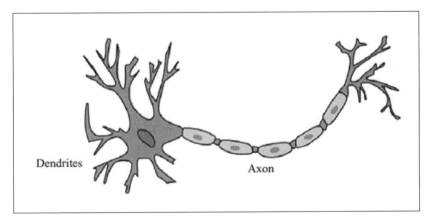

A neuron has several dendrites close to the nucleus of the cell and a single *axon* that transports signals from the nucleus of the cell. The dendrites are used to receive signals from other neurons and can be thought of as the input to the neuron. Similarly, the axon of the neuron is analogous to the output of the neuron. The neuron can thus be mathematically represented as a function that processes several inputs and produces a single output.

Several of these neurons are interconnected, and this network is termed as a **neural network**. A neuron essentially performs its function by relaying weak electrical signals from and to other neurons. The interconnecting space between two neurons is called a **synapse**.

An ANN comprises several interconnected neurons. Each neuron can be represented by a mathematical function that consumes several input values and produces an output value, as shown in the following diagram:

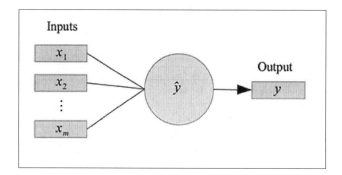

A single neuron can be illustrated by the preceding diagram. In mathematical terms, it's simply a function $\hat{y}$ that maps a set of input values $(x_1, x_2, \ldots x_m)$ to an output value y. The function $\hat{y}$ is called the **activation function** of the neuron, and its output value y is called the **activation of the neuron**. This representation of a neuron is termed as a **perceptron**. Perceptron can be used on its own and is effective enough to estimate supervised machine learning models, such as linear regression and logistic regression. However, complex nonlinear data can be better modeled with several interconnected perceptrons.

Generally, a bias input is added to the set of input values supplied to a perceptron. For the input values $(x_1, x_2, \ldots x_m)$, we add the term x_0 as a bias input such that $x_0 = 1$. A neuron with this added bias value can be illustrated by the following diagram:

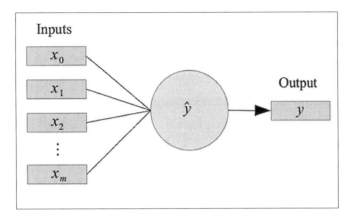

Each input value x_i supplied to the perceptron has an associated weight w_i. This weight is analogous to the coefficients of the features of a linear regression model. The activation function is applied to these weights and their corresponding input values. We can formally define the estimated output value $\hat{y}$ of the perceptron in terms of the input values, their weights, and the perceptron's activation function as follows:

$$\hat{y} = g\left(\sum_{i=0}^{m} x_i w_i\right), \text{ where } g(x, w) \text{ is the activation function}$$

The activation function to be used by the nodes of an ANN depends greatly on the sample data that has to be modeled. Generally, the **sigmoid** or **hyperbolic tangent** functions are used as the activation function for classification problems (for more information, refer to *Wavelet Neural Network (WNN) approach for calibration model building based on gasoline near infrared (NIR) spectr*). The sigmoid function is said to be *activated* for a given threshold input.

We can plot the variance of the sigmoid function to depict this behavior, as shown in the following plot:

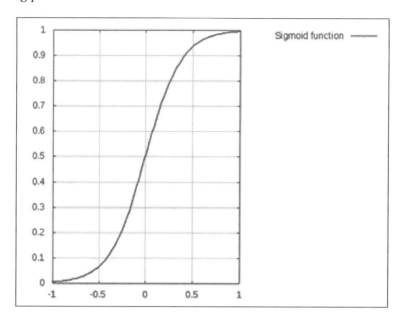

ANNs can be broadly classified into *feed-forward neural networks* and *recurrent neural networks* (for more information, refer to *Bidirectional recurrent neural networks*). The difference between these two types of ANNs is that in feed-forward neural networks, the connections between the nodes of the ANN do not form a directed cycle as opposed to recurrent neural networks where the node interconnections do form a directed cycle. Thus, in feed-forward neural networks, each node in a given layer of the ANN receives input only from the nodes in the immediate previous layer in the ANN.

There are several ANN models that have practical applications, and we will explore a few of them in this chapter.

Understanding multilayer perceptron ANNs

We now introduce a simple model of feed-forward neural networks — the **Multilayer Perceptron** model. This model represents a basic feed-forward neural network and is versatile enough to model regression and classification problems in the domain of supervised learning. All the input flows through a feed-forward neural network in a single direction. This is a direct consequence of the fact that there is no *feedback* from or to any layer in a feed-forward neural network.

By feedback, we mean that the output of a given layer is fed back as input to the perceptrons in a previous layer in the ANN. Also, using a single layer of perceptrons would mean using only a single activation function, which is equivalent to using *logistic regression* to model the given training data. This would mean that the model cannot be used to fit nonlinear data, which is the primary motivation of ANNs. We must note that we discussed logistic regression in *Chapter 3, Categorizing Data*.

A multilayer perceptron ANN can be illustrated by the following diagram:

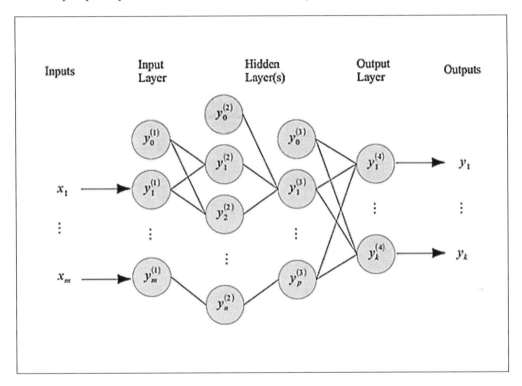

A multilayer perceptron ANN comprises several layers of perceptron nodes. It exhibits a single input layer, a single output layer, and several hidden layers of perceptrons. The input layer simply relays the input values to the first hidden layer of the ANN. These values are then propagated to the output layer through the other hidden layers, where they are weighted and summed using the activation function, to finally produce the output values.

Each sample in the training data is represented by the $\left(y^{(i)}, x^{(i)}\right)$ tuple, where $y^{(i)}$ is the expected output and $x^{(i)}$ is the input value of the ith training sample. The $x^{(i)}$ input vector comprises a number of values equal to the number of features in the training data.

The output of each node is termed as the **activation** of the node and is represented by the term $a_i^{(l)}$ for the ith node in the layer l. As we mentioned earlier, the activation function used to produce this value is the sigmoid function or the hyperbolic tangent function. Of course, any other mathematical function could be used to fit the sample data. The input layer of a multilayer perceptron network simply adds a bias input to the input values, and the set of inputs supplied to the ANN are relayed to the next layer. We can formally represent this equality as follows:

$$a_i^{(l)} = x_i$$

The synapses between every pair of layers in the ANN have an associated weight matrix. The number of rows in these matrices is equal to the number of input values, that is, the number of nodes in the layer closer to the input layer of the ANN and the number of columns equal to the number of nodes in the layer of the synapse that is closer to the output layer of the ANN. For a layer l, the weight matrix is represented by the term $\Theta^{(l)}$.

The activation values of a layer l can be determined using the activation function of the ANN. The activation function is applied on the products of the weight matrix and the activation values produced by the previous layer in the ANN. Generally, the activation function used for a multilayer perceptron is a sigmoid function. This equality can be formally represented as follows:

$$a^{(l)} = g\left(\Theta^{(l)}a^{(l-1)}\right), \text{where } g(x) \text{ is the activation function}$$

Generally, the activation function used for a multilayer perceptron is a sigmoid function. Note that we do not add a bias value in the output layer of an ANN. Also, the output layer can produce any number of output values. To model a *k-class* classification problem, we would require an ANN producing k output values.

To perform binary classification, we can only model a maximum of two classes of input data. The output value generated by an ANN used for binary classification is always 0 or 1. Thus, for $k = 2$ classes, $y \in \{0,1\}$.

We can also model a multiclass classification using the k binary output values, and thus, the output of the ANN is a $k \times 1$ matrix. This can be formally expressed as follows:

For k classes,

$$y_{C=1} = \begin{bmatrix} 1 \\ 0 \\ \vdots \\ 0 \end{bmatrix}, y_{C=2} = \begin{bmatrix} 0 \\ 1 \\ \vdots \\ 0 \end{bmatrix}, \ldots y_{C=k} = \begin{bmatrix} 0 \\ 0 \\ \vdots \\ 1 \end{bmatrix}, \text{where } |y| = k \times 1$$

Hence, we can use a multilayer perceptron ANN to perform binary and multiclass classifications. A multilayer perceptron ANN can be trained using the **backpropagation algorithm**, which we will study and implement later in this chapter.

Let's assume that we want to model the behavior of a logical XOR gate. An XOR gate can be thought of a binary classifier that requires two inputs and generates a single output. An ANN that models the XOR gate would have a structure as shown in the following diagram. Interestingly, linear regression can be used to model both AND and OR logic gates but cannot be used to model an XOR gate. This is due to the nonlinear nature of the output of an XOR gate, and thus, ANNs are used to overcome this limitation.

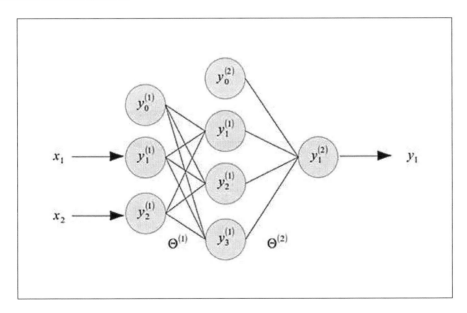

The multilayer perceptron illustrated in the preceding diagram has three nodes in the input layer, four nodes in the hidden layer, and one node in the output layer. Observe that every layer other than the output layer adds a bias input to the set of input values for the nodes in the next layer. There are two synapses in the ANN, shown in the preceding diagram, and they are associated with the weight matrices $\Theta^{(1)}$ and $\Theta^{(2)}$. Note that the first synapse is between the input layer and hidden layer, and the second synapse is between the hidden layer and the output layer. The weight matrix $\Theta^{(1)}$ has a size of 3×3, and the weight matrix $\Theta^{(2)}$ has a size of 4×1. Also, the term Θ is used to represent all the weight matrices in the ANN.

As the activation function of each node in a multilayer perceptron ANN is a sigmoid function, we can define the cost function of the weights of the nodes of the ANN similar to the cost function of a logistic regression model. The cost function of an ANN can be defined in terms of the weight matrices as follows:

$$J(\Theta) = -\frac{1}{N}\left[\sum_{i=1}^{N}\sum_{k=1}^{K} y_k^{(i)}\log\left(\hat{y}\left(x^{(i)}\right)_k\right) + \left(1 - y_k^{(i)}\right)\log\left(1 - \hat{y}\left(x^{(i)}\right)_k\right)\right]$$

The preceding cost function is essentially the average of the cost functions of each node in the output layer of an ANN (for more information, refer to *Neural Networks in Materials Science*). For a multilayer perceptron ANN with K output values, we perform the average over the K terms. Note that $y_k^{(i)}$ represents the kth output value of the ANN, $x^{(i)}$ represents the input variables of the ANN, and N is the number of sample values in the training data. The cost function is essentially that of logistic regression but is applied here for the K output values. We can add a regularization parameter to the preceding cost function and express the regularized cost function using the following equation:

$$J(\Theta) = -\frac{1}{N}\left[\sum_{i=1}^{N}\sum_{k=1}^{K} y_k^{(i)}\log\left(\hat{y}\left(x^{(i)}\right)_k\right) + \left(1 - y_k^{(i)}\right)\log\left(1 - \hat{y}\left(x^{(i)}\right)_k\right)\right] + \frac{\lambda}{2N}\sum_{l=1}^{L-1}\sum_{i=1}^{s_l}\sum_{j=1}^{s_{l+1}}\left(\Theta_{ij}^{(l)}\right)^2$$

The cost function defined in the preceding equation adds a regularization term similar to that of logistic regression. The regularization term is essentially the sum of the squares of all weights of all input values of the several layers of the ANN, excluding the weights for the added bias input. Also, the term s_l refers to the number of nodes in layer l of the ANN. An interesting point to note is that in the preceding regularized cost function, only the regularization term depends on the number of layers in the ANN. Hence, the *generalization* of the estimated model is based on the number of layers in the ANN.

Understanding the backpropagation algorithm

The **backpropagation learning** algorithm is used to train a multilayer perceptron ANN from a given set of sample values. In brief, this algorithm first calculates the output value for a set of given input values and also calculates the amount of error in the output of the ANN. The amount of error in the ANN is determined by comparing the predicted output value of the ANN to the expected output value for the given input values from the training data provided to the ANN. The calculated error is then used to modify the weights of the ANN. Thus, after training the ANN with a reasonable number of samples, the ANN will be able to predict the output value for a set of input values. The algorithm comprises of three distinct phases. They are as follows:

- A forward propagation phase
- A backpropagation phase
- A weight update phase

The weights of the synapses in the ANN are first initialized to random values within the ranges $-\varepsilon$ and ε. We initialize the weights to values within this range to avoid a symmetry in the weight matrices. This avoidance of symmetry is called **symmetry breaking,** and it is performed so that each iteration of the backpropagation algorithm produces a noticeable change in the weights of the synapses in the ANN. This is desirable in an ANN as each of its node should learn independently of other nodes in the ANN. If all the nodes were to have identical weights, the estimated learning model will be either overfit or underfit.

Also, the backpropagation learning algorithm requires two additional parameters, which are the learning rate P and the learning momentum Λ. We will see the effects of these parameters in the example later in this section.

The forward propagation phase of the algorithm simply calculates the activation values of all nodes in the various layers of the ANN. As we mentioned earlier, the activation values of the nodes in the input layer are the input values and the bias input of the ANN. This can be formally defined by using the following equation:

$$a_i^{(l)} = x_i$$

Using these activation values from the input layer of the ANN, the activation of the nodes in the other layers of the ANN is determined. This is done by applying the activation function to the products of the weight matrix of a given layer and the activation values from the previous layer in the ANN. This can be formally expressed as follows:

$$a^{(l)} = g\left(\Theta^{(l)} a^{(l-1)}\right)$$

The preceding equation explains that the activation value of a layer l is equal to the activation function applied to the output (or activation) values of the previous layer and the given layer's weight matrix. Next, the activation values of the output layer are *backpropagated*. By this, we mean that that the activation values are traversed from the output layer through the hidden layers to the input layer of the ANN. During this phase, we determine the amount of error or delta in each node in the ANN. The delta values of the output layer are determined by calculating the difference between the expected output values, $y^{(i)}$, and the activation values of the output layer, $a^{(L)}$. This difference calculation can be summarized by the following equation:

$$\delta^{(L)} = a^{(L)} - y^{(i)}$$

The term $\delta^{(l)}$ of a layer l is a matrix of size $j \times 1$ where j is the number of nodes in layer l. This term can be formally defined as follows:

$$\delta^{(l)} = \left[\delta_j^{(l)}\right], \text{where } j \in \{\text{nodes in layer } l\}$$

The delta terms of the layers other than the output layer of the ANN are determined by the following equality:

$$\delta^{(l)} = \left(\Theta^{(l)}\right)^T \delta^{(l+1)} .* g'\left(a^{(l)}\right), \text{where } g'\left(a^{(l)}\right) = a^{(l)} .* \left(1 - a^{(l)}\right)$$

In the preceding equation, the binary operation .* is used to represent an element-wise multiplication of two matrices of equal size. Note that this operation is different from matrix multiplication, and an element-wise multiplication will return a matrix composed of the products of the elements with the same position in two matrices of equal size. The term $g'(x)$ represents the derivative of the activation function used in the ANN. As we are using the sigmoid function as our activation function, the term $g'(a^{(l)})$ has the value $a^{(l)} .* (1 - a^{(l)})$.

Thus, we can calculate the delta values of all nodes in the ANN. We can use these delta values to determine the gradients of the synapses of the ANN. We now move on to the final weight update phase of the backpropagation algorithm.

The gradients of the various synapses are first initialized to matrices with all the elements as 0. The size of a gradient matrix of a given synapse is the same size as the weight matrix of the synapse. The gradient term $\Delta^{(l)}$ represents the gradients of the synapse layer that is present immediately after layer l in the ANN. The initialization of the gradients of the synapses in the ANN is formally expressed as follows:

$$\Delta^{(l)} = [0]$$

For each sample value in the training data, we calculate the deltas and activation values of all nodes in the ANN. These values are added to the gradients of the synapses using the following equation:

$$\Delta^{(l)} := \Delta^{(l)} + \delta^{(l+1)} \left(a^{(l)} \right)^T$$

We then calculate the average of the gradients for all the sample values and use the delta and gradient values of a given layer to update the weight matrix as follows:

$$W^{(l)} := W^{(l)} - \left(\rho \Delta^{(l)} + \Lambda \delta^{(l)} \right)$$

Thus, the learning rate and learning momentum parameters of the algorithm come into play only in the weight update phase. The preceding three equations represent a single iteration of the backpropagation algorithm. A large number of iterations must be performed until the overall error in the ANN converges to a small value. We can now summarize the backpropagation learning algorithm using the following steps:

1. Initialize the weights of the synapses of the ANN to random values.

2. Select a sample value and forward propagate the sample values through several layers of the ANN to generate the activations of every node in the ANN.

3. Backpropagate the activations generated by the last layer of the ANN through the hidden layers and to the input layer of the ANN. Through this step, we calculate the error or delta of every node in the ANN.

4. Calculate the product of the errors generated from step 3 with the synapse weights or input activations for all the nodes in the ANN. This step produces the gradient of weight for each node in the network. Each gradient is represented by a ratio or percentage.

5. Calculate the changes in the weights of the synapse layers in the ANN using the gradients and deltas of a given layer in the ANN. These changes are then subtracted from the weights of the synapses in the ANN. This is essentially the weight update step of the backpropagation algorithm.

6. Repeat steps 2 to 5 for the rest of the samples in the training data.

There are several distinct parts in the backpropagation learning algorithm, and we will now implement each part and combine it into a complete implementation. As the deltas and weights of the synapses and activations in an ANN can be represented by matrices, we can write a vectorized implementation of this algorithm.

 Note that for the following example, we require functions from the `incanter.core` namespace from the Incanter library. The functions in this namespace actually use the Clatrix library for the representation of a matrix and its manipulation.

Let's assume that we need to implement an ANN to model a logical XOR gate. The sample data is simply the truth table of the XOR gate and can be represented as a vector, shown as follows:

```
;; truth table for XOR logic gate
(def sample-data [[[0 0] [0]]
                  [[0 1] [1]]
                  [[1 0] [1]]
                  [[1 1] [0]]]])
```

Each element defined in the preceding vector `sample-data` is itself a vector comprising other vectors for the input and output values of an XOR gate. We will use this vector as our training data for building an ANN. This is essentially a classification problem, and we will use ANNs to model it. In abstract terms, an ANN should be capable of performing both binary and multiclass classifications. We can define the protocol of an ANN as follows:

```
(defprotocol NeuralNetwork
  (run       [network inputs])
  (run-binary [network inputs])
  (train-ann  [network samples]))
```

The `NeuralNetwork` protocol defined in the preceding code has three functions. The `train-ann` function can be used to train the ANN and requires some sample data. The `run` and `run-binary` functions can be used on this ANN to perform multiclass and binary classifications, respectively. Both the `run` and `run-binary` functions require a set of input values.

The first step of the backpropagation algorithm is the initialization of the weights of the synapses of the ANN. We can use the `rand` and `matrix` functions to generate these weights as a matrix, shown as follows:

```
(defn rand-list
  "Create a list of random doubles between
  -epsilon and +epsilon."
  [len epsilon]
  (map (fn [x] (- (rand (* 2 epsilon)) epsilon))
       (range 0 len)))

(defn random-initial-weights
  "Generate random initial weight matrices for given layers.
  layers must be a vector of the sizes of the layers."
  [layers epsilon]
  (for [i (range 0 (dec (length layers)))]
    (let [cols (inc (get layers i))
          rows (get layers (inc i))]
      (matrix (rand-list (* rows cols) epsilon) cols))))
```

The `rand-list` function shown in the preceding code creates a list of random elements in the positive and negative range of `epsilon`. As we described earlier, we choose this range to break the symmetry of the weight matrix.

The `random-initial-weights` function generates several weight matrices for different layers of the ANN. As defined in the preceding code, the `layers` argument must be a vector of the sizes of the layers of the ANN. For an ANN with two nodes in the input layer, three nodes in the hidden layer, and one node in the output layer, we pass `layers` as [2 3 1] to the `random-initial-weights` function. Each weight matrix has a number of columns equal to the number of inputs and number of rows equal to the number of nodes in the next layer of the ANN. We set the number of columns in a weight matrix of a given layer to the number of inputs, plus an extra input for the bias of the neural layer. Note that we use a slightly different form of the `matrix` function. This form takes a single vector and partitions this vector into a matrix that has a number of columns as specified by second argument to this function. Thus, the vector passed to this form of the `matrix` function must have (`* rows cols`) elements, where `rows` and `cols` are the number of rows and columns, respectively, in the weight matrix.

As we will need to apply the sigmoid function to all the activations of a layer in the ANN, we must define a function that applies the sigmoid function on all the elements in a given matrix. We can use the `div`, `plus`, `exp`, and `minus` functions from the `incanter.core` namespace to implement such a function, as shown in the following code:

```
(defn sigmoid
  "Apply the sigmoid function 1/(1+exp(-z)) to all
  elements in the matrix z."
  [z]
  (div 1 (plus 1 (exp (minus z)))))
```

 Note that all of the previously defined functions apply the corresponding arithmetic operation on all the elements in a given matrix and returns a new matrix.

We will also need to implicitly add a bias node to each layer in an ANN. This can be done by wrapping around the `bind-rows` function, which adds a row of elements to a matrix, as shown in the following code:

```
(defn bind-bias
  "Add the bias input to a vector of inputs."
  [v]
  (bind-rows [1] v))
```

Since the bias value is always 1, we specify the row of elements as `[1]` to the `bind-rows` function.

Using the functions defined earlier, we can implement forward propagation. We essentially have to multiply the weights of a given synapse between two layers in an ANN and then apply the sigmoid function on each of the generated activation values, as shown in the following code:

```
(defn matrix-mult
  "Multiply two matrices and ensure the result is also a matrix."
  [a b]
  (let [result (mmult a b)]
    (if (matrix? result)
      result
      (matrix [result]))))

(defn forward-propagate-layer
  "Calculate activations for layer l+1 given weight matrix
```

```
    of the synapse between layer l and l+1 and layer l activations."
    [weights activations]
    (sigmoid (matrix-mult weights activations))))

(defn forward-propagate
  "Propagate activation values through a network's
  weight matrix and return output layer activation values."
  [weights input-activations]
  (reduce #(forward-propagate-layer %2 (bind-bias %1))
          input-activations weights))
```

In the preceding code, we first define a matrix-mult function, which performs
matrix multiplication and ensures that the result is a matrix. Note that to define
matrix-mult, we use the mmult function instead of the mult function that multiplies
the corresponding elements in two matrices of the same size.

Using the matrix-mult and sigmoid functions, we can implement the
forward propagation step between two layers in the ANN. This is done in the
forward-propagate-layer function, which simply multiplies the matrices
representing the weights of the synapse between two layers in the ANN and the
input activation values while ensuring that the returned value is always a matrix.
To propagate a given set of values through all the layers of an ANN, we must add
a bias input and apply the forward-propagate-layer function for each layer.
This can be done concisely using the reduce function over a closure of the
forward-propagate-layer function as shown in the forward-propagate
function defined in the preceding code.

Although the forward-propagate function can determine the output activations
of the ANN, we actually require the activations of all the nodes in the ANN to use
backpropagation. We can do this by translating the reduce function to a recursive
function and introducing an accumulator variable to store the activations of every
layer in the ANN. The forward-propagate-all-activations function, which
is defined in the following code, implements this idea and uses the loop form to
recursively apply the forward-propagate-layer function:

```
(defn forward-propagate-all-activations
  "Propagate activation values through the network
  and return all activation values for all nodes."
  [weights input-activations]
  (loop [all-weights     weights
         activations     (bind-bias input-activations)
         all-activations [activations]]
    (let [[weights
```

```
              & all-weights']    all-weights
              last-iter?         (empty? all-weights')
              out-activations    (forward-propagate-layer
                                   weights activations)
              activations'       (if last-iter? out-activations
                                       (bind-bias out-activations))
              all-activations' (conj all-activations activations')]
          (if last-iter? all-activations'
              (recur all-weights' activations' all-activations')))))))
```

The `forward-propagate-all-activations` function defined in the preceding code requires all the weights of the nodes in the ANN and the input values to pass through the ANN as activation values. We first use the `bind-bias` function to add the bias input to the input activations of the ANN. We then store this value in an accumulator, that is, the variable `all-activations`, as a vector of all the activations in the ANN. The `forward-propagate-layer` function is then applied over the weight matrices of the various layers of the ANN, and each iteration adds a bias input to the input activations of the corresponding layer in the ANN.

 Note that we do not add the bias input in the last iteration as it computes the output layer of the ANN. Thus, the `forward-propagate-all-activations` function applies forward propagation of input values through an ANN and returns the activations of every node in the ANN. Note that the activation values in this vector are in the order of the layers of the ANN.

We will now implement the backpropagation phase of the backpropagation learning algorithm. First, we would have to implement a function to calculate the error term $\delta^{(l)}$ from the equation $\delta^{(l)} = \left(\Theta^{(l)}\right)^T \delta^{(l+1)} \times \left(a^{(l)}\left(1-a^{(l)}\right)\right)$. We will do this with the help of the following code:

```
(defn back-propagate-layer
  "Back propagate deltas (from layer l+1) and
  return layer l deltas."
  [deltas weights layer-activations]
  (mult (matrix-mult (trans weights) deltas)
        (mult layer-activations (minus 1 layer-activations))))
```

The `back-propagate-layer` function defined in the preceding code calculates the errors, or deltas, of a synapse layer *l* in the ANN from the weights of the layer and the deltas of the next layer in the ANN.

Note that we only use matrix multiplication to calculate the term $\left(\Theta^{(i)}\right)^{T}\delta^{(i+1)}$ via the `matrix-mult` function. All other multiplication operations are element-wise multiplication of matrices, which is done using the `mult` function.

Essentially, we have to apply this function from the output layer to the input layer through the various hidden layers of an ANN to produce the delta values of every node in the ANN. These delta values can then be added to the activations of the nodes, thus producing the gradient values by which we must adjust the weights of the nodes in the ANN. We can do this in a manner similar to the `forward-propagate-all-activations` function, that is, by recursively applying the `back-propagate-layer` function over the various layers of the ANN. Of course, we have to traverse the layers of the ANN in the reverse order, that is, starting from the output layer, through the hidden layers, to the input layer. We will do this with the help of the following code:

```
(defn calc-deltas
  "Calculate hidden deltas for back propagation.
  Returns all deltas including output-deltas."
  [weights activations output-deltas]
  (let [hidden-weights     (reverse (rest weights))
        hidden-activations (rest (reverse (rest activations)))]
    (loop [deltas          output-deltas
           all-weights     hidden-weights
           all-activations hidden-activations
           all-deltas      (list output-deltas)]
      (if (empty? all-weights) all-deltas
        (let [[weights
               & all-weights']     all-weights
              [activations
               & all-activations'] all-activations
              deltas'              (back-propagate-layer
                                     deltas weights activations)
              all-deltas'          (cons (rest deltas')
                                         all-deltas)]
          (recur deltas' all-weights'
                 all-activations' all-deltas'))))))
```

The `calc-deltas` function determines the delta values of all the perceptron nodes in the ANN. For this calculation, the input and output activations are not needed. Only the hidden activations, bound to the `hidden-activations` variable, are needed to calculate the delta values. Also, the weights of the input layer are skipped as they are bound to the `hidden-weights` variable. The `calc-deltas` function then applies the `back-propagate-layer` function to all the weight matrices of each synapse layer in the ANN, thus determining the deltas of all the nodes in the matrix. Note that we don't add the delta of the bias nodes to a computed set of deltas. This is done using the `rest` function, `(rest deltas')`, on the calculated deltas of a given synapse layer, as the first delta is that of a bias input in a given layer.

By definition, the gradient vector terms for a given synapse layer $\Delta^{(l)}$ are determined by multiplying the matrices $\delta^{(l+1)}$ and $a^{(l)}$, which represent the deltas of the next layer and activations of the given layer respectively. We will do this with the help of the following code:

```
(defn calc-gradients
  "Calculate gradients from deltas and activations."
  [deltas activations]
  (map #(mmult %1 (trans %2)) deltas activations))
```

The `calc-gradients` function shown in the preceding code is a concise implementation of the term $\delta^{(l+1)}\left(a^{(l)}\right)^{T}$. As we will be dealing with a sequence of delta and activation terms, we use the `map` function to apply the preceding equality to the corresponding deltas and activations in the ANN. Using the `calc-deltas` and `calc-gradient` functions, we can determine the total error in the weights of all nodes in the ANN for a given training sample. We will do this with the help of the following code:

```
(defn calc-error
  "Calculate deltas and squared error for given weights."
  [weights [input expected-output]]
  (let [activations    (forward-propagate-all-activations
                         weights (matrix input))
        output         (last activations)
        output-deltas  (minus output expected-output)
        all-deltas     (calc-deltas
                         weights activations output-deltas)
        gradients      (calc-gradients all-deltas activations)]
    (list gradients
       (sum (pow output-deltas 2)))))
```

The `calc-error` function defined in the preceding code requires two parameters—the weight matrices of the synapse layers in the ANN and a sample training value, which is shown as `[input expected-output]`. The activations of all the nodes in the ANN are first calculated using the `forward-propagate-all-activations` function, and the delta value of the last layer is calculated as the difference of the expected output value and the actual output value produced by the ANN. The output value calculated by the ANN is simply the last activation value produced by the ANN, shown as `(last activations)` in the preceding code. Using the calculated activations, the deltas of all the perceptron nodes are determined via the `calc-deltas` function. These delta values are in turn used to determine the gradients of weights in the various layers of the ANN using the `calc-gradients` function. The **Mean Square Error (MSE)** of the ANN for the given sample value is also calculated by adding the squares of the delta values of the output layer of the ANN.

For a given weight matrix of a layer in the ANN, we must initialize the gradients for the layer as a matrix with the same dimensions as the weight matrix, and all the elements in the gradient matrix must be set to `0`. This can be implemented using a composition of the `dim` function, which returns the size of a matrix as a vector, and a variant form of the `matrix` function, as shown in the following code:

```
(defn new-gradient-matrix
  "Create accumulator matrix of gradients with the
  same structure as the given weight matrix
  with all elements set to 0."
  [weight-matrix]
  (let [[rows cols] (dim weight-matrix)]
    (matrix 0 rows cols)))
```

In the `new-gradient-matrix` function defined in the preceding code, the `matrix` function expects a value, the number of rows and the number of columns to initialize a matrix. This function produces an initialized gradient matrix with the same structure as the supplied weight matrix.

We now implement the `calc-gradients-and-error` function to apply the `calc-error` function on a set of weight matrices and sample values. We must basically apply the `calc-error` function to each sample and accumulate the sum of the gradient and the MSE values. We then calculate the average of these accumulated values to return the gradient matrices and total MSE for the given sample values and weight matrices. We will do this with the help of the following code:

```
(defn calc-gradients-and-error' [weights samples]
  (loop [gradients   (map new-gradient-matrix weights)
         total-error 1
         samples     samples]
```

```
      (let [[sample
              & samples']      samples
             [new-gradients
              squared-error]  (calc-error weights sample)
             gradients'       (map plus new-gradients gradients)
             total-error'     (+ total-error squared-error)]
        (if (empty? samples')
          (list gradients' total-error')
          (recur gradients' total-error' samples')))))

(defn calc-gradients-and-error
  "Calculate gradients and MSE for sample
  set and weight matrix."
  [weights samples]
  (let [num-samples    (length samples)
        [gradients
         total-error]  (calc-gradients-and-error'
                          weights samples)]
    (list
      (map #(div % num-samples) gradients)    ; gradients
      (/ total-error num-samples))))          ; MSE
```

The `calc-gradients-and-error` function defined in the preceding code relies on the `calc-gradients-and-error'` helper function. The `calc-gradients-and-error'` function initializes the gradient matrices, performs the application of the `calc-error` function, and accumulates the calculated gradient values and MSE. The `calc-gradients-and-error` function simply calculates the average of the accumulated gradient matrices and MSE returned from the `calc-gradients-and-error'` function.

Now, the only missing piece in our implementation is modifying the weights of the nodes in the ANN using calculated gradients. In brief, we must repeatedly update the weights until a convergence in the MSE is observed. This is actually a form of gradient descent applied to the nodes of an ANN. We will now implement this variant of gradient descent in order to train the ANN by repeatedly modifying the weights of the nodes in the ANN, as shown in the following code:

```
(defn gradient-descent-complete?
  "Returns true if gradient descent is complete."
  [network iter mse]
  (let [options (:options network)]
    (or (>= iter (:max-iters options))
        (< mse (:desired-error options)))))
```

The `gradient-descent-complete?` function defined in the preceding code simply checks for the termination condition of gradient descent. This function assumes that the ANN, represented as a network, is a map or record that contains the `:options` keyword. The value of this key is in turn another map that contains the various configuration options of the ANN. The `gradient-descent-complete?` function checks whether the total MSE of the ANN is less than the desired MSE, which is specified by the `:desired-error` option. Also, we add another condition to check if the number of iterations performed exceeds the maximum number of iterations specified by the `:max-iters` option.

Now, we will implement a `gradient-descent` function for multilayer perceptron ANNs. In this implementation, the changes in weights are calculated by the `step` function provided by the gradient descent algorithm. These calculated changes are then simply added to the existing weights of the synapse layers of the ANN. We will implement the `gradient-descent` function for multilayer perceptron ANNs with the help of the following code:

```
(defn apply-weight-changes
  "Applies changes to corresponding weights."
  [weights changes]
  (map plus weights changes))


(defn gradient-descent
  "Perform gradient descent to adjust network weights."
  [step-fn init-state network samples]
  (loop [network network
         state init-state
         iter 0]
    (let [iter       (inc iter)
          weights    (:weights network)
          [gradients
           mse]      (calc-gradients-and-error weights samples)]
      (if (gradient-descent-complete? network iter mse)
        network
        (let [[changes state] (step-fn network gradients state)
              new-weights     (apply-weight-changes
                                weights changes)
              network         (assoc network
                                :weights new-weights)]
          (recur network state iter))))))
```

The `apply-weight-changes` function defined in the preceding code simply adds the weights and the calculated changes in the weights of the ANN. The `gradient-descent` function requires a `step` function (specified as `step-fn`), the initial state of the ANN, the ANN itself, and the sample data to train the ANN. This function must calculate the weight changes from the ANN, the initial gradient matrices, and the initial state of the ANN. The `step-fn` function also returns the changed state of the ANN. The weights of the ANN are then updated using the `apply-weight-changes` function, and this iteration is repeatedly performed until the `gradient-descent-complete?` function returns as `true`. The weights of the ANN are specified by the `:weights` keyword in the `network` map. These weights are then updated by simply overwriting the value on the `network` specified by the `:weights` keyword.

In the context of the backpropagation algorithm, we need to specify the learning rate and learning momentum by which the ANN must be trained. These parameters are needed to determine the changes in the weights of the nodes in the ANN. A function implementing this calculation must then be specified as the `step-fn` parameter to the `gradient-descent` function, as shown in the following code:

```
(defn calc-weight-changes
  "Calculate weight changes:
  changes = learning rate * gradients +
            learning momentum * deltas."
  [gradients deltas learning-rate learning-momentum]
  (map #(plus (mult learning-rate %1)
              (mult learning-momentum %2))
       gradients deltas))


(defn bprop-step-fn [network gradients deltas]
  (let [options             (:options network)
        learning-rate       (:learning-rate options)
        learning-momentum   (:learning-momentum options)
        changes             (calc-weight-changes
                              gradients deltas
                              learning-rate learning-momentum)]
    [(map minus changes) changes]))


(defn gradient-descent-bprop [network samples]
  (let [gradients (map new-gradient-matrix (:weights network))]
    (gradient-descent bprop-step-fn gradients
                      network samples)))
```

The `calc-weight-changes` function defined in the preceding code calculates the change of weights, termed as $\rho\Delta^{(i)} + \Lambda\delta^{(i)}$, from the gradient values and deltas of a given layer in the ANN. The `bprop-step-fn` function extracts the learning rate and learning momentum parameters from the ANN that is represented by `network` and uses the `calc-weight-changes` function. As the weights will be added with the changes by the `gradient-descent` function, we return the changes in weights as negative values using the `minus` function.

The `gradient-descent-bprop` function simply initializes the gradient matrices for the given weights of the ANN and calls the `gradient-descent` function by specifying `bprop-step-fn` as the `step` function to be used. Using the `gradient-descent-bprop` function, we can implement the abstract `NeuralNetwork` protocol we had defined earlier, as follows:

```
(defn round-output
  "Round outputs to nearest integer."
  [output]
  (mapv #(Math/round ^Double %) output))

(defrecord MultiLayerPerceptron [options]
  NeuralNetwork

  ;; Calculates the output values for the given inputs.
  (run [network inputs]
    (let [weights (:weights network)
          input-activations (matrix inputs)]
      (forward-propagate weights input-activations)))

  ;; Rounds the output values to binary values for
  ;; the given inputs.
  (run-binary [network inputs]
    (round-output (run network inputs)))

  ;; Trains a multilayer perceptron ANN from sample data.
  (train-ann [network samples]
    (let [options         (:options network)
          hidden-neurons  (:hidden-neurons options)
          epsilon         (:weight-epsilon options)
          [first-in
           first-out]     (first samples)
          num-inputs      (length first-in)
          num-outputs     (length first-out)
```

```
        sample-matrix    (map #(list (matrix (first %))
                                     (matrix (second %)))
                             samples)
        layer-sizes      (conj (vec (cons num-inputs
                                          hidden-neurons))
                               num-outputs)
        new-weights      (random-initial-weights
                           layer-sizes epsilon)
        network          (assoc network :weights new-weights)]
    (gradient-descent-bprop network sample-matrix)))))
```

The MultiLayerPerceptron record defined in the preceding code trains a multilayer perceptron ANN using the gradient-descent-bprop function. The train-ann function first extracts the values for the number of hidden neurons and the constant ε from the options map specified to the ANN. The sizes of the various synapse layers in the ANN are first determined from the sample data and bound to the layer-sizes variable. The weights of the ANN are then initialized using the random-initial-weights function and updated in the record network using the assoc function. Finally, the gradient-descent-bprop function is called to train the ANN using the backpropagation learning algorithm.

The ANN defined by the MultiLayerPerceptron record also implements two other functions, run and run-binary, from the NeuralNetwork protocol. The run function uses the forward-propagate function to determine the output values of a trained MultiLayerPerceptron ANN. The run-binary function simply rounds the value of the output returned by the run function for the given set of input values.

An ANN created using the MultiLayerPerceptron record requires a single options parameter containing the various options we can specify for the ANN. We can define the default options for such an ANN as follows:

```
(def default-options
  {:max-iters 100
   :desired-error 0.20
   :hidden-neurons [3]
   :learning-rate 0.3
   :learning-momentum 0.01
   :weight-epsilon 50})

(defn train [samples]
  (let [network (MultiLayerPerceptron. default-options)]
    (train-ann network samples)))
```

The map defined by the `default-options` variable contains the following keys that specify the options for the `MultiLayerPerceptron` ANN:

- `:max-iter`: This key specifies the maximum number of iterations to run the `gradient-descent` function.

- `:desired-error`: This variable specifies the expected or acceptable MSE in the ANN.

- `:hidden-neurons`: This variable specifies the number of hidden neural nodes in the network. The value [3] represents a single hidden layer with three neurons.

- `:learning-rate` and `:learning-momentum`: These keys specify the learning rate and learning momentum for the weight update phase of the backpropagation learning algorithm.

- `:epsilon`: This variable specifies the constant used by the `random-initial-weights` function to initialize the weights of the ANN.

We also define a simple helper function `train` to create an ANN of the `MultiLayerPerceptron` type and train the ANN using the `train-ann` function and the sample data specified by the `samples` parameter. We can now create a trained ANN from the training data specified by the `sample-data` variable as follows:

```
user> (def MLP (train sample-data))
#'user/MLP
```

We can then use the trained ANN to predict the output of some input values. The output generated by the ANN defined by MLP closely matches the output of an XOR gate as follows:

```
user> (run-binary MLP  [0 1])
[1]
user> (run-binary MLP  [1 0])
[1]
```

However, the trained ANN produces incorrect outputs for some set of inputs as follows:

```
user> (run-binary MLP  [0 0])
[0]
user> (run-binary MLP  [1 1])  ;; incorrect output generated
[1]
```

There are several measures we can implement in order to improve the accuracy of the trained ANN. First, we can regularize the calculated gradients using the weights matrices of the ANN. This modification will produce a noticeable improvement in the preceding implementation. We can also increase the maximum number of iterations to be performed. We can also tune the algorithm to perform better by tweaking the learning rate, the learning momentum, and the number of hidden nodes in the ANN. These modifications are skipped as they have to be done by the reader.

The **Enclog** library (`http://github.com/jimpil/enclog`) is a Clojure wrapper library for the **Encog** library for machine learning algorithms and ANNs. The Encog library (`http://github.com/encog`) has two primary implementations: one in Java and one in .NET. We can use the Enclog library to easily generate customized ANNs to model both supervised and unsupervised machine learning problems.

The Enclog library can be added to a Leiningen project by adding the following dependency to the `project.clj` file:

```
[org.encog/encog-core "3.1.0"]
[enclog "0.6.3"]
```

Note that the Enclog library requires the Encog Java library as a dependency.

For the example that will follow, the namespace declaration should look similar to the following declaration:

```
(ns my-namespace
  (:use [enclog nnets training]))
```

We can create an ANN from the Enclog library using the `neural-pattern` and `network` functions from the `enclog.nnets` namespace. The `neural-pattern` function is used to specify a neural network model for the ANN. The `network` function accepts a neural network model returned from the `neural-pattern` function and creates a new ANN. We can provide several options to the `network` function depending on the specified neural network model. A feed-forward multilayer perceptron network is defined as follows:

```
(def mlp (network (neural-pattern :feed-forward)
                  :activation :sigmoid
                  :input      2
                  :output     1
                  :hidden     [3]))
```

For a feed-forward neural network, we can specify the activation function with the `:activation` key to the `network` function. For our example, we used the sigmoid function, which is specified as `:sigmoid`, as the activation function for the ANNs nodes. We also specified the number of nodes in the input, output, and hidden layers of the ANN using the `:input`, `:output`, and `:hidden` keys.

To train an ANN created by the `network` function with some sample data, we use the `trainer` and `train` functions from the `enclog.training` namespace. The learning algorithm to be used to train the ANN must be specified as the first parameter to the `trainer` function. For the backpropagation algorithm, this parameter is the `:back-prop` keyword. The value returned by the trainer function represents an ANN as well as the learning algorithm to be used to train the ANN. The `train` function is then used to actually run the specified training algorithm on the ANN. We will do this with the help of the following code:

```
(defn train-network [network data trainer-algo]
  (let [trainer (trainer trainer-algo
                         :network network
                         :training-set data)]
    (train trainer 0.01 1000 [])))  ;; 0.01 is the expected error
```

The `train-network` function defined in the preceding code takes three parameters. The first parameter is an ANN created by the network function, the second parameter is the training data to be used to train the ANN, and the third parameter specifies the learning algorithm by which the ANN must be trained. As shown in the preceding code, we can specify the ANN and the training data to the `trainer` function using the key parameters, `:network` and `:training-set`. The `train` function is then used to run the training algorithm on the ANN using the sample data. We can specify the expected error in the ANN and the maximum number of iterations to run the training algorithm as the first and second parameters to the `train` function. In the preceding example, the desired error is `0.01`, and the maximum number of iterations is 1000. The last parameter passed to the `train` function is a vector specifying the behaviors of the ANN, and we ignore it by passing it as an empty vector.

The training data to be used to run the training algorithm on the ANN can be created using Enclog's data function. For example, we can create a training data for a logical XOR gate using the data function as follows:

```
(def dataset
  (let [xor-input [[0.0 0.0] [1.0 0.0] [0.0 1.0] [1.0 1.0]]
        xor-ideal [[0.0]     [1.0]     [1.0]     [0.0]]]
    (data :basic-dataset xor-input xor-ideal)))
```

The data function requires the type of data as the first parameter of the function, followed by the input and output values of the training data as vectors. For our example, we will use the :basic-dataset and :basic parameters. The :basic-dataset keyword can be used to create training data, and the :basic keyword can be used to specify a set of input values.

Using the data defined by the dataset variable and the train-network function, we can train the ANN's MLP to model the output of an XOR gate as follows:

```
user> (def MLP (train-network mlp dataset :back-prop))
Iteration # 1 Error: 26.461526% Target-Error: 1.000000%
Iteration # 2 Error: 25.198031% Target-Error: 1.000000%
Iteration # 3 Error: 25.122343% Target-Error: 1.000000%
Iteration # 4 Error: 25.179218% Target-Error: 1.000000%
...
...
Iteration # 999 Error: 3.182540% Target-Error: 1.000000%
Iteration # 1,000 Error: 3.166906% Target-Error: 1.000000%
#'user/MLP
```

As shown by the preceding output, the trained ANN has an error of about 3.16 percent. We can now use the trained ANN to predict the output of a set of input values. To do this, we use the Java compute and getData methods, which are specified by .compute and .getData respectively. We can define a simple helper function to call the .compute method for a vector of input values and round the output to a binary value as follows:

```
(defn run-network [network input]
  (let [input-data (data :basic input)
        output     (.compute network input-data)
        output-vec (.getData output)]
    (round-output output-vec)))
```

We can now use the `run-network` function to test the trained ANN using a vector of input values, as follows:

```
user> (run-network MLP [1 1])
[0]
user> (run-network MLP [1 0])
[1]
user> (run-network MLP [0 1])
[1]
user> (run-network MLP [0 0])
[0]
```

As shown in the preceding code, the trained ANN represented by `MLP` completely matches the behavior of an XOR gate.

In conclusion, the Enclog library gives us a small set of powerful functions that can be used to build ANNs. In the preceding example, we explored a feed-forward multilayer perceptron model. The library provides several other ANN models, such as **Adaptive Resonance Theory (ART)**, **Self-Organizing Maps (SOM)**, and Elman networks. The Enclog library also allows us to customize the activation function of the nodes in a particular neural network model. For the feed-forward network in our example, we've used the sigmoid function. Several mathematical functions, such as sine, hyperbolic tan, logarithmic, and linear functions, are also supported by the library. There are also several machine learning algorithms supported by the Enclog library that can be used to train an ANN.

Understanding recurrent neural networks

We will now switch our focus to recurrent neural networks and study a simple recurrent neural network model. An **Elman neural network** is a simple recurrent ANN with a single input, output, and hidden layer. There is also an extra *context layer* of neural nodes. Elman neural networks are used to simulate short-term memory in supervised and unsupervised machine learning problems. Enclog does include support for Elman neural networks, and we will demonstrate how we can build an Elman neural network using the Enclog library.

The context layer of an Elman neural network receives unweighted inputs from the hidden layer of the ANN. In this way, the ANN can remember the previous values that we generated using the hidden layer and use these values to affect the predicted value. Thus, the context layer serves as a type of short-term memory for the ANN. An Elman neural network can be illustrated by the following diagram:

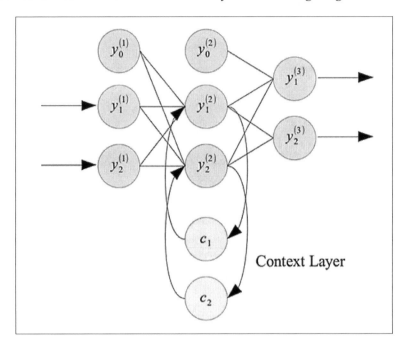

The structure of an Elman network, as depicted by the preceding diagram, resembles that of a feed-forward multilayer perceptron ANN. An Elman network adds an extra context layer of neural nodes to the ANN. The Elman network illustrated in the preceding diagram takes two inputs and produces two outputs. The input and hidden layers of the Elman network add an extra bias input, similar to a multilayer perceptron. The activations of the hidden layers' neurons are fed directly to the two context nodes c_1 and c_2. The values stored in these context nodes are then used later by the nodes in the hidden layer of the ANN to recollect the previous activations to determine the new activation values.

We can create an Elman network that specifies the :elman keyword to the neural-pattern function from the Enclog library as follows:

```
(def elman-network (network (neural-pattern :elman)
                            :activation :sigmoid
                            :input     2
                            :output    1
                            :hidden    [3]))
```

To train the Elman network, we can use the resilient propagation algorithm (for more information, refer to *Empirical Evaluation of the Improved Rprop Learning Algorithm*). This algorithm can also be used to train other recurrent networks supported by Enclog. Interestingly, the resilient propagation algorithm can be used to train feed-forward networks as well. This algorithm also performs significantly better than the backpropagation learning algorithm. Although a complete description of this algorithm is beyond the scope of this book, the reader is encouraged to learn more about this learning algorithm. The resilient propagation algorithm is specified as the :resilient-prop keyword to the train-network function, which we had defined earlier. We can train the Elman neural network using the train-network function and the dataset variable as follows:

```
user> (def EN (train-network elman-network dataset
                             :resilient-prop))
Iteration # 1 Error: 26.461526% Target-Error: 1.000000%
Iteration # 2 Error: 25.198031% Target-Error: 1.000000%
Iteration # 3 Error: 25.122343% Target-Error: 1.000000%
Iteration # 4 Error: 25.179218% Target-Error: 1.000000%
...
...
Iteration # 99 Error: 0.979165% Target-Error: 1.000000%
#'user/EN
```

As shown in the preceding code, the resilient propagation algorithm requires a relatively smaller number of iterations in comparison to the backpropagation algorithm. We can now use this trained ANN to simulate an XOR gate just like we did in the previous example.

In summary, recurrent neural network models and training algorithms are the other useful models that can be used to model classification or regression problems using ANNs.

Building SOMs

SOM (pronounced as **ess-o-em**) is another interesting ANN model that is useful for unsupervised learning. SOMs are used in several practical applications such as handwriting and image recognition. We will also revisit SOMs when we discuss clustering in *Chapter 7, Clustering Data*.

In unsupervised learning, the sample data contains no expected output values, and the ANN must recognize and match patterns from the input data entirely on its own. SOMs are used for *competitive learning*, which is a special class of unsupervised learning in which the neurons in the output layer of the ANN compete among themselves for activation. The activated neuron determines the final output value of the ANN, and hence, the activated neuron is also termed as a **winning neuron**.

Neurobiological studies have shown that different sensory inputs sent to the brain are mapped to the corresponding areas of the brain's *cerebral cortex* in an orderly pattern. Thus, neurons that deal with closely related operations are kept close together. This is known as the **principle of topographic formation**, and SOMs are, in fact, modeled on this behavior.

An SOM essentially transforms input data with a large number of dimensions to a low-dimensional discrete map. The SOM is trained by placing the neurons at the nodes of this map. This internal map of the SOM usually has one or two dimensions. The neurons in the SOM become *selectively tuned* to the patterns in the input values. When a particular neuron in the SOM is activated for a particular input pattern, its neighboring neurons tend to get more excited and more tuned to the pattern in the input values. This behavior is termed as **lateral interaction** of a set of neurons. An SOM, thus, finds patterns in the input data. When a similar pattern is found in a set of inputs, the SOM recognizes this pattern. The layers of neural nodes in an SOM can be illustrated as follows:

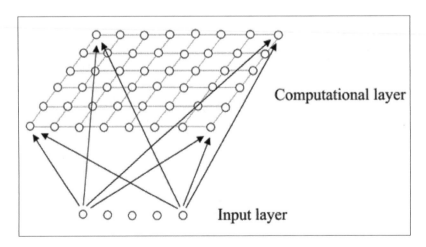

An SOM has an input layer and a computational layer, as depicted by the preceding diagram. The computational layer is also termed as the **feature map** of the SOM. The input nodes map the input values to several neurons in the computational layer. Each node in the computational layer has its output connected to its neighboring node, and each of these connections has a weight associated with it. These weights are termed as the **connection weights** of the feature map. The SOM remembers patterns in the input values by adjusting the connection weights of the nodes in its computational layer.

The self-organizing process of an SOM can be described as follows:

1. The connection weights are first initialized to random values.
2. For each input pattern, the neural nodes in the computational layer compute a value using a discriminant function. These values are then used to decide the winning neuron.
3. The neuron with the least value for the discriminant function is selected, and the connection weights to its surrounding neurons are modified to be activated for similar patterns in the input data.

The weights must be modified such that the value produced by the discriminant function for the neighboring nodes is reduced for the given pattern in the input. Thus, the winning node and its surrounding nodes produce higher output or activation values for similar patterns in the input data. The amount of change by which the weights are adjusted depends on the learning rate specified to the training algorithm.

For a given number of dimensions D in the input data, the discriminant function can be formally defined as follows:

$$d_j(x) = \sum_{i=0}^{D} (x_i - w_j)^2$$

In the preceding equation, the term w_j is the weight vector of the jth neuron in the SOM. The length of the vector w_j is equal to the number of neurons connected to the jth neuron.

Once we have selected the winning neuron in an SOM, we must select the neighboring neurons of the winning neuron. We must adjust the weights of these neighboring neurons along with the weight of the winning neuron. A variety of schemes can be used for the selection of the winning neuron's neighboring nodes. In the simplest case, we can select a single neighboring neuron.

We can alternatively use the `bubble` function or the `radial bias` function to select a group of neighboring neurons surrounding the winning neuron (for more information, refer to *Multivariable functional interpolation and adaptive networks*).

To train an SOM, we must perform the following steps as part of the training algorithm:

1. Set the weights of the nodes in the computational layer to random values.

2. Select a sample input pattern from the training data.

3. Find the winning neuron for the selected set of input patterns.

4. Update the weights of the winning neuron and its surrounding nodes.

5. Repeat steps 2 to 4 for all the samples in the training data.

The Enclog library does support the SOM neural network model and training algorithm. We can create and train an SOM from the Enclog library as follows:

```
(def som (network (neural-pattern :som) :input 4 :output 2))

(defn train-som [data]
  (let [trainer (trainer :basic-som :network som
                         :training-set data
                         :learning-rate 0.7
                         :neighborhood-fn
             (neighborhood-F :single))]
    (train trainer Double/NEGATIVE_INFINITY 10 []))))
```

The `som` variable appearing in the preceding code represents an SOM. The `train-som` function can be used to train the SOM. The SOM training algorithm is specified as `:basic-som`. Note that we specify the learning rate as `0.7` using the `:learning-rate` key.

The `:neighborhood-fn` key passed to the `trainer` function in the preceding code specifies how we select the neighbors of the winning node in the SOM for a given set of input values. We specify that a single neighboring node of the winning node must be selected with the help of `(neighborhood-F :single)`. We can also specify different neighborhood functions. For example, we can specify the `bubble` function as `:bubble` or the `radial basis` function as `:rbf`.

We can use the `train-som` function to train the SOM with some input patterns. Note that the training data to be used to train the SOM will not have any output values. The SOM must recognize patterns in the input data on its own. Once the SOM is trained, we can use the Java `classify` method to detect patterns in the input. For the following example, we provide only two input patterns to train the SOM:

```
(defn train-and-run-som []
  (let [input [[-1.0, -1.0, 1.0, 1.0 ]
               [1.0, 1.0, -1.0, -1.0]]
        input-data (data :basic-dataset input nil) ;no ideal data
        SOM        (train-som input-data)
        d1         (data :basic (first input))
        d2         (data :basic (second input))]
    (println "Pattern 1 class:" (.classify SOM d1))
    (println "Pattern 2 class:" (.classify SOM d2))
    SOM))
```

We can run the `train-and-run-som` function defined in the preceding code and observe that the SOM recognizes the two input patterns in the training data as two distinct classes as follows:

```
user> (train-and-run-som)
Iteration # 1 Error: 2.137686% Target-Error: NaN
Iteration # 2 Error: 0.641306% Target-Error: NaN
Iteration # 3 Error: 0.192392% Target-Error: NaN
...
...
Iteration # 9 Error: 0.000140% Target-Error: NaN
Iteration # 10 Error: 0.000042% Target-Error: NaN
Pattern 1 class: 1
Pattern 2 class: 0
#<SOM org.encog.neural.som.SOM@19a0818>
```

In conclusion, SOMs are a great model for dealing with unsupervised learning problems. Also, we can easily build SOMs to model such problems using the Enclog library.

Summary

We have explored a few interesting ANN models in this chapter. These models can be applied to solve both supervised and unsupervised machine learning problems. The following are some of the other points that we covered:

- We have explored the necessity of ANNs and their broad types, that is, feed-forward and recurrent ANNs.

- We have studied the multilayer perceptron ANN and the backpropagation algorithm used to train this ANN. We've also provided a simple implementation of the backpropagation algorithm in Clojure using matrices and matrix operations.

- We have introduced the Enclog library that can be used to build ANNs. This library can be used to model both supervised and unsupervised machine learning problems.

- We have explored recurrent Elman neural networks, which can be used to produce ANNs with a small error in a relatively less number of iterations. We've also described how we can create and train such an ANN using the Enclog library.

- We introduced SOMs, which are neural networks that can be applied in the domain of unsupervised learning. We've also described how we can create and train an SOM using the Enclog library.

5
Selecting and Evaluating Data

In the previous chapter, we studied **Artificial Neural Networks** (**ANNs**) and how they can be used to effectively model nonlinear sample data. So far, we've discussed several machine learning techniques that can be used to model a given training set of data. In this chapter, we will explore the following topics that focus on how to select appropriate features from the sample data:

- We will study methods to evaluate or quantify how accurately a formulated model fits the supplied training data. These techniques will be useful when we have to extend or debug an existing model.

- We will also explore how we can use the `clj-ml` library to perform this process on a given machine learning model.

- Towards the end of the chapter, we will implement a working spam classifier that incorporates a model evaluation technique.

The term **machine learning diagnostic** is often used to describe a test that can be run to gain insight about what is and isn't working in a machine learning model. This information generated by the diagnostic can then be used to improve the performance of the given model. Generally, when designing a machine learning model, it's advisable to formulate a diagnostic for the model in parallel. Implementing a diagnostic for a given model can take around the same time as formulating the model itself, but implementing a diagnostic is a good investment of time since it would help in quickly determining what needs to be changed in the model in order to improve it. Thus, machine learning diagnostics are helpful in saving time with respect to debugging or improving a formulated learning model.

Another interesting aspect of machine learning is that without knowing the nature of the data we are trying to fit, we can make no assumption about which machine learning model we can use to fit the sample data. This axiom is known as the **No Free Lunch** theorem, and can be summarized as follows:

> *"Without prior assumptions about the nature of a learning algorithm, no learning algorithm is superior or inferior to any other (or even random guessing)."*

Understanding underfitting and overfitting

In the previous chapters, we've talked about minimizing the error or cost function of a formulated machine learning model. It's apt for the overall error of the estimated model to be low, but a low error is generally not enough to determine how well the model fits the supplied training data. In this section, we will revisit the concepts of *overfitting* and *underfitting*.

An estimated model is said to be **underfit** if it exhibits a large error in prediction. Ideally, we should strive to minimize this error in the model. However, a formulated model with a low error or cost function could also indicate that the model doesn't understand the underlying relationship between the given features of the model. Rather, the model is *memorizing* the supplied data, and this could even result in modeling random noise. In this case, the model is said to be **overfit**. A general symptom of an overfit model is failure to correctly predict the output variable from unseen data. An underfit model is also said to exhibit **high bias** and an overfit model is said to have **high variance**.

Suppose we are modeling a single dependent and independent variable in our model. Ideally, the model should fit the training data while generalizing on data that hasn't yet been observed in the training data.

The variance of the dependent variables with the independent variable in an underfit model can be represented using the following plot:

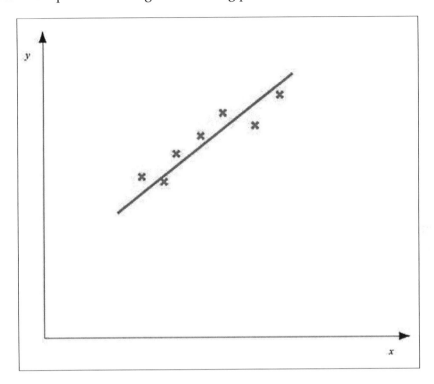

In the preceding diagram, the red crosses represent data points in our sample data. As shown in the diagram, an underfit model will exhibit a large overall error, and we must try to reduce this error by appropriately selecting the features for our model and using regularization.

On the other hand, a model could also be overfit, in which the overall error in the model has a low value, but the estimated model fails to correctly predict the dependent variable from previously unseen data. An overfit model can be depicted using the following plot:

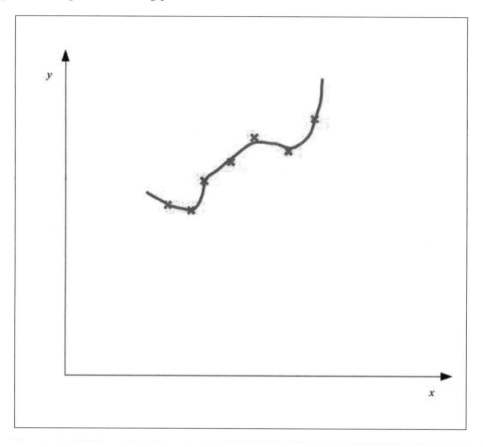

As shown in the preceding diagram, the estimated model plot closely but inappropriately fits the training data and thus has a low overall error. But, the model fails to respond correctly to new data.

The model that describes a good fit for the sample data will have a low overall error and can predict the dependent variable correctly from previously unseen values for the independent variables in our model. An appropriately fit model should have a plot similar to the following diagram:

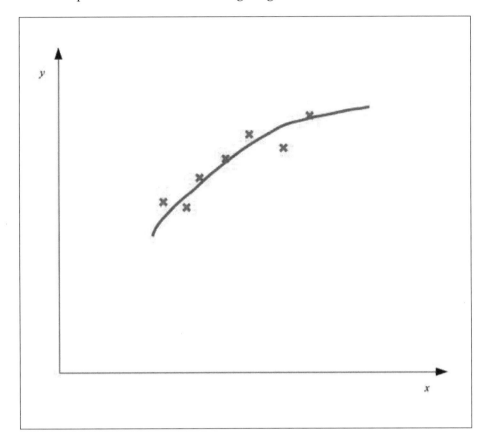

ANNs can also be underfit or overfit on the provided sample data. For example, an ANN with a few hidden nodes and layers could be an underfit model, while an ANN with a large number of hidden nodes and layers could exhibit overfitting.

Evaluating a model

We can plot the variance of the dependent and independent variables of a model to determine if the model is underfit or overfit. However, with a larger number of features, we need a better way to visualize how well the model generalizes the relationship of the dependent and independent variables of the model over the training data.

We can evaluate a trained machine learning model by determining the cost function of the model on some different data. Thus, we need to split the available sample data into two subsets—one for training the model and another for testing it. The latter subset is also called the **test set** of our model.

The cost function is then calculated for the N_{test} samples in the test set. This gives us a measure of the overall error in the model when used on previously unseen data. This value is represented by the term $J_{test}(\hat{y})$ of the estimated model $\hat{y}$ and is also called the **test error** of the formulated model. The overall error in the training data is called the **training error** of the model and is represented by the term $J_{train}(\hat{y})$. A linear regression model's test error can be calculated as follows:

$$J_{test}(\hat{y}) = \frac{1}{N_{test}} \sum_{i=1}^{N_{test}} \left(\hat{y}(X_i) - Y_i \right)^2$$

Similarly, the test error in a binary classification model can be formally expressed as follows:

$$J_{test}(\hat{y}) = \frac{1}{N_{test}} \sum_{i=1}^{N_{test}} err\left(\hat{y}(X_i), Y_i \right)$$

$$where\ err\left(\hat{y}(X_i), Y_i \right) = 1\ if\ \hat{y}(X_i) \geq 0.5$$

$$and\ err\left(\hat{y}(X_i), Y_i \right) = 0\ if\ \hat{y}(X_i) < 0.5$$

The problem of determining the features of a model such that the test error is low is termed as **model selection** or **feature selection**. Also, to avoid overfitting, we must measure how well the model generalizes over the training data. The test error on its own is an optimistic estimate of the generalization error in the model over the training data. However, we must also measure the generalization error in data that hasn't yet been seen by the model. If the model has a low error over unseen data as well, we can be certain that the model does not overfit the data. This process is termed as **cross-validation**.

Thus, to ensure that the model can perform well on unseen data, we will require an additional set of data, called the **cross-validation set**. The number of samples in the cross-validation set is represented by the term N_{cv}. Typically, the sample data is partitioned into the training, test, and cross-validation sets such that the number of samples in the training data are significantly greater than those in the test and cross-validate sets. The error in generalization, or rather the cross-validation error $J_{cv}(\hat{y})$, thus indicates how well the estimated model fits unseen data. Note that we don't modify the estimated model when we use the cross-validation and test sets on it. We will study more about cross-validation in the following sections of this chapter. As we will see later, we can also use cross-validation to determine the features of a model from some sample data.

For example, suppose we have 100 samples in our training data. We partition this sample data into three sets. The first 60 samples will be used to estimate a model that fits the data appropriately. Out of the 40 remaining samples, 20 will be used to cross-validate the estimated model, and the other 20 will be used to finally test the cross-validated model.

In the context of classification, a good representation of the accuracy of a given classifier is a *confusion matrix*. This representation is often used to visualize the performance of a given classifier based on a supervised machine learning algorithm. Each column in this matrix represents the number of samples that belong to a particular class as predicted by the given classifier. The rows of the confusion matrix represent the actual classes of the samples. The confusion matrix is also called the **contingency matrix** or the **error matrix** of the trained classifier.

For example, say we have two classes in a given classification model. The confusion matrix of this model might look like the following:

		Predicted class	
		A	B
Actual class	A	45	15
	B	30	10

In a confusion matrix, the predicted classes in our model are represented by vertical columns and the actual classes are represented by horizontal rows. In the preceding example of a confusion matrix, there are a total of 100 samples. Out of these, 45 samples from class A and 10 samples from class B were predicted to have the correct class. However, 15 samples of class A have been classified as class B and similarly 30 samples of class B have been predicted to have class A.

Let's consider the following confusion matrix of a different classifier that uses the same data as the previous example:

		Predicted class	
		A	B
Actual class	A	45	5
	B	0	50

In the preceding confusion matrix, the classifier classifies all samples of class B correctly. Also, only 5 samples of class A are classified incorrectly. Thus, this classifier better understands the distinction between the two classes of data when compared to the classifier used in the previous example. In practice, we must strive to train a classifier such that it has values close to *0* for all the elements other than the diagonal elements in its confusion matrix.

Understanding feature selection

As we mentioned earlier, we need to determine an appropriate set of features from the sample data on which we must base our model. We can use cross-validation to determine which set of features to use from the training data, which can be explained as follows.

For each set or combination of feature variables, we determine the training and cross-validation error of a model based on the selected set of features. For example, we might want to add polynomial features derived from the independent variables of our model. We evaluate the training and cross-validation errors for each set of features depending on the highest degree of polynomial used to model the training data. We can plot the variance of these error functions over the degree of polynomial used, similar to the following diagram:

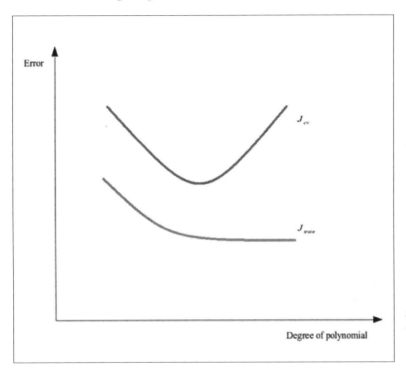

From the preceding diagram, we can determine which set of features produce an underfit or overfit estimated model. If a selected model has a high value for both the training and cross-validation errors, which is found towards the left of the plot, then the model is underfitting the supplied training data. On the other hand, a low training error and a high cross-validation error, as shown towards the right of the plot, indicates that the model is overfit. Ideally, we must select the set of features with the lowest possible values of the training and cross-validation errors.

Varying the regularization parameter

To produce a better fit of the training data, we can use regularization to avoid the problem of overfitting our data. The value of the regularization parameter λ of a given model must be appropriately selected depending on the behavior of the model. Note that a high regularization parameter could result in a high training error, which is an undesirable effect. We can vary the regularization parameter in a formulated machine learning model to produce the following plot of the error values over the value of the regularization parameter in our model:

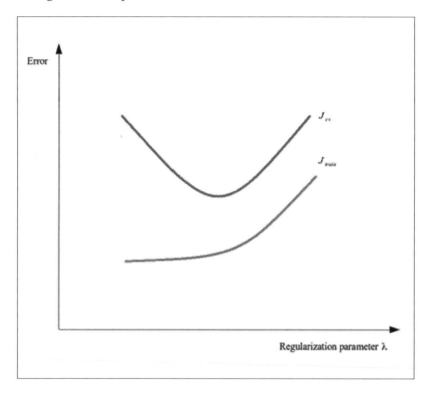

Thus, as shown in the preceding plot, we can also minimize the training and cross-validation error in the model by changing the regularization parameter. If a model exhibits a high value for both these error values, we must consider reducing the value of the regularization parameter until both the error values are significantly low for the supplied sample data.

Understanding learning curves

Another useful way to visualize the performance of a machine learning model is to use learning curves. A **learning curve** is essentially a plot of the error values in a model over the number of samples by which it is trained and cross-validated. For example, a model could have the following learning curve for the training and cross-validation errors:

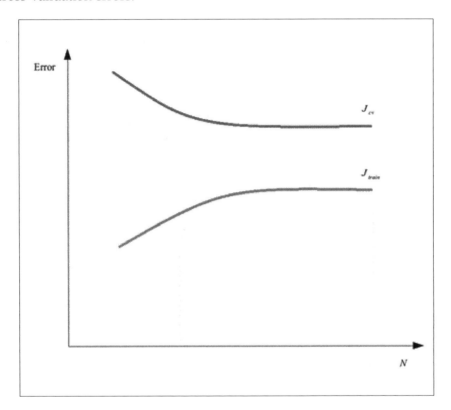

Learning curves can be used to diagnose an underfit and overfit model. For example, the training error could be observed to increase quickly and converge towards a value close to the cross-validation with the number of samples provided to the model. Also, both the error values in our model have a significantly high value. A model that exhibits this kind of variance of error with the number of samples is underfit and has a learning curve similar to the following plot:

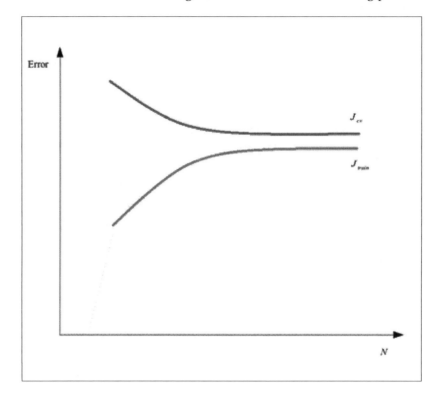

On the other hand, a model's training error could be observed to increase slowly with the number of samples provided to the model, and there might also be a large difference between the training and cross-validation errors in the model. This model is said to be overfit and has a learning curve similar to the following plot:

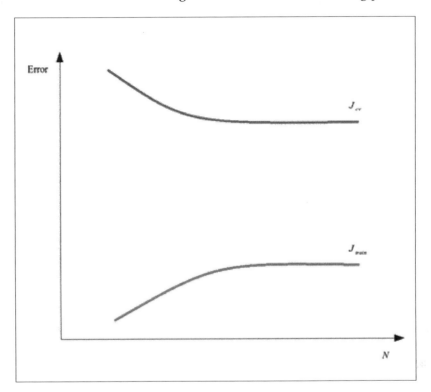

Thus, learning curve is a good supplementary tool to cross-validation for determining what is not working and what needs to be changed in a given machine learning model.

Improving a model

Once we have determined whether a model is underfit or overfit over the given sample data, we must decide on how to improve the model's understanding of the relationship between the independent and dependent variables in our model. Let's briefly discuss a few of these techniques, as follows:

- Add or remove some features. As we will explore later, this technique can be used to improve both an underfit and an overfit model.

- Vary the value of the regularization parameter λ. Like adding or removing features, this method can be applied to both underfit and overfit models.

- Gather more training data. This method is a fairly obvious solution for improving an overfit model as it's needed to formulate a more generalized model to fit the training data.

- Add features which are polynomial terms of other features in the model. This method can be used to improve an underfit model. For example, if we are modeling two independent feature variables, x_1 and x_2, we could add the terms x_1^2, x_2^2 and $x_1 x_2$ as additional features to improve the model. The polynomial terms could be of even higher degrees, such as x_1^3 and $x_1^2 x_2^4$, although this could result in overfitting the training data.

Using cross-validation

As we briefly mentioned earlier, cross-validation is a common validation technique that can be used to evaluate machine learning models. Cross-validation essentially measures how well the estimated model will generalize some given data. This data is different from the training data supplied to our model, and is called the **cross-validation set**, or simply **validation set**, of our model. Cross-validation of a given model is also called **rotation estimation**.

If an estimated model performs well during cross-validation, we can assume that the model can understand the relationship between its various independent and dependent variables. The goal of cross-validation is to provide a test to determine if a formulated model is overfit on the training data. In the perspective of implementation, cross-validation is a kind of unit test for a machine learning system.

A single round of cross-validation generally involves partitioning all the available sample data into two subsets and then performing training on one subset and validation and/or testing on the other subset. Several such rounds, or *folds*, of cross-validation must be performed using different sets of data to reduce the variance of the overall cross-validation error of the given model. Any particular measure of the cross-validation error should be calculated as the average of this error over the different folds in cross-validation.

There are several types of cross-validation we can implement as a diagnostic for a given machine learning model or system. Let's briefly explore a few of them as follows:

- A common type is *k-fold* cross-validation, in which we partition the cross-validation data into k equal subsets. The training of the model is then performed on $k - 1$ subsets of the data and the cross-validation is performed on a single subset.

- A simple variation of *k-fold* cross-validation is *2-fold* cross-validation, which is also called the *holdout method*. In *2-fold* cross-validation, the training and cross-validation subsets of data will be almost equal in proportion.

- **Repeated random subsampling** is another simple variant of cross-validation in which the sample data is first randomized or shuffled and then used as training and cross-validation data. This method is notably not dependent on the number of folds used for cross-validation.

- Another form of *k-fold* cross-validation is **leave-one-out** cross-validation, in which only a single record from the available sample data is used for cross-validation. Leave-one-out cross-validation is essentially *k-fold* cross-validation in which k is equal to the number of samples or observations in the sample data.

Cross-validation basically treats the estimated model as a black box, that is, it makes no assumptions about the implementation of the model. We can also use cross-validation to select features in a given model by using cross-validation to determine the feature set that produces the best fit model over the given sample data. Of course, there are a couple of limitations of classification, which can be summarized as follows:

- If a given model is needed to perform feature selection internally, we must perform cross-validation for each selected feature set in the given model. This can be computationally expensive depending on the amount of available sample data.

- Cross-validation is not very useful if the sample data comprises exactly or nearly equal samples.

In summary, it's a good practice to implement cross-validation for any machine learning system that we build. Also, we can choose an appropriate cross-validation technique depending on the problem we are trying to model as well as the nature of the collected sample data.

 For the example that will follow, the namespace declaration should look similar to the following declaration:

```
(ns my-namespace
  (:use [clj-ml classifiers data]))
```

We can use the `clj-ml` library to cross-validate the classifier we built for the fish packaging plant in *Chapter 3, Categorizing Data*. Essentially, we built a classifier to determine whether a fish is a salmon or a sea bass using the `clj-ml` library. To recap, a fish is represented as a vector containing the category of the fish and values for the various features of the fish. The attributes of a fish are its length, width, and lightness of skin. We also described a template for a sample fish, which is defined as follows:

```
(def fish-template
  [{:category [:salmon :sea-bass]}
   :length :width :lightness])
```

The `fish-template` vector defined in the preceding code can be used to train a classifier with some sample data. For now, we will not bother about which classification algorithm we have used to model the given training data. We can only assume that the classifier was created using the `make-classifier` function from the `clj-ml` library. This classifier is stored in the `*classifier*` variable as follows:

```
(def *classifier* (make-classifier ...))
```

Suppose the classifier was trained with some sample data. We must now evaluate this trained classification model. To do this, we must first create some sample data to cross-validate. For the sake of simplicity, we will use randomly generated data in this example. We can generate this data using the `make-sample-fish` function, which we defined in *Chapter 3, Categorizing Data*. This function simply creates a new vector of some random values representing a fish. Of course, we must not forget the fact that the `make-sample-fish` function has an in-built partiality, so we create a meaningful pattern in a number of samples created using this function as follows:

```
(def fish-cv-data
  (for [i (range 3000)] (make-sample-fish)))
```

We will need to use a dataset from the `clj-ml` library, and we can create one using the `make-dataset` function, as shown in the following code:

```
(def fish-cv-dataset
  (make-dataset "fish-cv" fish-template fish-cv-data))
```

To cross-validate the classifier, we must use the `classifier-evaluate` function from the `clj-ml.classifiers` namespace. This function essentially performs *k-fold* cross-validation on the given data. Other than the classifier and the cross-validation dataset, this function requires the number of folds that we must perform on the data to be specified as the last parameter. Also, we will first need to set the class field of the records in `fish-cv-dataset` using the `dataset-set-class` function. We can define a single function to perform these operations as follows:

```
(defn cv-classifier [folds]
  (dataset-set-class fish-cv-dataset 0)
  (classifier-evaluate *classifier* :cross-validation
                       fish-cv-dataset folds))
```

We will use 10 folds of cross-validation on the classifier. Since the `classifier-evaluate` function returns a map, we bind this return value to a variable for further use, as follows:

```
user> (def cv (cv-classifier 10))
#'user/cv
```

We can fetch and print the summary of the preceding cross-validation using the `:summary` keyword as follows:

```
user> (print (:summary cv))

Correctly Classified Instances        2986               99.5333 %
Incorrectly Classified Instances        14                0.4667 %
Kappa statistic                       0.9888
Mean absolute error                   0.0093
Root mean squared error               0.0681
Relative absolute error               2.2248 %
Root relative squared error          14.9238 %
Total Number of Instances             3000
nil
```

As shown in the preceding code, we can view several statistical measures of performance for our trained classifier. Apart from the correctly and incorrectly classified records, this summary also describes the **Root Mean Squared Error (RMSE)** and several other measures of error in our classifier. For a more detailed view of the correctly and incorrectly classified instances in the classifier, we can print the confusion matrix of the cross-validation using the `:confusion-matrix` keyword, as shown in the following code:

```
user> (print (:confusion-matrix cv))
=== Confusion Matrix ===

    a     b    <-- classified as
 2129     0 |    a = salmon
    9   862 |    b = sea-bass
nil
```

As shown in the preceding example, we can use the `clj-ml` library's `classifier-evaluate` function to perform a *k-fold* cross-validation on any given classifier. Although we are restricted to using classifiers from the `clj-ml` library when using the `classifier-evaluate` function, we must strive to implement similar diagnostics in any machine learning system we build.

Building a spam classifier

Now that we are familiar with cross-validation, we will build a working machine learning system that incorporates cross-validation. The problem at hand will be that of **spam classification**, in which we will have to determine the likelihood of a given e-mail being a spam e-mail. Essentially, the problem boils down to binary classification with a few tweaks to make the machine learning system more sensitive to spam (for more information, refer to *A Plan for Spam*). Note that we will not be implementing a classification engine that is integrated with an e-mail server, but rather we will be concentrating on the aspects of training the engine with some data and classifying a given e-mail.

The way this would be used in practice can be briefly explained as follows. A user will receive and read a new e-mail, and will decide whether to mark the e-mail as spam or not. Depending on the user's decision, we must train the e-mail service's spam engine using the new e-mail as data.

In order to train our spam classifier in a more automated manner, we'll have to simply gather data to feed into the classifier. We will need a large amount of data to effectively train a classifier with the English language. Luckily for us, sample data for spam classification can be found easily on the Web. For this implementation, we will use data from the **Apache SpamAssassin** project.

The Apache SpamAssassin project is an open source implementation of a spam classification engine in Perl. For our implementation, we will use the sample data from this project. You can download this data from `http://spamassassin.apache.org/publiccorpus/`. For our example, we have used the `spam_2` and `easy_ham_2` datasets. A Clojure Leiningen project housing our spam classifier implementation will require that these datasets be extracted and placed in the `ham/` and `spam/` subdirectories of the `corpus/` folder. The `corpus/` folder should be placed in the root directory of the Leiningen project that is the same folder of the `project.clj` file.

The features of our spam classifier will be the number of occurrences of all previously encountered words in spam and ham e-mails. By the term **ham**, we mean "not spam". Thus, there are effectively two independent variables in our model. Also, each word has an associated probability of occurrence in e-mails, which can be calculated from the number of times it's found in spam and ham e-mails and the total number of e-mails processed by the classifier. A new e-mail would be classified by finding all known words in the e-mail's header and body and then somehow combining the probabilities of occurrences of these words in spam and ham e-mails.

For a given word feature in our classifier, we must calculate the total probability of occurrence of the word by taking into account the total number of e-mails analyzed by the classifier (for more information, refer to *Better Bayesian Filtering*). Also, an unseen term is neutral in the sense that it is neither spam nor ham. Thus, the initial probability of occurrence of any word in the untrained classifier is 0.5. Hence, we use a **Bayesian probability** function to model the occurrence of a particular word.

In order to classify a new e-mail, we also need to combine the probabilities of occurrences of all the known words found in it. For this implementation, we will use **Fisher's method**, or **Fisher's combined probability test**, to combine the calculated probabilities. Although the mathematical proof of this test is beyond the scope of this book, it's important to know that this method essentially estimates the probabilities of several independent probabilities in a given model as a χ^2 (pronounced as **chi-squared**) distribution (for more information, refer to *Statistical Methods for Research Workers*). Such a distribution has an associated number of degrees of freedom. It can be shown that an χ^2 distribution with degrees of freedom equal to twice the number of combined probabilities k can be formally expressed as follows:

$$-2\sum_{i=1}^{k} \log p_i \sim \chi^2_{2k}$$

This means that using an χ^2 distribution with $2k$ degrees of freedom, the **Cumulative Distribution Function (CDF)**, of the probabilities of the e-mail being a spam or a ham can be combined to reflect a total probability that is high when there are a large number of probabilities with values close to 1.0. Thus, an e-mail is classified as spam only when most of the words in the e-mail have been previously found in spam e-mails. Similarly, a large number of ham keywords would indicate the e-mail is in fact a ham e-mail. On the other hand, a low number of occurrences of spam keywords in an e-mail would have a probability closer to 0.5, in which case the classifier will be unsure of whether the e-mail is spam or ham.

For the example that will follow, we will require the `file` and `cdf-chisq` functions from the `clojure.java.io` and Incanter libraries, respectively. The namespace declaration of the example should look similar to the following declaration:

```
(ns my-namespace
    (:use [clojure.java.io :only [file]]
          [incanter.stats :only [cdf-chisq]]))
```

A classifier trained using Fisher's method, as described earlier, will be very sensitive to new spam e-mails. We represent the dependent variable of our model by the probability of a given e-mail being spam. This probability is also termed as the **spam score** of the e-mail. A low score indicates that an e-mail is ham, while a high score indicates that the e-mail is spam. Of course, we must also include a third class to represent an unknown value in our model. We can define some reasonable limits for the scores of these categories as follows:

```
(def min-spam-score 0.7)
(def max-ham-score 0.4)

(defn classify-score [score]
  [(cond
     (<= score max-ham-score)  :ham
     (>= score min-spam-score) :spam
     :else :unsure)
   score])
```

As defined earlier, if an e-mail has a score of 0.7 or more, it's a spam e-mail. And a score of 0.5 or less indicates that the e-mail is ham. Also, if the score lies between these two values, we can't effectively decide whether the e-mail is spam or not. We represent these three categories using the keywords `:ham`, `:spam`, and `:unsure`.

The spam classifier must read several e-mails, determine all the words, or *tokens*, in the e-mails' text and header, and store this information as empirical knowledge to use later. We need to store the number of occurrences a particular word is found in spam and ham e-mails. Thus, every word that the classifier has encountered represents a feature. To represent this information for a single word, we will use a record with three fields as shown in the following code:

```
(defrecord TokenFeature [token spam ham])

(defn new-token [token]
  (TokenFeature. token 0 0))

(defn inc-count [token-feature type]
  (update-in token-feature [type] inc))
```

The record `TokenFeature` defined in the preceding code can be used to store the needed information for our spam classifier. The `new-token` function simply creates a new record for a given token by invoking the records, constructor. Obviously, a word is initially seen zero times in both spam and ham e-mails. We will also need to update these values, and we define the `inc-count` function to perform an update on the record using the `update-in` function. Note that the `update-in` function expects a function to apply to a particular field in the record as the last parameter. We are already dealing with a small amount of a mutable state in our implementation, so let's delegate access to this state through an agent. We would also like to keep track of the total number of ham and spam e-mails; so, we'll wrap these values with agents as well, as shown in the following code:

```
(def feature-db
  (agent {} :error-handler #(println "Error: " %2)))

(def total-ham (agent 0))
(def total-spam (agent 0))
```

The `feature-db` agent defined in the preceding code will be used to store all word features. We define a simple error handler for this agent using the `:error-handler` keyword parameter. The agent's `total-ham` and `total-spam` functions will keep track of the total number of ham and spam e-mails, respectively. We will now define a couple of functions to access these agents as follows:

```
(defn clear-db []
  (send feature-db (constantly {}))
  (send total-ham  (constantly 0))
  (send total-spam (constantly 0)))
```

```
(defn update-feature!
  "Looks up a TokenFeature record in the database and
  creates it if it doesn't exist, or updates it."
  [token f & args]
  (send feature-db update-in [token]
        #(apply f (if %1 %1 (new-token token))
                args)))
```

In case you are not familiar with agents in Clojure, we can use the `send` function to alter the value contained in an agent. This function expects a single argument, that is, the function to apply to its encapsulated value. The agent applies this function on its contained value and updates it if there are no errors. The `clear-db` function simply initializes all the agents we've defined with an initial value. This is done by using the `constantly` function that wraps a value in a function that returns the same value. The `update-feature!` function modifies the value of a given token in the `feature-db` map and creates a new token if the supplied token is not present in the map of `feature-db`. Since we will only be incrementing the number of occurrences of a given token, we will pass the `inc-count` function as a parameter to the `update-feature!` function.

Now, let's define how the classifier will extract words from a given e-mail. We'll use regular expressions to do this. If we want to extract all the words from a given string, we can use the regular expression `[a-zA-Z]{3,}`. We can define this regular expression using a literal syntax in Clojure, as shown in the following code. Note that we could also use the `re-pattern` function to create a regular expression. We will also define all the MIME header fields from which we should also extract tokens. We will do all this with the help of the following code:

```
(def token-regex #"[a-zA-Z]{3,}")

(def header-fields
  ["To:"
   "From:"
   "Subject:"
   "Return-Path:"])
```

To match tokens with the regular expression defined by `token-regex`, we will use the `re-seq` function, which returns all matching tokens in a given string as a sequence of strings. For the MIME headers of an e-mail, we need to use a different regular expression to extract tokens. For example, we can extract tokens from the "From" MIME header as follows:

```
user> (re-seq #"From:(.*)\n"
              "From: someone@host.org\n")
(["From: someone@host.org\n" " someone@host.org"])
```

Note the use of the newline character at the end of the regular expression, which is used to indicate the end of a MIME header in an e-mail.

We can then proceed to extract words from the values returned by matching the regular expression defined in the preceding code. Let's define the following few functions to extract tokens from a given e-mail's headers and body using this logic:

```
(defn header-token-regex [f]
  (re-pattern (str f "(.*)\n")))

(defn extract-tokens-from-headers [text]
  (for [field header-fields]
    (map #(str field %1)    ; prepends field to each word from line
         (mapcat (fn [x] (->> x second (re-seq token-regex)))
                 (re-seq (header-token-regex field)
                         text)))))

(defn extract-tokens [text]
  (apply concat
         (re-seq token-regex text)
         (extract-tokens-from-headers text)))
```

The `header-token-regex` function defined in the preceding code returns a regular expression for a given header, such as `From:(.*)\n` for the `"From"` header. The `extract-tokens-from-headers` function uses this regular expression to determine all words in the various header fields of an e-mail and appends the header name to all the tokens found in the header text. The `extract-tokens` function applies the regular expression over the text and headers of an e-mail and then flattens the resulting lists into a single list using the `apply` and `concat` functions. Note that the `extract-tokens-from-headers` function returns empty lists for the headers defined in `header-fields`, which are not present in the supplied e-mail header. Let's try this function out in the REPL with the help of the following code:

```
user> (def sample-text
        "From: 12a1mailbot1@web.de
         Return-Path: <12a1mailbot1@web.de>
         MIME-Version: 1.0")

user> (extract-tokens-from-headers sample-text)
(() ("From:mailbot" "From:web")
 () ("Return-Path:mailbot" "Return-Path:web"))
```

Using the `extract-tokens-from-headers` function and the regular expression defined by `token-regex`, we can extract all words comprising of three or more characters from an e-mail's header and text. Now, let's define a function to apply the `extract-tokens` function on a given e-mail and update the feature map using the `update-feature!` function with all the words found in the e-mail. We will do all this with the help of the following code:

```
(defn update-features!
  "Updates or creates a TokenFeature in database
  for each token in text."
  [text f & args]
  (doseq [token (extract-tokens text)]
    (apply update-feature! token f args)))
```

Using the `update-features!` function in the preceding code, we can train our spam classifier with a given e-mail. In order to keep track of the total number of spam and ham e-mails, we will have to send the `inc` function to the `total-spam` or `total-ham` agents depending on whether a given e-mail is spam or ham. We will do this with the help of the following code:

```
(defn inc-total-count! [type]
  (send (case type
          :spam total-spam
          :ham total-ham)
        inc))

(defn train! [text type]
  (update-features! text inc-count type)
  (inc-total-count! type))
```

The `inc-total-count!` function defined in the preceding code updates the total number of spam and ham e-mails in our feature database. The `train!` function simply calls the `update-features!` and `inc-total-count!` functions to train our spam classifier with a given e-mail and its type. Note that we pass the `inc-count` function to the `update-features!` function. Now, in order to classify a new e-mail as spam or ham, we must first define how to extract the known features from a given e-mail using our trained feature database. We will do this with the help of the following code:

```
(defn extract-features
  "Extracts all known tokens from text"
  [text]
  (keep identity (map #(@feature-db %1) (extract-tokens text))))
```

The `extract-features` function defined in the preceding code looks up all known features in a given e-mail by dereferencing the map stored in `feature-db` and applying it as a function to all the values returned by the `extract-tokens` function. As mapping the closure `#(@feature-db %1)` can return `()` or `nil` for all tokens that are not present in a `feature-db` agent, we will need to remove all empty values from the list of extracted features. To do this, we will use the `keep` function, which expects a function to apply to the non-nil values in a collection and the collection from which all nil values must be filtered out. Since we do not intend to transform the known features from the e-mail, we will pass the `identity` function, which returns its argument itself as the first parameter to the `keep` function.

Now that we have extracted all known features from a given e-mail, we must calculate all the probabilities of these features occurring in a spam e-mail. We must then combine these probabilities using Fisher's method we described earlier to determine the spam score of a new e-mail. Let's define the following functions to implement the Bayesian probability and Fisher's method:

```
(defn spam-probability [feature]
  (let [s (/ (:spam feature) (max 1 @total-spam))
        h (/ (:ham feature) (max 1 @total-ham))]
    (/ s (+ s h))))

(defn bayesian-spam-probability
  "Calculates probability a feature is spam on a prior
  probability assumed-probability for each feature,
  and weight is the weight to be given to the prior
  assumed (i.e. the number of data points)."
  [feature & {:keys [assumed-probability weight]
              :or  {assumed-probability 1/2 weight 1}}]
  (let [basic-prob (spam-probability feature)
        total-count (+ (:spam feature) (:ham feature))]
    (/ (+ (* weight assumed-probability)
          (* total-count basic-prob))
       (+ weight total-count))))
```

The `spam-probability` function defined in the preceding code calculates the probability of occurrence of a given word feature in a spam e-mail using the number of occurrences of the word in spam and ham e-mails and the total number of spam and ham e-mails processed by the classifier. To avoid division-by-zero errors, we ensure that the value of the number of spam and ham e-mails is at least 1 before performing division. The `bayesian-spam-probability` function uses this probability returned by the `spam-probability` function to calculate a weighted average with the initial probability of 0.5 or *1/2*.

We will now implement Fisher's method of combining the probabilities returned by the `bayesian-spam-probability` function for all the known features found in an e-mail. We will do this with the help of the following code:

```
(defn fisher
  "Combines several probabilities with Fisher's method."
  [probs]
  (- 1 (cdf-chisq
         (* -2 (reduce + (map #(Math/log %1) probs)))
         :df (* 2 (count probs)))))
```

The `fisher` function defined in the preceding code uses the `cdf-chisq` function from the `Incanter` library to calculate the CDF of the several probabilities transformed by the expression $-2\sum_{i=1}^{k}\log p_i$. We specify the number of degrees of freedom to this function using the `:df` optional parameter. We now need to apply the `fisher` function to the combined Bayesian probabilities of an e-mail being spam or ham, and combine these values into a final spam score. These two probabilities must be combined such that only a high number of occurrences of high probabilities indicate a strong probability of spam or ham. It has been shown that the simplest way to do this is to average the probability of a spam e-mail and the negative probability of a ham e-mail (or 1 minus the probability of a ham e-mail). We will do this with the help of the following code:

```
(defn score [features]
  (let [spam-probs (map bayesian-spam-probability features)
        ham-probs (map #(- 1 %1) spam-probs)
        h (- 1 (fisher spam-probs))
        s (- 1 (fisher ham-probs))]
    (/ (+ (- 1 h) s) 2)))
```

Hence, the `score` function will return the final spam score of a given e-mail. Let's define a function to extract the known word features from a given e-mail, combine the probabilities of occurrences of these features to produce the e-mail's spam score, and finally classify this spam score as a ham or spam e-mail, represented by the keywords `:ham` and `:spam` respectively, as shown in the following code:

```
(defn classify
  "Returns a vector of the form [classification score]"
  [text]
  (-> text
      extract-features
      score
      classify-score))
```

So far, we have implemented how we train our spam classifier and use it to classify a new e-mail. Now, let's define some functions to load the sample data from the project's `corpus/` folder and use this data to train and cross-validate our classifier, as follows:

```
(defn populate-emails
  "Returns a sequence of vectors of the form [filename type]"
  []
  (letfn [(get-email-files [type]
            (map (fn [f] [(.toString f) (keyword type)])
                 (rest (file-seq (file (str "corpus/" type))))))]
    (mapcat get-email-files ["ham" "spam"])))
```

The `populate-emails` function defined in the preceding code returns a sequence of vectors to represent all the ham e-mails from the `ham/` folder and the spam e-mails from the `spam/` folder in our sample data. Each vector in this returned sequence has two elements. The first element in this vector is a given e-mail's relative file path and the second element is either `:spam` or `:ham` depending on whether the e-mail is spam or ham. Note the use of the `file-seq` function to read the files in a directory as a sequence.

We will now use the `train!` function to feed the content of all e-mails into our spam classifier. To do this, we can use the `slurp` function to read the content of a file as a string. For cross-validation, we will classify each e-mail in the supplied cross-validation data using the `classify` function and return a list of maps representing the test result of the cross-validation. We will do this with the help of the following code:

```
(defn train-from-corpus! [corpus]
  (doseq [v corpus]
    (let [[filename type] v]
      (train! (slurp filename) type))))

(defn cv-from-corpus [corpus]
  (for [v corpus]
    (let [[filename type] v
          [classification score] (classify (slurp filename))]
      {:filename filename
       :type type
       :classification classification
       :score score})))
```

The `train-from-corpus!` function defined in the preceding code will train our spam classifier with all e-mails found in the `corpus/` folder. The `cv-from-corpus` function classifies the supplied e-mails as spam or ham using the trained classifier and returns a sequence of maps indicating the results of the cross-validation process. Each map in the sequence returned by the `cv-from-corpus` function contains the file of the e-mail, the actual type (spam or ham) of the e-mail, the predicted type of the e-mail, and the spam score of the e-mail. Now, we need to call these two functions on two appropriately partitioned subsets of the sample data as follows:

```
(defn test-classifier! [corpus cv-fraction]
  "Trains and cross-validates the classifier with the sample
  data in corpus, using cv-fraction for cross-validation.
  Returns a sequence of maps representing the results
  of the cross-validation."
  (clear-db)
  (let [shuffled (shuffle corpus)
        size (count corpus)
        training-num (* size (- 1 cv-fraction))
        training-set (take training-num shuffled)
        cv-set (nthrest shuffled training-num)]
    (train-from-corpus! training-set)
    (await feature-db)
    (cv-from-corpus cv-set)))
```

The `test-classifier!` function defined in the preceding code will randomly shuffle the sample data and select a specified fraction of this randomized data as the cross-validation set for our classifier. The `test-classifier!` function then calls the `train-from-corpus!` and `cv-from-corpus` functions to train and cross-validate the data. Note that the use of the `await` function is to wait until the `feature-db` agent has finished applying all functions that have been sent to it via the `send` function.

Now we need to analyze the results of cross-validation. We must first determine the number of incorrectly classified and missed e-mails from the actual and expected class of a given e-mail as returned by the `cv-from-corpus` function. We will do this with the help of the following code:

```
(defn result-type [{:keys [filename type classification score]}]
  (case type
    :ham (case classification
           :ham :correct
           :spam :false-positive
           :unsure :missed-ham)
```

```
:spam (case classification
          :spam :correct
          :ham :false-negative
          :unsure :missed-spam)))
```

The `result-type` function will determine the number of incorrectly classified and missed e-mails in the cross-validation process. We can now apply the `result-type` function to all the maps in the results returned by the `cv-from-corpus` function and print a summary of the cross-validation results with the help of the following code:

```
(defn analyze-results [results]
  (reduce (fn [map result]
            (let [type (result-type result)]
              (update-in map [type] inc)))
          {:total (count results) :correct 0 :false-positive 0
           :false-negative 0 :missed-ham 0 :missed-spam 0}
          results))

(defn print-result [result]
  (let [total (:total result)]
    (doseq [[key num] result]
      (printf "%15s : %-6d%6.2f %%%n"
              (name key) num (float (* 100 (/ num total)))))))
```

The `analyze-results` function defined in the preceding code simply applies the `result-type` function to all the map values in the sequence returned by the `cv-from-corpus` function, while maintaining the total number of incorrectly classified and missed e-mails. The `print-result` function simply prints the analyzed result as a string. Finally, let's define a function to load all the e-mails using the `populate-emails` function and then use this data to train and cross-validate our spam classifier. Since the `populate-emails` function will return an empty list, or `nil` when there are no e-mails, we will check this condition to avoid failing at a later stage in our program:

```
(defn train-and-cv-classifier [cv-frac]
  (if-let [emails (seq (populate-emails))]
    (-> emails
        (test-classifier! cv-frac)
        analyze-results
        print-result)
    (throw (Error. "No mails found!"))))
```

In the `train-and-cv-classifier` function shown in the preceding code, we first call the `populate-emails` function and convert the result to a sequence using the `seq` function. If the sequence has any elements, we train and cross-validate the classifier. If there are no e-mails found, we simply throw an error. Note that the `if-let` function is used to check whether the sequence returned by the `seq` function has any elements.

We have all the parts needed to create and train a spam classifier. Initially, as the classifier hasn't seen any e-mails, the probability of any e-mail or text being spam is 0.5. This can be verified by using the `classify` function, as shown in the following code, which initially classifies any text as the `:unsure` type:

```
user> (classify "Make money fast")
[:unsure 0.5]
user> (classify "Job interview today! Programmer job position for GNU
project")
[:unsure 0.5]
```

We now train the classifier and cross-validate it using the `train-and-cv-classifier` function. We will use one-fifth of all the available sample data as our cross-validation set. This is shown in the following code:

```
user> (train-and-cv-classifier 1/5)
          total : 600     100.00 %
        correct : 585      97.50 %
 false-positive : 1         0.17 %
 false-negative : 1         0.17 %
     missed-ham : 9         1.50 %
    missed-spam : 4         0.67 %
nil
```

Cross-validating our spam classifier asserts that it's appropriately classifying e-mails. Of course, there is still a small amount of error, which can be corrected by using more training data. Now, let's try to classify some text using our trained spam classifier, as follows:

```
user> (classify "Make money fast")
[:spam 0.9720416490829515]
user> (classify "Job interview today! Programmer job position for GNU
project")
[:ham 0.19095646757667556]
```

Interestingly, the text "Make money fast" is classified as spam and the text "Job interview ... GNU project" is classified as ham, as shown in the preceding code. Let's have a look at how the trained classifier extracts features from some text using the extract-features function. Since the classifier will initially have read no tokens, this function will obviously return an empty list or nil when the classifier is untrained, as follows:

```
user> (extract-features "some text to extract")
(#clj_ml5.spam.TokenFeature{:token "some", :spam 91, :ham 837}
 #clj_ml5.spam.TokenFeature{:token "text", :spam 907, :ham 1975}
 #clj_ml5.spam.TokenFeature{:token "extract", :spam 3, :ham 5})
```

As shown in the preceding code, each TokenFeature record will contain the number of times a given word is seen in spam and ham e-mails. Also, the word "to" is not recognized as a feature since we only consider words comprising of three or more characters.

Now, let's check how sensitive to spam e-mail our spam classifier actually is. We'll first have to select some text or a particular term that is classified as neither spam nor ham. For the training data selected for this example, the word "Job" fits this requirement, as shown in the following code. Let's train the classifier with the word "Job" while specifying the type of the text as ham. We can do this using the train! function, as follows:

```
user> (classify "Job")
[:unsure 0.6871002132196162]
user> (train! "Job" :ham)
#<Agent@1f7817e: 1993>
user> (classify "Job")
[:unsure 0.6592140921409213]
```

After training the classifier with the given text as ham, the probability of the term being spam is observed to decrease by a small amount. If the term "Job" occurred in several more e-mails that were ham, the classifier would eventually classify this word as ham. Thus, the classifier doesn't show much of a reaction to a new ham e-mail. On the contrary, the classifier is observed to be very sensitive to spam e-mails, as shown in the following code:

```
user> (train! "Job" :spam)
#<Agent@1f7817e: 1994>
user> (classify "Job")
[:spam 0.7445135045480734]
```

An occurrence of a particular word in a single spam e-mail is observed to greatly increase a classifier's predicted probability of the given term belonging to a spam e-mail. The term "Job" will subsequently be classified as spam by our classifier, at least until it's seen to appear in a sufficiently large number of ham e-mails. This is due to the nature of the chi-squared distribution that we are modeling.

We can also improve the overall error of our spam classifier by supplying it with more training data. To demonstrate this, let's cross-validate the classifier with only one-tenth of the sample data. Thus, the classifier would be effectively trained with nine-tenths of the available data, as follows:

```
user> (train-and-cv-classifier 1/10)
          total : 300     100.00 %
        correct : 294      98.00 %
 false-positive : 0         0.00 %
 false-negative : 1         0.33 %
     missed-ham : 3         1.00 %
    missed-spam : 2         0.67 %
nil
```

As shown in the preceding code, the number of misses and wrongly classified e-mails is observed to reduce when we use more training data. Of course, this is only shown as an example, and we should instead collect more e-mails to feed into the classifier as training data. Using a significant amount of the sample data for cross-validation is a good practice.

In summary, we have effectively built a spam classifier that is trained using Fisher's method. We have also implemented a cross-validation diagnostic, which serves as a kind of unit test for our classifier.

Note that the exact values produced by the `train-and-cv-classifier` function will vary depending on the spam and ham emails used as training data.

Summary

In this chapter, we have explored techniques that can be used to diagnose and improve a given machine learning model. The following are some of the other points that we have covered:

- We have revisited the problems of underfitting and overfitting of sample data and also discussed how we can evaluate a formulated model to diagnose whether it's underfit or overfit.

- We have explored cross-validation and how it can be used to determine how well a formulated model will respond to previously unseen data. We have also seen that we can use cross-validation to select the features and the regularization parameter of a model. We also studied a few kinds of cross-validation that we can implement for a given model.

- We briefly explored learning curves and how they can be used to diagnose the underfit and overfit models.

- We've explored the tools provided by the `clj-ml` library to cross-validate a given classifier.

- Lastly, we've built an operational spam classifier that incorporates cross-validation to determine whether the classifier is appropriately classifying e-mails as spam.

In the following chapters, we will continue exploring more machine learning models, and we'll also study **Support Vector Machines (SVMs)** in detail.

6
Building Support Vector Machines

In this chapter, we will explore **Support Vector Machines (SVMs)**. We will study several SVM implementations in Clojure that can be used to build and train an SVM using some given training data.

SVMs are supervised learning models that are used for both regression and classification. In this chapter, however, we will focus on the problem of classification within the context of SVMs. SVMs find applications in text mining, chemical classification, and image and handwriting recognition. Of course, we should not overlook the fact that the overall performance of a machine learning model mostly depends on the amount and nature of the training data and is also affected by which machine learning model we use to model the available data.

In the simplest form, an SVM separates and predicts two classes of data by estimating the optimal vector plane or **hyperplane** between these two classes represented in vector space. A **hyperplane** can be simply defined as a plane that has one less dimension than the ambient space. For a three-dimensional space, we would obtain a two-dimensional hyperplane.

A basic SVM is a non-probabilistic binary classifier that uses linear classification. In addition to linear classification, SVMs can also be used to perform nonlinear classification over several classes. An interesting aspect of SVMs is that the estimated vector plane will have a substantially large and distinct gap between the classes of input values. Due to this, SVMs often have a good generalization performance and also implement a kind of automatic complexity control to avoid overfitting. Hence, SVMs are also called **large margin classifiers**. In this chapter, we will also study how SVMs achieve this large margin between classes of input data, when compared to other classifiers. Another interesting fact about SVMs is that they scale very well with the number of features being modeled and thus, SVMs are often used in machine learning problems that deal with a large number of features.

Understanding large margin classification

As we previously mentioned, SVMs classify input data across large margins. Let's examine how this is achieved. We use our definition of a logistic classification model, which we previously described in *Chapter 3, Categorizing Data*, as a basis for reasoning about SVMs.

We can use the logistic or *sigmoid* function to separate two classes of input values, as we described in *Chapter 3, Categorizing Data*. This function can be formally defined as a function of an input variable X as follows:

$$Y = \frac{1}{1 + e^{-\beta^T X}}$$

In the preceding equation, the output variable Y depends not only on the variable X, but also on the coefficient β. The variable X is analogous to the vector of input values in our model, and the term β is the parameter vector of the model. For binary classification, the value of Y must exist in the range of 0 and 1. Also, the class of a set of input values is determined by whether the output variable Y is closer to 0 or 1. For these values of Y, the term $\beta^T X$ is either much greater than or much less than 0. This can be formally expressed as follows:

$$\text{If } Y \approx 1, \beta^T X \gg 0$$
$$Y \approx 0, \beta^T X \ll 0$$

For N sample with input values X_i and output values Y_i, we define the cost function $J(\beta)$ as follows:

$$J(\beta) = \frac{-1}{N} \sum_{i=0}^{N} \left(Y_i \log \hat{Y}_i + (1 - Y_i) \log(1 - \hat{Y}_i) \right)$$

 Note that the term $\hat{Y}_i$ represents the output variable calculated from the estimated model.

For a logistic classification model, $\hat{Y}_i$ is the value of logistic function when applied to a set of input values X_i. We can simplify and expand the summation term $Y_i \log Y_i + (1 - \hat{Y}_i) \log(1 - \hat{Y}_i)$ in the cost function defined in the preceding equation, as follows:

$$-\left(Y \log Y + \left(1 - \hat{Y}\right) \log \left(1 - \hat{Y}\right)\right)$$

$$= -Y \log\left(\frac{1}{1 + e^{-\beta^T X}}\right) - (1 - Y) \log\left(1 - \frac{1}{1 + e^{-\beta^T X}}\right)$$

It's obvious that the cost function shown in the preceding expression depends on the two logarithmic terms in the expression. Thus, we can represent the cost function as a function of these two logarithmic terms, represented by the terms $cost_0$ and $cost_1$. Now, let's assume the two terms as shown the following equation:

$$\text{Let } cost_0 = -\log\left(\frac{1}{1 + e^{\beta^T X}}\right) \text{ and } cost_1 = -\log\left(1 - \frac{1}{1 + e^{\beta^T X}}\right)$$

Both the functions $cost_0$ and $cost_1$ are composed using the logistic function. A classifier that models the logistic function must be trained such that these two functions are minimized over all possible values of the parameter vector β. We can use the **hinge-loss** function to approximate the desired behavior of a linear classifier that uses the logistic function (for more information, refer to "Are Loss Functions All the Same?"). We will now study the hinge-loss function by comparing it to the logistic function. The following diagram depicts how the $cost_0$ function must vary with respect to the term $\beta^T X$ and how it can be modeled using the logistic and hinge-loss functions:

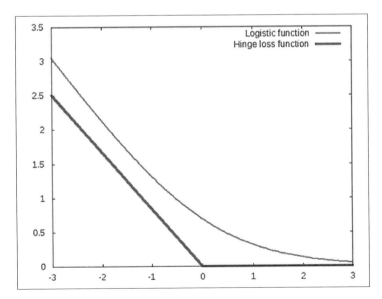

In the plot shown in the preceding diagram, the logistic function is represented as a smooth curve. The function is seen to decrease rapidly before a given point and then decreases at a lower rate. In this example, the point at which this change of rate of the logistic function occurs is found to be $x = 0$. The hinge-loss function approximates this by using two line segments that meet at the point $x = 0$. Interestingly, both these functions model a behavior that changes at a rate that is inversely proportional to the input value x. Similarly, we can approximate the effect of the $cost_1$ function using the hinge-loss function as follows:

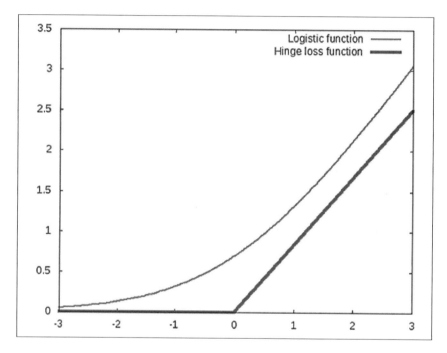

Note that the $cost_1$ function is directly proportional to the term $\beta^T X$. Thus, we can achieve the classification ability of the logistic function by modelling the hinge-loss function and a classifier built using the hinge-loss function will perform equally well as a classifier using the logistic function.

As seen in the preceding diagram, the hinge-loss function only changes its value at the point $\beta^T X = 0$. This applies to both the functions $cost_0$ and $cost_1$. Thus, we can use the hinge loss function to separate two classes of data depending on whether the value of $\beta^T X$ is greater or less than 0. In this case, there's virtually no margin of separation between these two classes. To improve the margin of classification, we can modify the hinge-loss function such that its value is greater than 0 only when $\beta^T X \leq -1$ or $\beta^T X \geq 1$.

The modified hinge-loss functions can be plotted for the two classes of data as follows. The following plot describes the case where $\beta^T X \geq 1$:

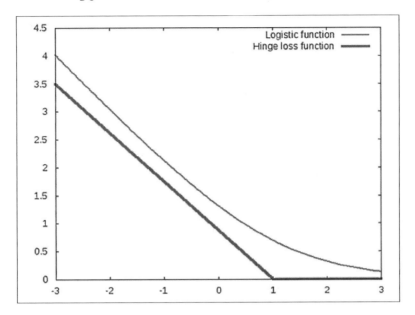

Similarly, the modified hinge-loss function for the case $\beta^T X \leq -1$ can be illustrated by the following plot:

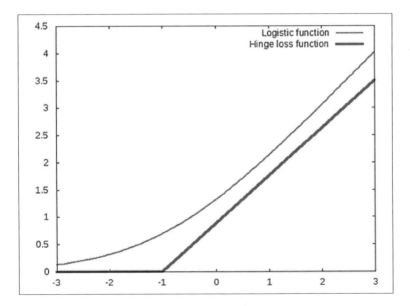

Note that the *hinge* occurs at *-1* in the case of $\beta^T X \le -1$.

If we substitute the hinge-loss functions in place of the $cost_0$ and $cost_1$ functions, we arrive at an optimization problem of SVMs (for more information, refer to "Support-vector networks"), which can be formally written as follows:

$$\arg \min_{\beta} \left[\sum_{i=1}^{N} Y_i cost_0 \left(\beta^T X_i \right) + \left(1 - Y_i \right) cost_1 \left(\beta^T X_i \right) + \frac{\lambda}{2N} \sum_{j=0}^{N} \left[\beta_j^2 \right] \right]$$

In the preceding equation, the term λ is the regularization parameter. Also, when $Y_i \approx 1$, the behavior of the SVM is affected more by the $cost_0$ function than the $cost_1$ function, and vice versa when $Y_i \approx 0$. In some contexts, the regularization parameter λ of the model is added to the optimization problem as a constant C, where C is analogous to $\frac{1}{\lambda}$. This representation of the optimization problem can be formally expressed as follows:

$$\arg \min_{\beta} \left[C \sum_{i=1}^{N} Y_i cost_0 \left(\beta^T X_i \right) + \left(1 - Y_i \right) cost_1 \left(\beta^T X_i \right) + \frac{1}{2} \sum_{j=0}^{N} \left[\beta_j^2 \right] \right]$$

As we only deal with two classes of data in which Y_i is either 0 or 1, we can rewrite the optimization problem described previously, as follows:

$$\min_{\beta} \frac{1}{2} \sum_{i} \beta_i^2, \text{ subject to}$$

$$\beta^T X_i \ge 1 \text{ if } Y_i = 1$$

$$\beta^T X_i \le -1 \text{ if } Y_i = 0$$

Let's try to visualize the behavior of an SVM on some training data. Suppose we have two input variables x_1 and x_2 in our training data. The input values and their classes can represented by the following plot diagram:

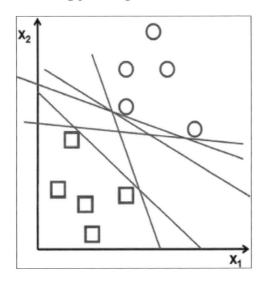

In the preceding plot diagram, the two classes in the training data are represented as circles and squares. A linear classifier will attempt to partition these sample values into two distinct classes and will produce a decision boundary that can be represented by any one of the lines in the preceding plot diagram. Of course, the classifier should strive to minimize the overall error of the formulated model, while also finding a model that generalizes the data well. An SVM will also attempt to partition the sample data into two classes just as any other classification model. However, the SVM manages to determine a hyperplane of separation that is observed to have the largest possible margin between the two classes of input data.

This behavior of an SVM can be illustrated using the following plot:

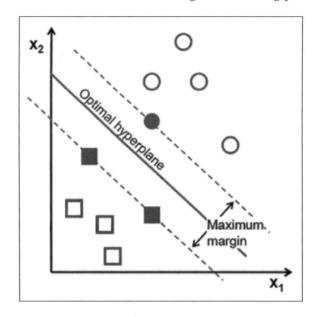

As shown in the preceding plot diagram, an SVM will determine the optimal hyperplane that separates the two classes of data with the maximum possible margin between these two classes. From the optimization problem of an SVM, which we previously described, we can prove that the equation of the hyperplane of separation estimated by the SVM is as follows:

$$\left(\beta^T X + \beta_0\right) = 1$$

[Note that in the preceding equation, the constant β_0 is simply the y-intercept of the hyperplane.]

To understand more about how an SVM achieves this large margin of separation, we need to use some elementary vector arithmetic. Firstly, we can define the length of a given vector as follows:

$$If\ U\ is\ a\ vector\ with\ elements\ \left[u_i\right]$$

$$\|U\|, Length\ of\ vector\ U = \sqrt{\sum_i u_i}$$

Another operation that is often used to describe SVMs is the inner product of the two vectors. The inner product of two given vectors can be formally defined as follows:

For two vectors $U = [u_i]$ and $V = [v_i]$ of the same length,

$$\langle U, V \rangle = \text{Inner Product of vectors } U \text{ and } V = U \cdot V = \sum_{i=0}^{n} u_i v_i$$

 Note that the inner product of two vectors only exists if the two vectors are of the same length.

As shown in the preceding equation, the inner product $\langle U, V \rangle$ of the two vectors U and V is equal to the dot product of the transpose of U and the vector V. Another way to represent the inner product of two vectors is in terms of the projection of one vector onto another, which is given as follows:

$$\langle U, V \rangle = U \cdot V = P \cdot \|U\|, \text{where } P \text{ is the projection of V onto U}$$

Note that the term $U \cdot V$ is equivalent to the vector product $U^T V$ of the vector V and the transpose of the vector U. Since the expression $P \cdot \|U\|$ is equivalent to the product $U^T \cdot V$ of the vectors, we can rewrite the optimization problem, which we described earlier in terms of the projection of the input variables onto the output variable. This can be formally expressed as follows:

$$\arg \min_{\beta} \frac{1}{2} \sum_i \beta_i^2, \text{subject to}$$
$$P_i \cdot \|\beta\| \geq 1 \text{ if } Y_i = 1$$
$$P_i \cdot \|\beta\| \leq -1 \text{ if } Y_i = 0$$
$$\text{where } P_i \text{ is the projection of } X_i \text{ onto } Y_i$$

Hence, an SVM attempts to minimize the squared sum of the elements in the parameter vector β while ensuring that the optimal hyperplane that separates the two classes of data is present in between the two planes and $P_i \cdot \|\beta\| = -1$ and $P_i \cdot \|\beta\| = 1$. These two planes are called the **support vectors** of the SVM. Since we must minimize the values of the elements in the parameter vector β, the projection P_i must be large enough to ensure that $P_i \cdot \|\beta\| > -1$ and $P_i \cdot \|\beta\| < 1$:

If $\beta \ll 0$, then P_i must be $\gg 0$

Thus, the SVM will ensure that the projection of the input variable X_i onto the output variable Y_i is as large as possible. This implies that the SVM will find the largest possible margin between the two classes of input values in the training data.

Alternative forms of SVMs

We will now describe a couple of alternative forms to represent an SVM. The remainder of this section can be safely skipped, but the reader is advised to know these forms as they also widely used notations of SVMs.

If w is the normal to hyperplane estimated by an SVM, we can represent this hyperplane of separation using the following equation:

$$w \cdot X - b = 0$$

 Note that in the preceding equation, the term b is the y-intercept of the hyperplane and is analogous to the term β_0 in the equation of the hyperplane that we previously described.

The two peripheral support vectors of this hyperplane have the following equations:

$$w \cdot X - b = 1 \ and \ w \cdot X - b = -1$$

We can use the expression $w \cdot X - b$ to determine the class of a given set of input values. If the value of this expression is less than or equal to -1, then we can say that the input values belong to one of the two classes of data. Similarly, if the value of the expression $w \cdot X - b$ is greater than or equal to 1, the input values are predicted to belong to the second class. This can be formally expressed as follows:

$$For \ \hat{Y}_i \approx 1, w \cdot X_i - b \geq 1$$
$$\hat{Y}_i \approx -1, w \cdot X_i - b \leq -1$$

The two inequalities described in the preceding equation can be combined into a single inequality, as follows:

$$\hat{Y}_i \left(w \cdot X_i - b \right) \geq 1$$

Thus, we can concisely rewrite the optimization problem of SVMs as follows:

$$\arg\min_{w,b}\left[\frac{1}{2}\|w\|^2\right], subject\ to\ Y_i\left(w\cdot X_i-b\right)\geq1$$

In the constrained problem defined in the preceding equation, we use the normal w instead of the parameter vector β to parameterize the optimization problem. By using Lagrange multipliers α, we can express the optimization problem as follows:

$$\arg\min_{w,b}\max_{\alpha}\left[\frac{1}{2}\|w\|^2-\sum_{i=0}^{N}\alpha_i\left(Y_i\left(w\cdot X_i-b\right)-1\right)\right]$$

This form of the optimization problem of an SVM is known as the **primal form**. Note that in practice, only a few of the Lagrange multipliers will have a value greater than 0. Also, this solution can be expressed as a linear combination of the input vectors X_i and the output variable Y_i, as follows:

$$w=\sum_{i=0}^{N}\alpha_iY_iX_i$$

We can also express the optimization problem of an SVM in the *dual form*, which is a constrained representation that can be described as follows:

$$\arg\max_{\alpha}\left[\sum_{i=0}^{N}\alpha_i-\frac{1}{2}\sum_{i,j}\alpha_i\alpha_jY_iY_jK\left(X_i,X_j\right)\right]$$

$$subject\ to\ \sum_{i=0}^{N}\alpha_iY_i=0, and\ \alpha_i\geq0\ for\ i\in\left(1,N\right)$$

In the constrained problem described in the preceding equation, the function $K\left(X_i,X_j\right)$ is called the **kernel function** and we will discuss more about the role of this function in SVMs in the later sections of this chapter.

Linear classification using SVMs

As we previously described, SVMs can be used to perform linear classification over two distinct classes. An SVM will attempt to find a hyperplane that separates the two classes such that the estimated hyperplane describes the maximum achievable margin of separation between the two classes in our model.

For example, an estimated hyperplane between two classes of data can be visualized using the following plot diagram:

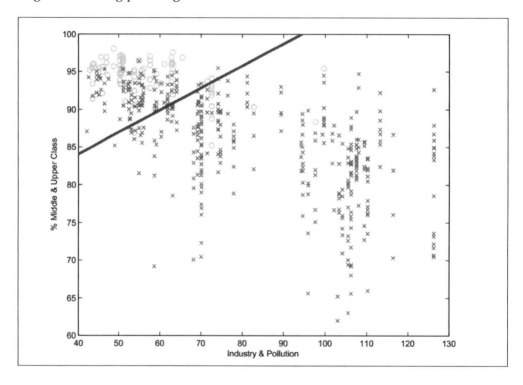

As depicted in the graph shown in the preceding plot diagram, the circles and crosses are used to represent the two classes of input values in the sample data. The line represents the estimated hyperplane of an SVM.

In practice, it's often more efficient to use an implemented SVM rather than implement our own SVM. There are several libraries that implement SVMs that have been ported to multiple programming languages. One such library is **LibLinear** (http://www.csie.ntu.edu.tw/~cjlin/liblinear/), which implements a linear classifier using an SVM. The Clojure wrapper for LibLinear is clj-liblinear (https://github.com/lynaghk/clj-liblinear) and we will now explore how we can use this library to easily build a linear classifier.

> The clj-liblinear library can be added to a Leiningen project by adding the following dependency to the project.clj file:
>
> [clj-liblinear "0.1.0"]
>
> For the example that will follow, the namespace declaration should look similar to the following declaration:
>
> (ns my-namespace
>   (:use [clj-liblinear.core :only [train predict]]))

Firstly, let's generate some training data, such that we have two classes of input values. For this example, we will model two input variables, as follows:

```
(def training-data
  (concat
   (repeatedly
    500 #(hash-map :class 0
                   :data {:x (rand)
                          :y (rand)}))
   (repeatedly
    500 #(hash-map :class 1
                   :data {:x (- (rand))
                          :y (- (rand))}))))
```

Using the repeatedly function as shown in the preceding code, we generate two sequences of maps. Each map in these two sequences contains the keys :class and :data. The value of the :class key represents the class of category of the input values and the value of the :data key is itself another map with the keys :x and :y. The values of the keys :x and :y represent the two input variables in our training data. These values for the input variables are randomly generated using the rand function. The training data is generated such that the class of a set of input values is 0 if both the input values are positive, and the class of a set of input values is 1 if both the input values are negative. As shown in the preceding code, a total of a 1,000 samples are generated for two classes as two sequences using the repeatedly function, and then combined into a single sequence using the concat function. We can inspect some of these input values in the REPL, as follows:

```
user> (first training-data)
{:class 0,
 :data {:x 0.054125811753944264, :y 0.23575052637986382}}
user> (last training-data)
{:class 1,
 :data {:x -0.8067872409710037, :y -0.6395480020409928}}
```

We can create and train an SVM using the training data we've generated.
To do this, we use the `train` function. The `train` function accepts two arguments, which include a sequence of input values and a sequence of output values. Both sequences are assumed to be in the same order. For the purpose of classification, the output variable can be set to the class of a given set of input values as shown in the following code:

```
(defn train-svm []
  (train
   (map :data training-data)
   (map :class training-data)))
```

The `train-svm` function defined in the preceding code will instantiate and train an SVM with the `training-data` sequence. Now, we can use the trained SVM to perform classification using the `predict` function, as shown in the following code:

```
user> (def svm (train-svm))
#'user/svm
user> (predict svm {:x 0.5 :y 0.5})
0.0
user> (predict svm {:x -0.5 :y 0.5})
0.0
user> (predict svm {:x -0.4 :y 0.4})
0.0
user> (predict svm {:x -0.4 :y -0.4})
1.0
user> (predict svm {:x 0.5 :y -0.5})
1.0
```

The `predict` function requires two parameters, which are an instance of an SVM and a set of input values.

As shown in the preceding code, we use the `svm` variable to represent a trained SVM. We then pass the `svm` variable to the `predict` function, along with a new set of input values whose class we intend to predict. It's observed that the output of the `predict` function agrees with the training data. Interestingly, the classifier predicts the class of any set of input values as 0 as long as the input value `:y` is positive, and conversely the class of a set of input values whose `:y` feature is negative is predicted as 1.

In the previous example, we used an SVM to perform classification. However, the output variable of the trained SVM was always a number. Thus, we could also use the `clj-liblinear` library in the same way as described in the preceding code to train a regression model.

The `clj-liblinear` library also supports more complex types for the features of an SVM, such as vectors, maps, and sets. We will now demonstrate how we can train a classifier that uses sets as input variables, instead of plain numbers as shown in the previous example. Suppose we have a stream of tweets from a given user's Twitter feed. Assume that the user will manually classify these tweets into a specific category, which is selected from a set of predefined categories. This processed sequence of tweets can be represented as follows:

```
(def tweets
  [{:class 0 :text "new lisp project released"}
   {:class 0 :text "try out this emacs package for common lisp"}
   {:class 0 :text "a tutorial on guile scheme"}

   {:class 1 :text "update in javascript library"}
   {:class 1 :text "node.js packages are now supported"}
   {:class 1 :text "check out this jquery plugin"}

   {:class 2 :text "linux kernel news"}
   {:class 2 :text "unix man pages"}
   {:class 2 :text "more about linux software"}])
```

The tweets vector defined in the preceding code contains several maps, each of which have the keys `:class` and `:text`. The `:text` key contains the text of a tweet, and we will train an SVM using the value contained by the `:text` keyword. But we can't use the text in verbatim, since some words might be repeated in a tweet. Also, we need some way of dealing with the case of the letters in this text. Let's define a function to convert this text into a set as follows:

```
(defn extract-words [text]
  (->> #" "
       (split text)
       (map lower-case)
       (into #{})))
```

The `extract-words` function defined in the preceding code will convert any string, represented by the parameter `text`, into a set of words that are all in lower case. To create a set, we use the `(into #{})` form. By definition, this set will not contain any duplicate values. Note the use of the `->>` threading macro in the definition of the `extract-words` function.

 In the `extract-words` function, the `->>` form can be equivalently written as `(into #{} (map lower-case (split text #" ")))`.

We can inspect the behavior of the `extract-words` function in the REPL, as follows:

```
user> (extract-words "Some text to extract some words")
#{"extract" "words" "text" "some" "to"}
```

Using the `extract-words` function, we can effectively train an SVM with a set of strings as a feature variable. As we mentioned earlier, this can be done using the `train` function, as follows:

```
(defn train-svm []
  (train (->> tweets
              (map :text)
              (map extract-words))
         (map :class tweets)))
```

The `train-svm` function defined in the preceding code will create and train an SVM with the processed training data in the tweets variable using the `train` and `extract-words` functions. We now need to compose the `predict` and `extract-words` functions in the following code so that we can predict the class of a given tweet:

```
(defn predict-svm [svm text]
  (predict
    svm (extract-words text)))
```

The `predict-svm` function defined in the preceding code can be used to classify a given tweet. We can verify the predicted classes of the SVM for some arbitrary tweets in the REPL, as follows:

```
user> (def svm (train-svm))
#'user/svm
user> (predict-svm svm "a common lisp tutorial")
0.0
user> (predict-svm svm "new javascript library")
1.0
user> (predict-svm svm "new linux kernel update")
2.0
```

In conclusion, the `clj-liblinear` library allows us to easily build and train an SVM with most Clojure data types. The only restriction that is imposed by this library is that the training data must be linearly separable into the classes of our model. We will study how we can build more complex classifiers in the following sections of this chapter.

Using kernel SVMs

In some cases, the available training data is not linearly separable and we would not be able to model the data using linear classification. Thus, we need to use different models to fit nonlinear data. As described in *Chapter 4, Building Neural Networks*, ANNs can be used to model this kind of data. In this section, we will describe how we can fit an SVM on nonlinear data using kernel functions. An SVM that incorporates kernel function is termed as a **kernel support vector machine**. Note that, in this section, the terms SVM and kernel SVM are used interchangeably. A kernel SVM will classify data based on a nonlinear decision boundary, and the nature of the decision boundary depends on the kernel function that is used by the SVM. To illustrate this behavior, a kernel SVM will classify the training data into two classes as described by the following plot diagram:

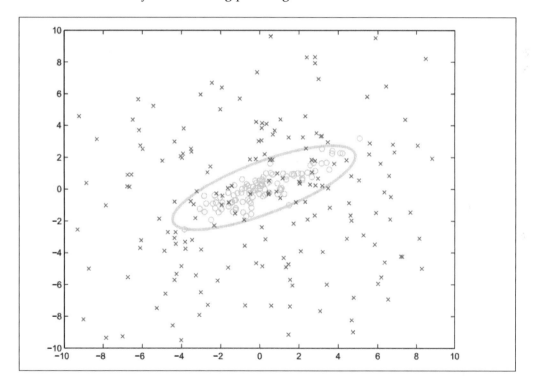

The concept of using kernel functions in SVMs is actually based on mathematical transformation. The role of the kernel function in an SVM is to transform the input variables in the training data such that the transformed features are linearly separable. Since an SVM linearly partitions the input data based on a large margin, this large gap of separation between the two classes of data will also be observable in a nonlinear space.

The kernel function is written as $K(X_i, X_j)$, where X_i is a vector of input values from the training data and X_j is the transformed vector of X_i. The function $K(X_i, X_j)$ represents the similarity of these two vectors and is equivalent to the inner product of these two vectors in the transformed space. If the input vector X_i has a given class, then the class of the vector X_j is the same as that of the vector X_i when the kernel function of these two vectors has a value close to 1, that is, when $K(X_i, X_j) \approx 1$. A kernel function can be mathematically expressed as follows:

$$K(X_i, X_j) = \langle (X_i), (X_j) \rangle, \text{where } \phi : S \to V$$

In the preceding equation, the function ϕ performs the transformation from a nonlinear space S into a linear space V. Note that the explicit representation of ϕ is not required, and it's enough to know that V is an inner product space. Although we are free to choose any arbitrary kernel function to model the given training data, we must strive to reduce the problem of minimizing the cost function of the formulated SVM model. Thus, the kernel function is generally selected such that calculating the SVM's decision boundary only requires determining the dot products of vectors in the transformed feature space V.

A common choice for the kernel function of an SVM is the **polynomial kernel function**, also called the **polynomic kernel function**, which models the training data as polynomials of the original feature variables. As the reader may recall from *Chapter 5, Selecting and Evaluating Data*, we have discussed how polynomial features can greatly improve the performance of a given machine learning model. The polynomial kernel function can be thought of as an extension of this concept that applies to SVMs. This function can be formally expressed as follows.

$$K(X_i, X_j) = (X_i^T \cdot X_j + c)^d, \text{ where } d \text{ is the degree of the polynomial}$$

In the preceding equation, the term d represents the highest degree of the polynomial features. Also, when (the constant) $c = 0$, the kernel is termed to be **homogenous**.

Another widely used kernel function is the **Gaussian kernel function**. Most readers who are adept in linear algebra will need no introduction to the Gaussian function. It's important to know that this function represents a normal distribution of data in which the data points are closer to the mean of the data.

In the context of SVMs, the Gaussian kernel function can be used to represent a model in which one of the two classes in the training data has values for the input variables that are close to an arbitrary mean value. The Gaussian kernel function can be formally expressed as follows:

$$K\left(X_i, X_j\right) = exp\left(\frac{-\left\|X_j - X_i\right\|^2}{2\rho^2}\right)$$

In the Gaussian kernel function defined in the preceding equation, the term ρ represents the variance of the training data and represents the *width* of the Gaussian kernel.

Another popular choice for the kernel function is the **string kernel function** that operates on string values. By the term *string*, we mean a finite sequence of symbols. The string kernel function essentially measures the similarity between two given strings. If both the strings passed to the string kernel function are the same, the value returned by this function will be 1. Thus, the string kernel function is useful in modeling data where the features are represented as strings.

Sequential minimal optimization

The optimization problem of an SVM can be solved using **Sequential Minimal Optimization (SMO)**. The optimization problem of an SVM is the numerical optimization of the cost function across several dimensions in order to reduce the overall error of the trained SVM. In practice, this must be done through numerical optimization techniques. A complete discussion of the SMO algorithm is beyond the scope of this book. However, we must note that this algorithm solves the optimization problem by a *divide-and-conquer* technique. Essentially, SMO divides the optimization problem of multiple dimensions into several smaller two-dimensional problems that can be solved analytically (for more information, refer to *Sequential Minimal Optimization: A Fast Algorithm for Training Support Vector Machines*).

LibSVM is a popular library that implements SMO to train an SVM. The `svm-clj` library is a Clojure wrapper for LibSVM and we will now explore how we can use this library to formulate an SVM model.

The `svm-clj` library can be added to a Leiningen project by adding the following dependency to the `project.clj` file:

```
[svm-clj "0.1.3"]
```

For the example that will follow, the namespace declaration should look similar to the following declaration:

```
(ns my-namespace
  (:use svm.core))
```

This example will use a simplified version of the **SPECT Heart** dataset (http://archive.ics.uci.edu/ml/datasets/SPECT+Heart). This dataset describes the diagnosis of several heart disease patients using **Single Proton Emission Computed Tomography (SPECT)** images. The original dataset contains a total of 267 samples, in which each sample has 23 features. The output variable of the dataset describes a positive or negative diagnosis of a given patient, which is represented using either +1 or -1, respectively.

For this example, the training data is stored in a file named `features.dat`. This file must be placed in the `resources/` directory of the Leiningen project to make it available for use. This file contains several input features and the class of these input values. Let's have a look at one of the following sample values in this file:

```
+1 2:1 3:1 4:-0.132075 5:-0.648402 6:1 7:1 8:0.282443 9:1 10:0.5 11:1
12:-1 13:1
```

As shown in the preceding line of code, the first value +1 denotes the class of the sample and the other values represent the input variables. Note that the indexes of the input variables are also given. Also, the value of the first feature in the preceding sample is 0, as it is not mentioned using a 1: key. From the preceding line, it's clear that each sample will have a maximum of 12 features. All sample values must conform to this format, as dictated by LibSVM.

We can train an SVM using this sample data. To do this, we use the `train-model` function from the `svm-clj` library. Also, since we must first load the sample data from the file, we will need to first call the `read-dataset` function as well using the following code:

```
(def dataset (read-dataset "resources/features.dat"))

(def model (train-model dataset))
```

The trained SVM represented by the model variable as defined in the preceding code can now be used to predict the class of a set of input values. The `predict` function can be used for this purpose. For simplicity, we will use a sample value from the dataset variable itself as follows:

```
user> (def feature (last (first dataset)))
#'user/feature
user> feature
{1 0.708333, 2 1.0, 3 1.0, 4 -0.320755, 5 -0.105023,
  6 -1.0, 7 1.0, 8 -0.4198, 9 -1.0, 10 -0.2258, 12 1.0, 13 -1.0}
user> (feature 1)
0.708333
user> (predict model feature)
1.0
```

As shown in the REPL output in the preceding code, `dataset` can be treated as a sequence of maps. Each map contains a single key that represents the value of the output variable in the sample. The value of this key in the `dataset` map is another map that represents the input variables of the given sample. Since the `feature` variable represents a map, we can call it as a function, as shown by the `(feature 1)` call in the preceding code.

The predicted value agrees with the actual value of the output variable, or the class, of a given set of input values. In conclusion, the `svm-clj` library provides us with a simple and concise implementation of an SVM.

Using kernel functions

As we have mentioned earlier, we can choose a kernel function for an SVM when we need to fit some nonlinear data. We will now demonstrate how this is achieved in practice using the `clj-ml` library. Since this library has already been discussed in the previous chapters, we will not focus on the complete training of an SVM, but rather on how we can create an SVM that uses kernel functions.

For the example that will follow, the namespace declaration should look similar to the following declaration:

```
(ns my-namespace
    (:use [clj-ml classifiers kernel-functions]))
```

The function, `make-kernel-function`, from the `clj-ml.kernel-functions` namespace is used to create kernel functions that can be used for SVMs. For example, we can create a polynomial kernel function by passing the `:polynomic` keyword to this function, as follows:

```
(def K (make-kernel-function :polynomic {:exponent 3}))
```

As shown in the preceding line, the polynomial kernel function defined by the variable K has a polynomial degree of 3. Similarly, we can also create a string kernel function using the `:string` keyword, as follows:

```
(def K (make-kernel-function :string))
```

There are several such kernel functions available in the `clj-ml` library and the reader is encouraged to explore more kernel functions in this library. The documentation for this namespace is available at `http://antoniogarrote.github.io/clj-ml/clj-ml.kernel-functions-api.html`. We can create an SVM using the `make-classifier` function by specifying the `:support-vector-machine` and `:smo` keywords; and the kernel function with the keyword option `:kernel-function`, as follows:

```
(def classifier
  (make-classifier :support-vector-machine :smo
                   :kernel-function K))
```

We can now train the SVM represented by the variable classifier as we have done in the previous chapters. The `clj-ml` library, thus, allows us to create SVMs that exhibit a given kernel function.

Summary

In this chapter, we have explored SVMs and how they can be used to fit both linear and nonlinear data. The following are the other topics that we have covered:

- We have examined how SVMs are capable of large margin classification and the various forms of the optimization problem of SVMs

- We have discussed how we can use kernel functions and SMO to train an SVM with nonlinear sample data

- We have also demonstrated how we can use several Clojure libraries to build and train SVMs

We will shift our focus to unsupervised learning in the next chapter and we will explore clustering techniques to model these types of machine learning problems.

7
Clustering Data

We will now shift our focus to **unsupervised learning**. In this chapter, we will study several **clustering** algorithms, or **clusterers**, and how we can implement them in Clojure. We will also demonstrate several Clojure libraries that provide implementations of clustering algorithms. Towards the end of the chapter, we explore will **dimensionality reduction** and how it can be used to provide an understandable visualization of the supplied sample data.

Clustering or **cluster analysis** is basically a method of grouping data or samples together. As a form of unsupervised learning, a clustering model is trained using unlabeled data, by which we mean the samples in the training data will not contain the class or category of the input values. Rather, the training data does not describe values for the output variable of a given set of inputs. A clustering model must determine similarities between several input values and infer the classes of these input values on its own. The sample values can thus be partitioned into a number of clusters using such a model.

There are several practical applications of clustering in real-world problems. Clustering is often used in image analysis, image segmentation, software evolution systems, and social network analysis. Outside the domain of computer science, clustering algorithms are used in biological classification, gene analysis, and crime analysis.

There are several clustering algorithms that have been published till date. Each of these algorithms has a unique notion of how a cluster is defined and how input values are combined into new clusters. Unfortunately, there is no given solution for any clustering problem and each algorithm must be evaluated on a trial-and-error basis to determine which model is best suited for the supplied training data. Of course, this is one of the aspects of unsupervised learning, in the sense that there is no definite way to say that a given solution is the best fit for any given data.

This is due to the fact that the input data is unlabeled, and a simple yes/no based reward system to train cannot easily be inferred from data in which the output variable or class of the input values is unknown.

In this chapter, we will describe a handful of clustering techniques that can be applied on unlabeled data.

Using K-means clustering

The **K-means clustering** algorithm is a clustering technique that is based on vector quantization (for more information, refer to "Algorithm AS 136: A K-Means Clustering Algorithm"). This algorithm partitions a number of sample vectors into K clusters and hence derives its name. In this section, we will study the nature and implementation of the K-means algorithm.

Quantization, in signal processing, is the process of mapping a large set of values into a smaller set of values. For example, an analog signal can be quantized to 8 bits and the signal can be represented by 256 levels of quantization. Assuming that the bits represent values within the range of 0 to 5 volts, the 8-bit quantization allows a resolution of 5/256 volts per bit. In the context of clustering, quantization of input or output can be done for the following reasons:

- To restrict the clustering to a finite set of clusters.

- To accommodate a range of values in the sample data that need to have some level of tolerance while clustering is performed. This kind of flexibility is crucial in grouping together unknown or unexpected sample values.

The gist of the algorithm can be concisely described as follows. The K mean values, or *centroids*, are first randomly initialized. The distance of each sample value from each centroid is then calculated. A sample value is grouped into a given centroid's cluster depending on which centroid has the minimum distance from the given sample. In a multidimensional space for multiple features or input values, the distance of a sample input vector is measured by **Euclidean distance** between the input vector and a given centroid. This phase of the algorithm is termed as the **assignment step**.

The next phase in the K-means algorithm is the **update step**. The values of the centroids are adjusted based on the partitioned input values generated from the previous step. These two steps are then repeated until the difference between the centroid values in two consecutive iterations becomes negligible. Thus, the final result of the algorithm is the clusters or classes of each set of input values in the given training data.

The iterations performed by the *K*-means algorithm can be illustrated using the following plots:

Each of the plots depict the centroid and partitioned sample values produced by each iteration of the algorithm for a given set of input values. The clusters in a given iteration are shown in different colors in each plot. The final plot represents the final partitioned set of input values produced by the *K*-means algorithm.

The optimization objective of the *K*-means clustering algorithm can be formally defined as follows:

$$\arg\min_{s} \sum_{i=1}^{K} \sum_{X_j \in S_i} \left\| X_j - \mu_i \right\|^2$$

In the optimization problem defined in the preceding equation, the terms $\mu_1, \mu_2, \ldots \mu_K$ represent the *K*-mean values around which the input values are clustered. The *K*-means algorithm minimizes the size of the clusters and also determines the mean values for which these clusters can be minimized in size.

This algorithm requires N sample values and K initial mean values as inputs. In the assignment step, the input values are assigned to clusters around the initial mean values supplied to the algorithm. In the later update step, the new mean values are calculated from the input values. In most implementations, the new mean values are calculated as the mean of all input values that belongs to a given cluster.

Most implementations initialize the K initial mean values to some randomly chosen input values. This technique is called the **Forgy method** of random initialization.

The *K*-means algorithm is NP-hard when either the number of clusters K or the number of dimensions in the input data d is unbound. When both these values are fixed, the *K*-means algorithm has a time complexity of $O\left(n^{dK+1} \log n\right)$. There are several variations of this algorithm that vary on how the new mean values are calculated.

We will now demonstrate how we can implement the *K*-means algorithm in pure Clojure, while using no external libraries. We begin by defining bits and pieces of the algorithm, which are then later combined to provide a basic visualization of the *K*-means algorithm.

We can say that the distance between two numbers is the absolute difference between their values and this can be implemented as a distance function, as shown in the following code:

```
(defn distance [a b]
  (if (< a b) (- b a) (- a b)))
```

If we are given a number of mean values, we can calculate the closest mean from a given number by using a composition of the distance and sort-by functions, as shown in the following code:

```
(defn closest [point means distance]
  (first (sort-by #(distance % point) means)))
```

To demonstrate the closest function defined in the preceding code, we will first need to define some data, that is, a sequence of numbers and a couple of mean values, as shown in the following code:

```
(def data '(2 3 5 6 10 11 100 101 102))
(def guessed-means '(0 10))
```

We can now use the data and guessed-means variables with the closest function and an arbitrary number, as shown in the following REPL output:

```
user> (closest 2 guessed-means distance)
0
user> (closest 9 guessed-means distance)
10
user> (closest 100 guessed-means distance)
10
```

Given the means 0 and 10, the closest function returns 0 as the closest mean to 2, and 10 as that for 9 and 100. Thus, a set of data points can be grouped by the means, which are closest to them. We can implement a function that implements this grouping operation using the closest and group-by functions as follows:

```
(defn point-groups [means data distance]
  (group-by #(closest % means distance) data))
```

The point-groups function defined in the preceding code requires three arguments, namely the initial mean values, the collection of points to be grouped, and lastly a function that returns the distance of a point from a given mean. Note that the group-by function applies a function, which is passed as the first parameter, to a collection, which is then passed as the second parameter.

We can apply the `point-groups` function on the list of numbers represented by the `data` variable to group the given values by their distance from the guessed means, represented by `guessed-means` as shown in the following code:

```
user> (point-groups guessed-means data distance)
{0 [2 3 5], 10 [6 10 11 100 101 102]}
```

As shown in the preceding code, the `point-groups` function partitions the sequence `data` into two groups. To calculate the new set of mean values from these groups of input values, we must calculate their average value, which can be implemented using the `reduce` and `count` functions, as shown in the following code:

```
(defn average [& list]
  (/ (reduce + list)
     (count list)))
```

We implement a function to apply the `average` function defined in the preceding code to the previous mean values and the map of groups returned by the `point-groups` function. We will do this with the help of the following code:

```
(defn new-means [average point-groups old-means]
  (for [m old-means]
    (if (contains? point-groups m)
      (apply average (get point-groups m))
      m)))
```

In the `new-means` function defined in the preceding code, for each value in the previous mean values, we apply the `average` function to the points that are grouped by the mean value. Of course, the `average` function must be applied to the points of a given mean only if the mean has any points grouped by it. This is checked using the `contains?` function in the `new-means` function. We can inspect the value returned by the `new-means` function on our sample data in the REPL, as shown in the following output:

```
user> (new-means average
        (point-groups guessed-means data distance)
            guessed-means)
(10/3 55)
```

As shown in the preceding output, the new mean values are calculated as (10/3 55) from the initial mean values (0 10). To implement the *K*-means algorithm, we must apply the `new-means` function iteratively over the new mean values returned by it. This iteration can be performed using the `iterate` function, which requires a function that takes a single argument to be passed to it.

We can define a function to use with the `iterate` function by currying the `new-means` function over the old mean values passed to it, as shown in the following code:

```
(defn iterate-means [data distance average]
  (fn [means]
    (new-means average
               (point-groups means data distance)
               means)))
```

The `iterate-means` function defined in the preceding code returns a function that calculates the new mean values from a given set of initial mean values, as shown in the following output:

```
user> ((iterate-means data distance average) '(0 10))
(10/3 55)
user> ((iterate-means data distance average) '(10/3 55))
(37/6 101)
```

As shown in the preceding output, the mean value is observed to change on applying the function returned by the `iterate-means` function a couple of times. This returned function can be passed to the `iterate` function and we can inspect the iterated mean values using the `take` function, as shown in the following code:

```
user> (take 4 (iterate (iterate-means data distance average)
                       '(0 10)))
((0 10) (10/3 55) (37/6 101) (37/6 101))
```

It's observed that the mean value changes only in the first three iterations and converges to the value `(37/6 10)` for the sample data that we have defined. The termination condition of the *K*-means algorithm is the convergence of the mean values and thus we must iterate over the values returned by the `iterate-means` function until the returned mean value does not differ from the previously returned mean value. Since the `iterate` function lazily returns an infinite sequence, we must implement a function that limits this sequence by the convergence of the elements in the sequence. This behavior can be implemented by lazy realization using the `lazy-seq` and `seq` functions as shown in the following code:

```
(defn take-while-unstable
  ([sq] (lazy-seq (if-let [sq (seq sq)]
                    (cons (first sq)
                          (take-while-unstable
                           (rest sq) (first sq))))))
  ([sq last] (lazy-seq (if-let [sq (seq sq)]
                         (if (= (first sq) last)
                           nil
                           (take-while-unstable sq))))))
```

The `take-while-unstable` function defined in the preceding code splits a lazy sequence into its head and tail terms and then compares the first element of the sequence with the first element of the tail of the sequence to return an empty list, or `nil`, if the two elements are equal. However, if they are not equal, the `take-while-unstable` function is invoked again on the tail of the sequence. Note the use of the `if-let` macro, which is simply a `let` form with an `if` expression as its body to check if the sequence `sq` is empty. We can inspect the value returned by the `take-while-unstable` function in the REPL as shown in the following output:

```
user> (take-while-unstable
        '(1 2 3 4 5 6 7 7 7 7))
(1 2 3 4 5 6 7)
user> (take-while-unstable
        (iterate (iterate-means data distance average)
                 '(0 10)))
((0 10) (10/3 55) (37/6 101))
```

Using the final mean value we have calculated, we can determine the clusters of input values using the `vals` function on the map returned by the `point-groups` function, as shown in the following code:

```
(defn k-cluster [data distance means]
  (vals (point-groups means data distance)))
```

Note that the `vals` function returns all the values in a given map as a sequence.

The `k-cluster` function defined in the preceding code produces the final clusters of input values returned by the *K*-means algorithm. We can apply the `k-cluster` function on the final mean value `(37/6 101)` to return the final clusters of input values, as shown in the following output:

```
user> (k-cluster data distance '(37/6 101))
([2 3 5 6 10 11] [100 101 102])
```

To visualize the change in the clusters of input values, we can apply the `k-cluster` function on the sequence of values returned by composing the `iterate` and `iterate-means` functions. We must limit this sequence by convergence of the values in all clusters and this can be done using the `take-while-unstable` function, as shown in the following code:

```
user> (take-while-unstable
        (map #(k-cluster data distance %)
             (iterate (iterate-means data distance average)
               '(0 10))))
(([2 3 5] [6 10 11 100 101 102])
 ([2 3 5 6 10 11] [100 101 102]))
```

We can refactor the preceding expression into a function that requires only the initial set of guessed mean values by binding the `iterate-means` function to the sample data. The functions used to calculate the distance of a given input value from a mean value and the average mean value from a set of input values are as shown in the following code:

```
(defn k-groups [data distance average]
  (fn [guesses]
    (take-while-unstable
      (map #(k-cluster data distance %)
           (iterate (iterate-means data distance average)
                    guesses)))))
```

We can bind the `k-groups` function defined in the preceding code with our sample data and the `distance` and `average` functions, which operate on numeric values as shown in the following code:

```
(def grouper
  (k-groups data distance average))
```

Now, we can apply the `grouper` function on any arbitrary set of mean values to visualize the changes in the clusters over the various iterations of the *K*-means algorithm, as shown in the following code:

```
user> (grouper '(0 10))
(([2 3 5] [6 10 11 100 101 102])
 ([2 3 5 6 10 11] [100 101 102]))
user> (grouper '(1 2 3))
(([2] [3 5 6 10 11 100 101 102])
 ([2 3 5 6 10 11] [100 101 102])
 ([2 3] [5 6 10 11] [100 101 102])
 ([2 3 5] [6 10 11] [100 101 102])
 ([2 3 5 6] [10 11] [100 101 102]))
user> (grouper '(0 1 2 3 4))
(([2] [3] [5 6 10 11 100 101 102])
 ([2] [3 5 6 10 11] [100 101 102])
 ([2 3] [5 6 10 11] [100 101 102])
 ([2 3 5] [6 10 11] [100 101 102])
 ([2] [3 5 6] [10 11] [100 101 102])
 ([2 3] [5 6] [10 11] [100 101 102]))
```

As we mentioned earlier, if the number of mean values is greater than the number of inputs, we end up with a number of clusters equal to the number of input values, in which each cluster contains a single input value. This can be verified in the REPL using the grouper function, as shown in the following code:

```
user> (grouper (range 200))
(([2] [3] [100] [5] [101] [6] [102] [10] [11]))
```

We can extend the preceding implementation to apply to vector values and not just numeric values, by changing the distance and average distance, which are parameters to the k-groups function. We can implement these two functions for vector values as follows:

```
(defn vec-distance [a b]
  (reduce + (map #(* % %) (map - a b))))

(defn vec-average [& list]
  (map #(/ % (count list)) (apply map + list)))
```

The vec-distance function defined in the preceding code implements the squared Euclidean distance between two vector values as the sum of the squared differences between the corresponding elements in the two vectors. We can also calculate the average of some vector values by adding them together and dividing each resulting element by the number of vectors that were added together, as shown in the vec-average function defined in the preceding code. We can inspect the returned values of these functions in the REPL as shown in the following output:

```
user> (vec-distance [1 2 3] [5 6 7])
48
user> (vec-average  [1 2 3] [5 6 7])
(3 4 5)
```

We can now define some of the following vector values to use as sample data for our clustering algorithm:

```
(def vector-data
  '([1 2 3] [3 2 1] [100 200 300] [300 200 100] [50 50 50]))
```

We can now use the `k-groups` function with the `vector-data`, `vec-distance`, and `vec-average` variables to print the various clusters iterated through to produce the final set of clusters, as shown in the following code:

```
user> ((k-groups vector-data vec-distance vec-average)
       '([1 1 1] [2 2 2] [3 3 3]))
((([[1 2 3] [3 2 1]] [[100 200 300] [300 200 100] [50 50 50]])

 ([[1 2 3] [3 2 1] [50 50 50]]
  [[100 200 300] [300 200 100]])

 ([[1 2 3] [3 2 1]]
  [[100 200 300] [300 200 100]]
  [[50 50 50]])))
```

Another improvement we can add to this implementation is updating identical mean values by the `new-means` function. If we pass a list of identical mean values to the `new-means` function, both the mean values will get updated. However, in the classic *K*-means algorithm, only one mean from two identical mean values is updated. This behavior can be verified in the REPL, by passing a list of identical means such as `'(0 0)` to the `new-means` function, as shown in the following code:

```
user> (new-means average
                 (point-groups '(0 0) '(0 1 2 3 4) distance)
                 '(0 0))
(2 2)
```

We can avoid this problem by checking the number of occurrences of a given mean in the set of mean values and only updating a single mean value if multiple occurrences of it are found. We can implement this using the `frequencies` function, which returns a map with keys as elements from the original collection passed to the `frequencies` function and values as the frequencies of occurrences of these elements. We can thus redefine the `new-means` function, as shown in the following code:

```
(defn update-seq [sq f]
  (let [freqs (frequencies sq)]
    (apply concat
     (for [[k v] freqs]
       (if (= v 1)
         (list (f k))
         (cons (f k) (repeat (dec v) k)))))))
```

```
(defn new-means [average point-groups old-means]
  (update-seq
   old-means
   (fn [o]
     (if (contains? point-groups o)
       (apply average (get point-groups o)) o)))))
```

The `update-seq` function defined in the preceding code applies a function `f` to the elements in a sequence `sq`. The function `f` is only applied to a single element if the element is repeated in the sequence. We can now observe that only a single mean value changes when we apply the redefined `new-means` function on the sequence of identical means `'(0 0)`, as shown in the following output:

```
user> (new-means average
                  (point-groups '(0 0) '(0 1 2 3 4) distance)
                  '(0 0))
(2 0)
```

A consequence of the preceding redefinition of the `new-means` function is that the `k-groups` function now produces identical clusters when applied to both distinct and identical initial mean values, such as `'(0 1)` and `'(0 0)`, as shown in the following code:

```
user> ((k-groups '(0 1 2 3 4) distance average)
       '(0 1))
(([0] [1 2 3 4]) ([0 1] [2 3 4]))
user> ((k-groups '(0 1 2 3 4) distance average)
       '(0 0))
(([0 1 2 3 4]) ([0] [1 2 3 4]) ([0 1] [2 3 4]))
```

This new behavior of the `new-means` function with respect to identical initial mean values also extends to vector values as shown in the following output:

```
user> ((k-groups vector-data vec-distance vec-average)
       '([1 1 1] [1 1 1] [1 1 1]))
((([1 2 3] [3 2 1] [100 200 300] [300 200 100] [50 50 50]])
 ([[1 2 3] [3 2 1]] [[100 200 300] [300 200 100] [50 50 50]])
 ([[1 2 3] [3 2 1] [50 50 50]] [[100 200 300] [300 200 100]])
 ([[1 2 3] [3 2 1]] [[100 200 300] [300 200 100]] [[50 50 50]]))
```

In conclusion, the `k-cluster` and `k-groups` functions defined in the preceding example depict how *K*-means clustering can be implemented in idiomatic Clojure.

Clustering data using clj-ml

The `clj-ml` library provides several implementations of clustering algorithms derived from the Java Weka library. We will now demonstrate how we can use the `clj-ml` library to build a *K*-means clusterer.

> The `clj-ml` and Incanter libraries can be added to a Leiningen project by adding the following dependency to the `project.clj` file:
>
> ```
> [cc.artifice/clj-ml "0.4.0"]
> [incanter "1.5.4"]
> ```
>
> For the example that will follow, the namespace declaration should look similar to the following declaration:
>
> ```
> (ns my-namespace
>   (:use [incanter core datasets]
>         [clj-ml data clusterers]))
> ```

For the examples that use the `clj-ml library` in this chapter, we will use the **Iris** dataset from the Incanter library as our training data. This dataset is essentially a sample of 150 flowers and four feature variables that are measured for these samples. The features of the flowers that are measured in the Iris dataset are the width and length of petal and sepal of the flowers. The sample values are distributed over three species or categories, namely Virginica, Setosa, and Versicolor. The data is available as a 5×150 sized matrix in which the species of a given flower is represented as the last column in this matrix.

We can select the features from the Iris dataset as a vector using the `get-dataset`, `sel`, and `to-vector` functions from the Incanter library, as shown in the following code. We can then convert this vector into a `clj-ml` dataset using the `make-dataset` function from the `clj-ml` library. This is done by passing the keyword names of the feature values as a template to the `make-dataset` function as shown in the following code:

```
(def features [:Sepal.Length
               :Sepal.Width
               :Petal.Length
               :Petal.Width])

(def iris-data (to-vect (sel (get-dataset :iris)
                             :cols features)))

(def iris-dataset
  (make-dataset "iris" features iris-data))
```

We can print the `iris-dataset` variable defined in the preceding code in the REPL to give us some information on what it contains as shown in the following code and output:

```
user> iris-dataset
#<ClojureInstances @relation iris

@attribute Sepal.Length numeric
@attribute Sepal.Width numeric
@attribute Petal.Length numeric
@attribute Petal.Width numeric

@data
5.1,3.5,1.4,0.2
4.9,3,1.4,0.2
4.7,3.2,1.3,0.2
...
4.7,3.2,1.3,0.2
6.2,3.4,5.4,2.3
5.9,3,5.1,1.8>
```

We can create a clusterer using the `make-clusterer` function from the `clj-ml.clusterers` namespace. We can specify the type of cluster to create as the first argument to the `make-cluster` function. The second optional argument is a map of options to be used to create the specified clusterer. We can train a given clusterer using the `cluster-build` function from the `clj-ml` library. In the following code, we create a new *K*-means clusterer using the `make-clusterer` function with the `:k-means` keyword and define a simple helper function to help train this clusterer with any given dataset:

```
(def k-means-clusterer
  (make-clusterer :k-means
                  {:number-clusters 3}))

(defn train-clusterer [clusterer dataset]
  (clusterer-build clusterer dataset)
  clusterer)
```

The `train-clusterer` function can be applied to the clusterer instance defined by the `k-means-clusterer` variable and the sample data represented by the `iris-dataset` variable, as shown in the following code and output:

```
user> (train-clusterer k-means-clusterer iris-dataset)
#<SimpleKMeans
kMeans
```

```
======

Number of iterations: 6
Within cluster sum of squared errors: 6.982216473785234
Missing values globally replaced with mean/mode

Cluster centroids:
                                  Cluster#
Attribute         Full Data             0             1             2
                     (150)          (61)          (50)          (39)
==================================================================
Sepal.Length        5.8433        5.8885         5.006        6.8462
Sepal.Width         3.0573        2.7377         3.428        3.0821
Petal.Length         3.758        4.3967         1.462        5.7026
Petal.Width         1.1993         1.418         0.246        2.0795
```

As shown in the preceding output, the trained clusterer contains 61 values in the
first cluster (cluster 0), 50 values in the second cluster (cluster 1), and 39 values in the
third cluster (cluster 2). The preceding output also gives us some information about
the mean values of the individual features in the training data. We can now predict
the classes of the input data using the trained clusterer and the `clusterer-cluster`
function as shown in the following code:

```
user> (clusterer-cluster k-means-clusterer iris-dataset)
#<ClojureInstances @relation 'clustered iris'

@attribute Sepal.Length numeric
@attribute Sepal.Width numeric
@attribute Petal.Length numeric
@attribute Petal.Width numeric
@attribute class {0,1,2}

@data
5.1,3.5,1.4,0.2,1
4.9,3,1.4,0.2,1
4.7,3.2,1.3,0.2,1
...
6.5,3,5.2,2,2
6.2,3.4,5.4,2.3,2
5.9,3,5.1,1.8,0>
```

The `clusterer-cluster` function uses the trained clusterer to return a new dataset that contains an additional fifth attribute that represents the category of a given sample value. As shown in the preceding code, this new attribute has the values `0`, `1`, and `2`, and the sample values also contain valid values for this new feature. In conclusion, the `clj-ml` library provides a good framework for working with clustering algorithms. In the preceding example, we created a *K*-means clusterer using the `clj-ml` library.

Using hierarchical clustering

Hierarchical clustering is another method of cluster analysis in which input values from the training data are grouped together into a hierarchy. The process of creating the hierarchy can be done in a top-down approach, where in all observations are first part of a single cluster and are then divided into smaller clusters. Alternatively, we can group the input values using a bottom-up methodology, where each cluster is initially a sample value from the training data and these clusters are then combined together. The former top-down approach is termed as **divisive clustering** and the later bottom-up method is called **agglomerative clustering**.

Thus, in agglomerative clustering, we combine clusters into larger clusters, whereas we divide clusters into smaller ones in divisive clustering. In terms of performance, modern implementations of agglomerative clustering algorithms have a time complexity of $O(n^2)$, while those of divisive clustering have much higher complexity of $O(2^n)$.

Suppose we have six input values in our training data. In the following illustration, assume that these input values are positioned according to some two-dimensional metric to measure the overall value of a given input value:

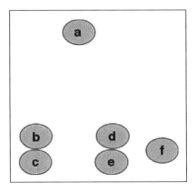

We can apply agglomerative clustering on these input values to produce the following hierarchy of clusters:

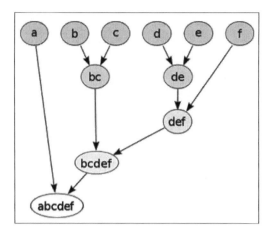

The values *b* and *c* are observed to be the closest to each other in the spatial distribution and are hence grouped into a cluster. Similarly, the nodes *d* and *e* are also grouped into another cluster. The final result of hierarchically clustering the input value is a single binary tree or a **dendogram** of the sample values. In effect, clusters such as *bc* and *def* are added to the hierarchy as binary subtrees of values or of other clusters. Although this process tends to appear very simple in a two-dimensional space, the solution to the problem of determining the distance and hierarchy between input values is much less trivial when applied over several dimensions of features.

In both agglomerative and divisive clustering techniques, the similarity between input values from the sample data has to be calculated. This can be done by measuring the distance between two sets of input values, grouping them into clusters using the calculated distance, and then determining the linkage or similarity between two clusters of input values.

The choice of the distance metric in a hierarchical clustering algorithm will determine the shape of the clusters that are produced by the algorithm. A couple of commonly used measures of the distance between two input vectors X and Y are the Euclidean distance $\|X - Y\|_2$ and the squared Euclidean distance $\|X - Y\|_2^2$, which can be formally expressed as follows:

$$\|X - Y\|_2 = \sqrt{\sum_i (x_i - y_i)^2}$$
$$\|X - Y\|_2^2 = \sum_i (x_i - y_i)^2$$

Another commonly used metric of the distance between input values is the maximum distance $\|X - Y\|_\infty$, which calculates the maximum absolute difference of corresponding elements in two given vectors. This function can be expressed as follows:

$$\|X - Y\|_\infty = \arg\max_i |x_i - y_i|$$

The second aspect of a hierarchical clustering algorithm is the linkage criteria, which is an effective measure of similarity or dissimilarity between two clusters of input values. Two commonly used methods of determining the linkage between two input values are **complete linkage clustering** and **single linkage clustering**. Both of these methods are forms of agglomerative clustering.

In agglomerative clustering, two input values or clusters with the shortest distance metric are combined into a new cluster. Of course, the definition of "shortest distance" is what is unique in any agglomerative clustering technique. In complete linkage clustering, input values farthest from each other are used to determine the grouping. Hence, this method is also termed as **farthest neighbor clustering**. This metric of the distance $D(X,Y)$ between two values can be formally expressed as follows:

$$\text{In complete linkage clustering, } D(X,Y) = \arg\max_{x \in X, y \in Y} d(x,y)$$

In the preceding equation, the function $d(x,y)$ is the selected metric of distance between two input vectors. Complete linkage clustering will essentially group together values or clusters that have the maximum value of the distance metric d. This operation of grouping together clusters is repeated until a single cluster is produced.

In single linkage clustering, values that are nearest to each other are grouped together. Hence, single linkage clustering is also called **nearest neighbor clustering**. This can be be formally stated using the following expression:

$$\text{In single linkage clustering, } D(X,Y) = \arg\min_{x \in X, y \in Y} d(x,y)$$

Another popular hierarchical clustering technique is the **Cobweb algorithm**. This algorithm is a form of **conceptual clustering**, in which a concept is created for each cluster produced by the clustering method used. By the term "concept", we mean a concise formal description of the data clustered together. Interestingly, conceptual clustering is closely related to decision tree learning, which we already discussed in *Chapter 3, Categorizing Data*. The Cobweb algorithm groups all clusters into a **classification tree**, in which each node contains a formal summary of the values or clusters that are its child nodes. This information can then be used to determine and predict the category of an input value with some missing features. In this sense, this technique can be used when some of the samples in the test data have missing or unknown features.

We now demonstrate a simple implementation of hierarchical clustering. In this implementation, we take a slightly different approach where we embed part of the required functionality into the standard vector data structure provided by the Clojure language.

 For the upcoming example, we require the `clojure.math.numeric-tower` library that can be added to a Leiningen project by adding the following dependency to the `project.clj` file:

`[org.clojure/math.numeric-tower "0.0.4"]`

The namespace declaration for the example should look similar to the following declaration:

```
(ns my-namespace
  (:use [clojure.math.numeric-tower :only [sqrt]]))
```

For this implementation, we will use the Euclidean distance between two points as a distance metric. We can calculate this distance from the sum of squares of the elements in an input vector, which can be computed using a composition of the `reduce` and `map` functions as follows:

```
(defn sum-of-squares [coll]
  (reduce + (map * coll coll)))
```

The `sum-of-squares` function defined in the preceding code will be used to determine the distance metric. We will define two protocols that abstract the operations we perform on a particular data type. From an engineering perspective, these two protocols could be combined into a single protocol, since both the protocols will be used in combination.

However, we use the following two protocols for this example for the sake of clarity:

```
(defprotocol Each
  (each [v op w]))

(defprotocol Distance
  (distance [v w]))
```

The each function defined in the Each protocol applies a given operation op on corresponding elements in two collections v and w. The each function is quite similar to the standard map function, but each allows the data type of v to decide how to apply the function op. The distance function defined in the Distance protocol calculates the distance between any two collections v and w. Note that we use the generic term "collection" since we are dealing with abstract protocols and not concrete implementations of the functions of these protocols. For this example, we will implement the preceding protocols as part of the vector data type. Of course, these protocols could also be extended to other data types such as sets and maps.

In this example, we will implement single linkage clustering as the linkage criteria. First, we will have to define a function to determine the two closest vectors from a set of vector values. To do this, we can apply the min-key function, which returns the key with the least associated value in a collection, on a vector. Interestingly, this is possible in Clojure since we can treat a vector as a map with the index values of the various elements in the vector as its keys. We will implement this with the help of the following code:

```
(defn closest-vectors [vs]
  (let [index-range (range (count vs))]
    (apply min-key
           (fn [[x y]] (distance (vs x) (vs y)))
           (for [i index-range
                 j (filter #(not= i %) index-range)]
             [i j])))))
```

The closest-vectors function defined in the preceding code determines all possible combinations of the indexes of the vector vs using the for form. Note that the vector vs is a vector of vectors. The distance function is then applied over the values of the possible index combinations and these distances are then compared using the min-key function. The function finally returns the index values of the two inner vector values that have the least distance from each other, thus implementing single linkage clustering.

We will also need to calculate the mean value of two vectors that have to be clustered together. We can implement this using the each function we had previously defined in the Each protocol and the reduce function, as follows:

```
(defn centroid [& xs]
  (each
   (reduce #(each %1 + %2) xs)
   *
   (double (/ 1 (count xs))))))
```

The centroid function defined in the preceding code will calculate the mean value of a sequence of vector values. Note the use of the double function to ensure that the value returned by the centroid function is a double-precision number.

We now implement the Each and Distance protocols as part of the vector data type, which is fully qualified as clojure.lang.PersistentVector. This is done using the extend-type function as follows:

```
(extend-type clojure.lang.PersistentVector
  Each
  (each [v op w]
    (vec
     (cond
      (number? w) (map op v (repeat w))
      (vector? w) (if (>= (count v) (count w))
                    (map op v (lazy-cat w (repeat 0)))
                    (map op (lazy-cat v (repeat 0)) w))))))
  Distance
  ;; implemented as Euclidean distance
  (distance [v w] (-> (each v - w)
                      sum-of-squares
                      sqrt)))
```

The each function is implemented such that it applies the op operation to each element in the v vector and a second argument w. The w parameter could be either a vector or a number. In case w is a number, we simply map the function op over v and the repeated value of the number w. If w is a vector, we pad the smaller vector with 0 values using the lazy-cat function and map op over the two vectors. Also, we wrap the entire expression in a vec function to ensure that the value returned is always a vector.

The distance function is implemented as the Euclidean distance between two vector values v and w using the sum-of-squares function that we previously defined and the sqrt function from the clojure.math.numeric-tower namespace.

We have all the pieces needed to implement a function that performs hierarchical clustering on vector values. We can implement hierarchical clustering primarily using the centroid and `closest-vectors` functions that we had previously defined, as follows:

```
(defn h-cluster
  "Performs hierarchical clustering on a
  sequence of maps of the form { :vec [1 2 3] } ."
  [nodes]
  (loop [nodes nodes]
    (if (< (count nodes) 2)
      nodes
      (let [vectors     (vec (map :vec nodes))
            [l r]       (closest-vectors vectors)
            node-range  (range (count nodes))
            new-nodes   (vec
                          (for [i node-range
                                :when (and (not= i l)
                                           (not= i r))]
                            (nodes i)))]
        (recur (conj new-nodes
                     {:left (nodes l) :right (nodes r)
                      :vec (centroid
                             (:vec (nodes l))
                             (:vec (nodes r)))})))))))
```

We can pass a vector of maps to the `h-cluster` function defined in the preceding code. Each map in this vector contains a vector as the value of the keyword `:vec`. The `h-cluster` function combines all the vector values from the `:vec` keywords in these maps and determines the two closest vectors using the `closest-vectors` function. Since the value returned by the `closest-vectors` function is a vector of two index values, we determine all the vectors with indexes other than the two index values returned by the `closest-vectors` function. This is done using a special form of the `for` macro that allows a conditional clause to be specified with the `:when` key parameter. The mean value of the two closest vectors is then calculated using the `centroid` function. A new map is created using the mean value and then added to the original vector to replace the two closest vector values. The process is repeated until the vector contains a single cluster, using the `loop` form. We can inspect the behavior of the `h-cluster` function in the REPL as shown in the following code:

```
user> (h-cluster [{:vec [1 2 3]} {:vec [3 4 5]} {:vec [7 9 9]}])
[{:left {:vec [7 9 9]},
  :right {:left {:vec [1 2 3]},
          :right {:vec [3 4 5]},
          :vec [2.0 3.0 4.0]},
  :vec [4.5 6.0 6.5] }]
```

When applied to three vector values [1 2 3], [3 4 5], and [7 9 9], as shown in the preceding code, the h-cluster function groups the vectors [1 2 3] and [3 4 5] into a single cluster. This cluster has the mean value of [2.0 3.0 4.0], which is calculated from the vectors [1 2 3] and [3 4 5]. This new cluster is then grouped with the vector [7 9 9] in the next iteration, thus producing a single cluster with a mean value of [4.5 6.0 6.5]. In conclusion, the h-cluster function can be used to hierarchically cluster vector values into a single hierarchy.

The clj-ml library provides an implementation of the Cobweb hierarchical clustering algorithm. We can instantiate such a clusterer using the make-clusterer function with the :cobweb argument.

```
(def h-clusterer (make-clusterer :cobweb))
```

The clusterer defined by the h-clusterer variable shown in the preceding code can be trained using the train-clusterer function and iris-dataset dataset, which we had previously defined, as follows: The train-clusterer function and iris-dataset can be implemented as shown in the following code:

```
user> (train-clusterer h-clusterer iris-dataset)
#<Cobweb Number of merges: 0
Number of splits: 0
Number of clusters: 3

node 0 [150]
|    leaf 1 [96]
node 0 [150]
|    leaf 2 [54]
```

As shown in the preceding REPL output, the Cobweb clustering algorithm partitions the input data into two clusters. One cluster has 96 samples and the other cluster has 54 samples, which is quite a different result compared to the *K*-means clusterer, we had previously used. In summary, the clj-ml library provides an easy-to-use implementation of the Cobweb clustering algorithm.

Using Expectation-Maximization

The **Expectation-Maximization (EM)** algorithm is a probabilistic approach for determining a clustering model that fits the supplied training data. This algorithm determines the **Maximum Likelihood Estimate (MLE)** of the parameters of a formulated clustering model (for more information, refer to *Maximum likelihood theory and applications for distributions generated when observing a function of an exponential family variable*).

Suppose we want to determine the probability of a coin toss being a head or a tail. If we flip the coin n times, we end up with h occurrences of heads and $n-h$ occurrences of tails. We can estimate the actual probability of occurrence of a head P as the ratio of the number of occurrences of a head to the total number of coin tosses performed, using the following equation:

$$\text{Estimated } \hat{p} = \frac{h}{n}$$

The probability $\hat{p}$ defined in the preceding equation is the MLE of the probability P. In the context of machine learning, the MLE can be maximized to determine the probability of occurrence of a given class or category. However, this estimated probability may not be statistically distributed in a well-defined way over the available training data, which makes it hard to determine the MLE efficiently. The problem is simplified by introducing a set of hidden values to account for the unobserved values in the training data. The hidden values are not directly measured from the data, but are determined from factors that influence the data. The likelihood function of the parameters β for a given set of observed values X and a set of hidden values Z is defined as the probability of occurrence of X and Z for a given set of parameters β. The likelihood is mathematically written as $L(\beta; X, Z)$, and can be expressed as follows:

$$L(\beta; X, Z) = P(X, Z \mid \beta)$$

The EM algorithm comprises two steps — the expectation step and the maximization step. In the expectation step, we calculate the expected value of the **log likelihood** function. This step determines a metric Q, which must be maximized in the next step, that is, the maximization step of the algorithm. These two steps can be formally summarized as follows:

$$\hat{\beta}_{i+1} = \arg \max_{\beta} Q(\beta, \hat{\beta}_i)$$

$$\text{where } Q(\beta, \hat{\beta}_i) = E_{Z|X,\hat{\beta}i} \left[\log L(\beta; X, Z) \right]$$

In the preceding equation, the value of β that maximizes the value of the function Q is iteratively calculated until it converges to a particular value. The term β_i represents the estimated parameters in the ith iteration of the algorithm. Also, the term E is the expected value of the log likelihood function.

The `clj-ml` library also provides an EM clusterer. We can create an EM clusterer using the `make-clusterer` function with the `:expectation-maximization` keyword as its argument, as shown in the following code:

```
(def em-clusterer (make-clusterer :expectation-maximization
                                  {:number-clusters 3}))
```

Note that we must also specify the number of clusters to produce as an option to the `make-clusterer` function.

We can train the clusterer defined by the `em-clusterer` variable in the preceding code using the `train-clusterer` function and `iris-dataset` dataset, which we had previously defined, as follows:

```
user> (train-clusterer em-clusterer iris-dataset)
#<EM
EM
==

Number of clusters: 3


                  Cluster
Attribute              0       1       2
                   (0.41)  (0.25)  (0.33)
=========================================
Sepal.Length
   mean            5.9275  6.8085   5.006
   std. dev.       0.4817  0.5339  0.3489

Sepal.Width
   mean            2.7503  3.0709   3.428
   std. dev.       0.2956  0.2867  0.3753

Petal.Length
   mean            4.4057  5.7233   1.462
   std. dev.       0.5254  0.4991  0.1719

Petal.Width
   mean            1.4131  2.1055   0.246
   std. dev.       0.2627  0.2456  0.1043
```

As shown in the preceding output, the EM clusterer partitions the given dataset into three clusters in which the clusters are distributed as approximately 41 percent, 25 percent, and 35 percent of the samples in the training data.

Using SOMs

As we mentioned earlier in *Chapter 4, Building Neural Networks*, SOMs can be used to model unsupervised machine learning problems such as clustering (for more information, refer to *Self-organizing Maps as Substitutes for K-Means Clustering*). To quickly recap, an SOM is a type of ANN that maps input values with a high number of dimensions to a low-dimensional output space. This mapping preserves patterns and topological relations between the input values. The neurons in the output space of an SOM will have higher activation values for input values that are spatially close to each other. Thus, SOMs are a good solution for clustering input data with a large number of dimensions.

The Incanter library provides a concise SOM implementation that we can use to cluster the input variables from the Iris dataset. We will demonstrate how we can use this SOM implementation for clustering in the example that will follow.

> The Incanter library can be added to a Leiningen project by adding the following dependency to the `project.clj` file:
>
> ```
> [incanter "1.5.4"]
> ```
>
> For the upcoming example, the namespace declaration should look similar to the following declaration:
>
> ```
> (ns my-namespace
>   (:use [incanter core som stats charts datasets]))
> ```

We first define the sample data to cluster using the `get-dataset`, `sel`, and `to-matrix` functions from the Incanter library as follows:

```
(def iris-features (to-matrix (sel (get-dataset :iris)
                            :cols [:Sepal.Length
                                   :Sepal.Width
                                   :Petal.Length
                                   :Petal.Width]))))
```

The `iris-features` variable defined in the preceding code is in fact a 150×4 sized matrix that represents the values of the four input variables that we have selected from the Iris dataset. Now, we can use the `som-batch-train` function from the `incanter.som` namespace to create and train an SOM using these selected features, as follows:

```
(def som (som-batch-train
           iris-features :cycles 10))
```

The som variable defined is actually a map with several key-value pairs. The :dims key in this map contains a vector that represents the dimensions in the lattice of neurons in the trained SOM, as shown in the following code and output:

```
user> (:dims som)
[10.0 2.0]
```

Thus, we can say that the neural lattice of the trained SOM is a 10×2 matrix. The :sets key of the map represented by the som variable gives us the positional grouping of the various indexes of the input values in the lattice of neurons of the SOM, as shown in the following output:

```
user> (:sets som)
{[4 1] (144 143 141 ... 102 100),
 [8 1] (149 148 147 ... 50),
 [9 0] (49 48 47 46 ... 0)}
```

As shown in the preceding REPL output, the input data is partitioned into three clusters. We can calculate the mean values of each feature using the mean function from the incanter.stats namespace as follows:

```
(def feature-mean
  (map #(map mean (trans
                    (sel iris-features :rows ((:sets som) %))))
       (keys (:sets som))))
```

We can implement a function to plot these mean values using the xy-plot, add-lines, and view functions from the Incanter library as follows:

```
(defn plot-means []
  (let [x (range (ncol iris-features))
        cluster-name #(str "Cluster " %)]
    (-> (xy-plot x (nth feature-mean 0)
                 :x-label "Feature"
                 :y-label "Mean value of feature"
                 :legend true
                 :series-label (cluster-name 0))
        (add-lines x (nth feature-mean 1)
                   :series-label (cluster-name 1))
        (add-lines x (nth feature-mean 2)
                   :series-label (cluster-name 2))
        view)))
```

The following linear plot is produced on calling the `plot-means` function defined in the preceding code:

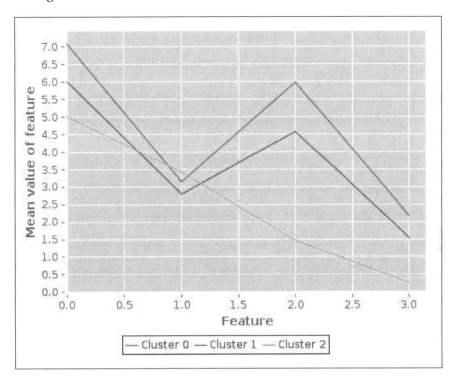

The preceding plot gives us an idea of the mean values of the various features in the three clusters determined by the SOM. The plot shows that two of the clusters (*Cluster 0* and *Cluster 1*) have similar features. The third cluster, however, has significantly different mean values for these set of features and is thus shown as a different shape in the plot. Of course, this plot doesn't give us much information about the distribution or variance of input values around these mean values. To visualize these features, we need to somehow transform the number of dimensions of the input data to two or three dimensions, which can be easily visualized. We will discuss more on this concept of reducing the number of features in the training data in the next section of this chapter.

We can also print the clusters and the actual categories of the input values using the `frequencies` and `sel` functions as follows:

```
(defn print-clusters []
  (doseq [[pos rws] (:sets som)]
    (println pos \:
             (frequencies
              (sel (get-dataset :iris)
                   :cols :Species :rows rws)))))
```

We can call the function `print-clusters` defined in the preceding code to produce the following REPL output:

```
user> (print-clusters)
[4 1] : {virginica 23}
[8 1] : {virginica 27, versicolor 50}
[9 0] : {setosa 50}
nil
```

As shown in the preceding output, the `virginica` and `setosa` species seem to be appropriately classified into two clusters. However, the cluster containing the input values of the `versicolor` species also contains 27 samples of the `virginica` species. This problem could be remedied by using more sample data to train the SOM or by modeling a higher number of features.

In conclusion, the Incanter library provides us with a concise implementation of an SOM, which we can train using the Iris dataset as shown in the preceding example.

Reducing dimensions in the data

In order to easily visualize the distribution of some unlabeled data in which the input values have multiple dimensions, we must reduce the number of feature dimensions to two or three. Once we have reduced the number of dimensions of the input data to two or three dimensions, we can trivially plot the data to provide a more understandable visualization of it. This process of reducing the number of dimensions in the input data is known as **dimensionality reduction**. As this process reduces the total number of dimensions used to represent the sample data, it is also useful for data compression.

Principal Component Analysis (PCA) is a form of dimensionality reduction in which the input variables in the sample data are transformed into linear uncorrelated variables (for more information, refer to *Principal Component Analysis*). These transformed features are called the **principal components** of the sample data.

PCA uses a covariance matrix and a matrix operation called **Singular Value Decomposition (SVD)** to calculate the principal components of a given set of input values. The covariance matrix denoted as Σ, can be determined from a set of input vectors X with N samples as follows:

$$\text{Covariance matrix } \Sigma = \frac{1}{N} X^T X$$

The covariance matrix is generally calculated from the input values after mean normalization, which is simply ensuring that each feature has a zero mean value. Also, the features could be scaled before determining the covariance matrix. Next, the SVD of the covariance matrix is determined as follows:

$$\text{By SVD, } M_{m \times n} = U_{m \times m} S_{m \times n} V_{n \times n}$$

SVD can be thought of as factorization of a matrix M with size $m \times n$ into three matrices U, S, and V. The matrix U has a size of $m \times m$, the matrix S has a size of $m \times n$, and the matrix V has a size of $n \times n$. The matrix M actually represents the n input vectors with m dimensions in the sample data. The matrix S is a diagonal matrix and is called the **singular value** of the matrix M, and the matrices U and V are called the **left and right singular vectors** of M, respectively. In the context of PCA, the matrix S is termed as the **reduction component** and the matrix U is termed as the **rotation component** of the sample data.

The PCA algorithm to reduce the m dimensions in the n input vectors to k dimensions can be summarized using the following steps:

1. Calculate the covariance matrix Σ from the input vectors X.

2. Calculate the matrices U, S, and V by applying SVD on the covariance matrix Σ.

3. From the $m \times m$ matrix U, select the first k columns to produce the matrix $U_{reduced}$, which is termed as the **reduced left singular vector** or **reduced rotation matrix** of the matrix Σ. This matrix represents the k principal components of the sample data and will have a size of $k \times m$.

4. Calculate the vectors with k dimensions, denoted by Z, as follows:

$$Z = U_{reduced}^{T} \times X$$

Note that the input to the PCA algorithm is the set of input vectors X from the sample data after mean normalization and feature scaling.

Since the matrix $U_{reduced}$ calculated in the preceding steps has k columns, the matrix Z will have a size of $k \times n$, which represents the n input vectors in k dimensions. We should note that a lower value of the number of dimensions k could result in a higher loss of variance in the data. Hence, we should choose k such that only a small fraction of the variance is lost.

The original input vectors X can be recreated from the matrix Z and the reduced left singular vector $U_{reduced}$ as follows:

$$X = U_{reduced} \times Z$$

The Incanter library includes some functions to perform PCA. In the example that will follow, we will use PCA to provide a better visualization of the Iris dataset.

> The namespace declaration of the upcoming example should look similar to the following declaration:
>
> ```
> (ns my-namespace
>     (:use [incanter core stats charts datasets]))
> ```

We first define the training data using the `get-dataset`, `to-matrix`, and `sel` functions, as shown in the following code:

```
(def iris-matrix (to-matrix (get-dataset :iris)))
(def iris-features (sel iris-matrix :cols (range 4)))
(def iris-species (sel iris-matrix :cols 4))
```

Similar to the previous example, we will use the first four columns of the Iris dataset as sample data for the input variables of the training data.

PCA is performed by the `principal-components` function from the `incanter.stats` namespace. This function returns a map that contains the rotation matrix U and the reduction matrix S from PCA, which we described earlier. We can select columns from the reduction matrix of the input data using the `sel` function as shown in the following code:

```
(def pca (principal-components iris-features))

(def U (:rotation pca))
(def U-reduced (sel U :cols (range 2)))
```

As shown in the preceding code, the rotation matrix of the PCA of the input data can be fetched using the `:rotation` keyword on the value returned by the `principal-components` function. We can now calculate the reduced features Z using the reduced rotation matrix and the original matrix of features represented by the `iris-features` variable, as shown in the following code:

```
(def reduced-features (mmult iris-features U-reduced))
```

The reduced features can then be visualized by selecting the first two columns of the `reduced-features` matrix and plotting them using the `scatter-plot` function, as shown in the following code:

```
(defn plot-reduced-features []
  (view (scatter-plot (sel reduced-features :cols 0)
                      (sel reduced-features :cols 1)
                      :group-by iris-species
                      :x-label "PC1"
                      :y-label "PC2")))
```

The following plot is generated on calling the `plot-reduced-features` function defined in the preceding code:

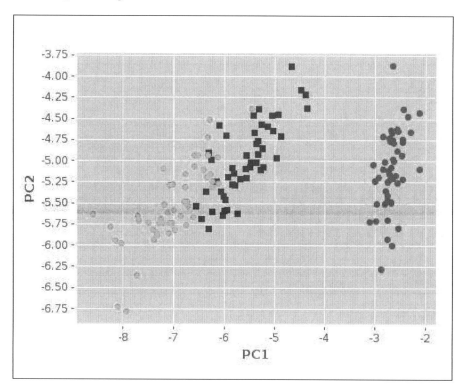

The scatter plot illustrated in the preceding diagram gives us a good visualization of the distribution of the input data. The blue and green clusters in the preceding plot are shown to have similar values for the given set of features. In summary, the Incanter library supports PCA, which allows for the easy visualization of some sample data.

Summary

In this chapter, we explored several clustering algorithms that can be used to model some unlabeled data. The following are some of the other points that we have covered:

- We explored the *K*-means algorithm and hierarchical clustering techniques while providing sample implementations of these methods in pure Clojure. We also described how we can leverage these techniques through the `clj-ml` library.

- We discussed the EM algorithm, which is a probabilistic clustering technique, and also described how we can use the `clj-ml` library to build an EM clusterer.

- We also explored how we can use SOMs to fit clustering problems with a high number of dimensions. We also demonstrated how we can use the Incanter library to build an SOM that can be used for clustering.

- Lastly, we studied dimensionality reduction and PCA, and how we can use PCA to provide a better visualization of the Iris dataset using the Incanter library.

In the following chapter, we will explore the concepts of anomaly detection and recommendation systems using machine learning techniques.

8

Anomaly Detection and Recommendation

In this chapter, we will study a couple of modern forms of applied machine learning. We will first explore the problem of *anomaly detection* and we will discuss *recommendation systems* later in this chapter.

Anomaly detection is a machine learning technique in which we determine whether a given set of values for some selected features that represent the system are unexpectedly different from the normally observed values of the given features. There are several applications of anomaly detection, such as detection of structural and operational defects in manufacturing, network intrusion detection systems, system monitoring, and medical diagnosis.

Recommendation systems are essentially information systems that seek to predict a given user's liking or preference for a given item. Over recent years, there have been a vast number of recommendation systems, or **recommender systems**, that have been built for several business and social applications to provide a better experience for their users. Such systems can provide a user with useful recommendations depending on the items that the user has previously rated or liked. Most existing recommendation systems today provide recommendations to users about online products, music, and social media. There are also a significant number of financial and business applications on the Web that use recommendation systems.

Interestingly, both anomaly detection and recommendation systems are applied forms of machine learning problems, which we have previously encountered in this book. Anomaly detection is in fact an extension of binary classification, and recommendation is actually an extended form of linear regression. We will study more about these similarities in this chapter.

Detecting anomalies

Anomaly detection is essentially the identification of items or observed values that do not conform to an expected pattern (for more information, refer to "A Survey of Outlier Detection Methodologies"). The pattern could be determined by values that have been previously observed, or by some limits across which the input values can vary. In the context of machine learning, anomaly detection can be performed in both supervised and unsupervised environments. Either way, the problem of anomaly detection is to find input values that are significantly different from other input values. There are several applications of this technique, and in the broad sense, we can use anomaly detection for the following reasons:

- To detect problems
- To detect a new phenomenon
- To monitor unusual behavior

The observed values that are found to be different from the other values are called outliers, anomalies, or exceptions. More formally, we define an **outlier** as an observation that lies outside the overall pattern of a distribution. By *outside*, we mean an observation that has a high numerical or statistical distance from the rest of the data.

Some examples of outliers can be depicted by the following plots, where the red crosses mark normal observations and the green crosses mark the anomalous observations:

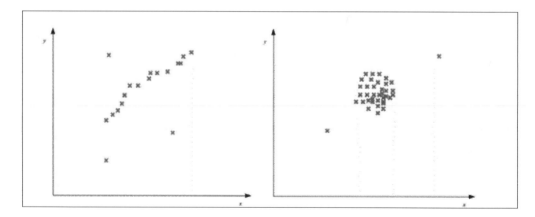

One possible approach to anomaly detection is to use a *probability distribution model*, which is built from the training data to detect anomalies. Techniques that use this approach are termed as *statistical methods* of anomaly detection. In this approach, an anomaly will have a low probability with respect to the overall probability distribution of the rest of the sample data. Hence, we try to fit a model onto the available sample data and use this formulated model to detect anomalies. The main problem with this approach is that it's hard to find a standard distribution model for stochastic data.

Another method that can be used to detect anomalies is a *proximity-based approach*. In this approach, we determine the proximity, or nearness, of a set of observed values with respect to the rest of the values in the sample data. For example, we could use the **K-Nearest Neighbors (KNN)** algorithm to determine the distances of a given observed value to its *k* nearest values. This technique is much simpler than estimating a statistical model over the sample data. This is because it's easier to determine a single measure, which is the proximity of an observed value, than it is to fit a standard model on the available training data. However, determining the proximity of a set of input values could be inefficient for larger datasets. For example, the KNN algorithm has a time complexity of $o(n^2)$, and computing the proximity of a given set of values to its *k* nearest values could be inefficient for a large value of *k*. Also, the KNN algorithm could be sensitive to the value of the neighbors *k*. If the value of *k* is too large, clusters of values with less than *k* individual sets of input values could be falsely classified as anomalies. On the other hand, if *k* is too small, some anomalies that have a few neighbors with a low proximity may not be detected.

We can also determine whether a given set of observed values is an anomaly based on the density of data around it. This approach is termed as the **density-based approach** to anomaly detection. A given set of input values can be classified as an anomaly if the data around the given values is low. In anomaly detection, the density-based and proximity-based approaches are closely related. In fact, the density of data is generally defined in terms of the proximity or distance of a given set of values with respect to the rest of the data. For example, if we use the KNN algorithm to determine the proximity or distance of a given set of values to the rest of the data, we can define the density as the reciprocal of the average distance to the *k* nearest values, as follows:

$$density(X,k) = \left(\frac{\sum_{i \in N(X,k)} distance(X,i)}{|N(X,k)|} \right)^{-1}$$

where $N(X,k)$ is the set of *k* nearest neighbors from X

Clustering-based approaches can also be used to detect anomalies. Essentially, clustering can be used to determine groups or clusters of values in the sample data. The items in a cluster can be assumed to be closely related, and anomalies are values that cannot be related to previously encountered values in the clusters in the sample data. Thus, we could determine all the clusters in the sample data and then mark the smallest clusters as anomalies. Alternatively, we can form clusters from the sample data and determine the clusters, if any, of a given set of previously unseen values.

If a set of input values does not belong to any cluster, it's definitely an anomalous observation. The advantage of clustering techniques is that they can be used in combination with other machine learning techniques that we previously discussed. On the other hand, the problem with this approach is that most clustering techniques are sensitive to the number of clusters that have been chosen. Also, algorithmic parameters of clustering techniques, such as the average number of items in a cluster and number of clusters, cannot be determined easily. For example, if we are modeling some unlabeled data using the KNN algorithm, the number of clusters K would have to be determined either by trial-and-error or by scrutinizing the sample data for obvious clusters. However, both these techniques are not guaranteed to perform well on unseen data.

In models where the sample values are all supposed to conform to some mean value with some allowable tolerance, the **Gaussian** or **normal distribution** is often used as the distribution model to train an anomaly detector. This model has two parameters—the mean μ and the variance σ^2. This distribution model is often used in statistical approaches to anomaly detection, where the input variables are normally found statistically close to some predetermined mean value.

The **Probability Density Function (PDF)** is often used by density-based methods of anomaly detection. This function essentially describes the likelihood that an input variable will take on a given value. For a random variable x, we can formally define the PDF as follows:

$$\text{PDF } f(x) = \frac{1}{\sqrt{2\pi}} e^{\frac{-x^2}{2}}$$

The PDF can also be used in combination with a normal distribution model for the purpose of anomaly detection. The PDF of a normal distribution is parameterized by the mean μ and variance σ^2 of the distribution, and can be formally expressed as follows:

$$\text{PDF } f(x; \mu, \sigma^2) = \frac{1}{\sigma\sqrt{2\pi}} e^{\frac{-1}{2}\left(\frac{x-\mu}{\sigma}\right)^2}$$

We will now demonstrate a simple implementation of an anomaly detector in Clojure, which is based on the PDF for a normal distribution as we previously discussed. For this example, we will use Clojure atoms to maintain all states in the model. Atoms are used to represent an atomic state in Clojure. By *atomic*, we mean that the underlying state changes completely or doesn't change at all — the changes in state are thus *atomic*.

We now define some functions to help us manipulate the features of the model. Essentially, we intend to represent these features and their values as a map. To manage the state of this map, we use an atom. Whenever the anomaly detector is fed a set of feature values, it must first check for any previous information on the features in the new set of values, and then it should start maintaining the state of any new features when it is necessary. As a function on its own cannot contain any external state in Clojure, we will use closures to bind state and functions together. In this implementation, almost all the functions return other functions, and the resulting anomaly detector will also be used just like a function. In summary, we will model the state of the anomaly detector using an atom, and then bind this atom to a function using a closure.

We start off by defining a function that initializes our model with some state. This state is essentially a map wrapped in an atom by using the `atom` function, as follows:

```
(defn update-totals [n]
  (comp #(update-in % [:count] inc)
        #(update-in % [:total] + n)
        #(update-in % [:sq-total] + (Math/pow n 2)))))


(defn accumulator []
  (let [totals (atom {:total 0, :count 0, :sq-total 0})]
    (fn [n]
      (let [result (swap! totals (update-totals n))
            cnt (result :count)
            avg (/ (result :total) cnt)]
        {:average avg
         :variance (- (/ (result :sq-total) cnt)
                      (Math/pow avg 2))}))))
```

The `accumulator` function defined in the preceding code initializes an atom and returns a function that applies the `update-totals` function to a value n. The value n represents a value of an input variable in our model. The `update-totals` function also returns a function that takes a single argument, and then it updates the state in the atom by using the `update-in` function. The function returned by the `accumulator` function will use the `update-totals` function to update the state of the mean and variance of the model.

We now implement the following PDF function for normal distribution that can be used to monitor sudden changes in the feature values of the model:

```
(defn density [x average variance]
  (let [sigma (Math/sqrt variance)
        divisor (* sigma (Math/sqrt (* 2 Math/PI)))
        exponent (/ (Math/pow (- x average) 2)
                    (if (zero? variance) 1
                        (* 2 variance)))]
    (/ (Math/exp (- exponent))
       (if (zero? divisor) 1
           divisor))))
```

The `density` function defined in the preceding code is a direct translation of the PDF function for normal distribution. It uses functions and constants from the `Math` namespace such as, `sqrt`, `exp`, and `PI` to find the PDF of the model by using the accumulated mean and variance of the model. We will define the the `density-detector` function as shown in the following code:

```
(defn density-detector []
  (let [acc (accumulator)]
    (fn [x]
      (let [state (acc x)]
        (density x (state :average) (state :variance))))))
```

The `density-detector` function defined in the preceding code initializes the state of our anomaly detector using the `accumulator` function, and it uses the `density` function on the state maintained by the accumulator to determine the PDF of the model.

Since we are dealing with maps wrapped in atoms, we can implement a couple of functions to perform this check by using the `contains?`, `assoc-in`, and `swap!` functions, as shown in the following code:

```
(defn get-or-add-key [a key create-fn]
  (if (contains? @a key)
    (@a key)
    ((swap! a #(assoc-in % [key] (create-fn))) key)))
```

The `get-or-add-key` function defined in the preceding code looks up a given key in an atom containing a map by using the `contains?` function. Note the use of the `@` operator to dereference an atom into its wrapped value. If the key is found in the map, we simply call the map as a function as `(@a key)`. If the key is not found, we use the `swap!` and `assoc-in` functions to add a new key-value pair to the map in the atom. The value of this key-value pair is generated from the `create-fn` parameter that is passed to the `get-or-add-key` function.

Using the `get-or-add-key` and `density-detector` functions we have defined, we can implement the following functions that return functions while detecting anomalies in the sample data so as to create the effect of maintaining the state of the PDF distribution of the model within these functions themselves:

```
(defn atom-hash-map [create-fn]
  (let [a (atom {})]
    (fn [x]
      (get-or-add-key a x create-fn))))


(defn get-var-density [detector]
  (fn [kv]
    (let [[k v] kv]
      ((detector k) v))))


(defn detector []
  (let [detector (atom-hash-map density-detector)]
    (fn [x]
      (reduce * (map (get-var-density detector) x)))))
```

The `atom-hash-map` function defined in the preceding code uses the `get-key` function with an arbitrary initialization function `create-fn` to maintain the state of a map in an atom. The detector function uses the `density-detector` function that we previously defined to initialize the state of every new feature in the input values that are fed to it. Note that this function returns a function that will accept a map with key-value parameters as the features. We can inspect the behavior of the implemented anomaly detector in the REPL as shown in the following code and output:

```
user> (def d (detector))
#'user/d
user> (d {:x 10 :y 10 :z 10})
1.0
user> (d {:x 10 :y 10 :z 10})
1.0
```

As shown in the preceding code and output, we created a new instance of our anomaly detector by using the `detector` function. The `detector` function returns a function that accepts a map of key-value pairs of features. When we feed the map with `{:x 10 :y 10 :z 10}`, the anomaly detector returns a PDF of `1.0` since all samples in the data so far have the same feature values. The anomaly detector will always return this value as long as the number of features and the values of these features remains the same in all sample inputs fed to it.

When we feed the anomaly detector with a set of features with different values, the PDF is observed to change to a finite number, as shown in the following code and output:

```
user> (d {:x 11 :y 9 :z 15})
0.0060352535208831985
user> (d {:x 10 :y 10 :z 14})
0.07930301229115849
```

When the features show a large degree of variation, the detector has a sudden and large decrease in the PDF of its distribution model, as shown in the following code and output:

```
user> (d {:x 100 :y 10 :z 14})
1.9851385000301642E-4
user> (d {:x 101 :y 9 :z 12})
5.589934974999084E-4
```

In summary, anomalous sample values can be detected when the PDF of the normal distribution model returned by the anomaly detector described previously has a large difference from its previous values. We can extend this implementation to check some kind of threshold value so that the result is quantized. The system thus detects an anomaly only when this threshold value of the PDF is crossed. When dealing with real-world data, all we would have to do is somehow represent the feature values we are modeling as a map and determine the threshold value to use via trial-and-error method.

Anomaly detection can be used in both supervised and unsupervised machine learning environments. In supervised learning, the sample data will be labeled. Interestingly, we could also use binary classification, among other supervised learning techniques, to model this kind of data. We can choose between anomaly detection and classification to model labeled data by using the following guidelines:

- Choose binary classification when the number of positive and negative examples in the sample data is almost equal. Conversely, choose anomaly detection if there are a very small number of positive or negative examples in the training data.

- Choose anomaly detection when there are many sparse classes and a few dense classes in the training data.

- Choose supervised learning techniques such as classification when positive samples that may be encountered by the trained model will be similar to positive samples that the model has already seen.

Building recommendation systems

Recommendation systems are information filtering systems whose goal is to provide its users with useful recommendations. To determine these recommendations, a recommendation system can use historical data about the user's activity, or it can use recommendations that other users liked (for more information, refer to "A Taxonomy of Recommender Agents on the Internet"). These two approaches are the basis of the two types of algorithms used by recommendation systems—**content-based filtering** and **collaborative filtering**. Interestingly, some recommendation systems even use a combination of these two techniques to provide users with recommendations. Both these techniques aim to recommend items, or domain objects that are managed or exchanged by user-centric applications, to its users. Such applications include several websites that provide users with online content and information, such as online shopping and media.

In *content-based filtering*, recommendations are determined by finding similar items by using a particular user's rating. Each item is represented as a set of discrete features or characteristics, and each item is also rated by several users. Thus, for each user, we have several sets of input variables to represent the characteristics of each item and a set of output variables that represent the user's rating for the item. This information can be used to recommend items with similar features or characteristics as items that were previously rated by a user.

Collaborative filtering methods are based on collecting data about a given user's behavior, activities, or preferences and using this information to recommend items to users. The recommendation is based on how similar a user's behavior is to that of other users. In effect, a user's recommendations are based on her past behavior as well as decisions made by other users in the system. A collaborative filtering technique will use the preferences of similar users to determine the features of all available items in the system, and then it will recommend items with similar features as the items that a given set of users are observed to like.

Content-based filtering

As we mentioned earlier, content-based filtering systems provide users with recommendations based on their past behavior as well as the characteristics of items that are positively rated or liked by the given user. We can also take into account the items that were disliked by the given user. An item is generally represented by several discrete attributes. These attributes are analogous to the input variables or features of a classification or linear regression based machine learning model.

For example, suppose we want to build a recommendation system that uses content-based filtering to recommend online products to its users. Each product can be characterized and identified by several known characteristics, and users can provide a rating for each characteristic of every product. The feature values of the products can have values between the 0 and 10, and the ratings provided by users for the products will have values within the range of 0 and 5. We can visualize the sample data for this recommendation system in a tabular representation, as follows:

Products	Users				Product Features			
	User 1	User 2	$\cdots$	User U	x_1	x_2	$\cdots$	x_N
Product 1	5	3	$\cdots$	?	6	9	$\cdots$	10
Product 2	?	4	$\cdots$	5	10	5	$\cdots$	8
$\vdots$	$\vdots$	$\vdots$	$\ddots$	$\vdots$	$\vdots$	$\vdots$	$\ddots$	$\vdots$
Product n	4	2	$\cdots$	2	4	10	$\cdots$	1

In the preceding table, the system has n products and U users. Each product is defined by N features, each of which will have a value in the range of 0 and 10, and each product is also rated by a user. Let the rating of each product i by a user u be represented as $Y_{u,i}$. Using the input values $x_{i,1}, x_{i,2}, \dots x_{i,N}$, or rather the input vector X_i, and the rating $Y_{u,i}$ of a user u, we can estimate a parameter vector β_u that we can use to to predict a user's rating. Thus, content-based filtering in fact applies a copy of linear regression to each user's rating and each product's feature values to estimate a regression model that can in turn be used to estimate the users rating for some unrated products. In effect, we learn the parameter β_u using the independent variables X_i and the dependent variable $Y_{u,i}$ and for all the users the system. Using the estimated parameter β_u and some given values for the independent variables, we can predict the value of the dependent variable for any given user. The optimization problem for content-based filtering can thus be expressed as follows:

$$\arg\min_{\beta_u} \left[\sum_{i:r(i,u)=1} \left((\beta_u)^T X_i - Y_{u,i} \right)^2 + \frac{\lambda}{2} \sum_{j=1}^{n} \beta_{u,j}^2 \right]$$

where $r(i,u) = 1$ if user u has rated product i

$= 0$ otherwise

and $\beta_{u,j}$ is the jth value in the vector β_u

The optimization problem defined in the preceding equation can be applied to all users of the system to produce the following optimization problem for U users:

$$\arg\min_{\beta_1,\beta_2,\ldots,\beta_u} \left[\sum_{u=1}^{U} \sum_{i:r(i,u)=1} \left(\left(\beta_u\right)^T X_i - Y_{u,i} \right)^2 + \frac{\lambda}{2} \sum_{u=1}^{U} \sum_{j=1}^{n} \beta_{u,j}^2 \right]$$

In simple terms, the parameter vector β tries to scale or transform the input variables to match the output variable of the model. The second term that is added is for *regularization*. Interestingly, the optimization problem defined in the receding equation is analogous to that of linear regression, and thus content-based filtering can be considered as an extension of linear regression.

The key issue with content-based filtering is whether a given recommendation system can learn from a user's preferences or ratings. Direct feedback can be used by asking for the rating of items in the system that they like, although these ratings can also be implied from a user's past behavior. Also, a content-based filtering system that is trained for a set of users and a specific category of items cannot be used to predict the same user's ratings for a different category of items. For example, it's a difficult problem to use a user's preference for news to predict the user's liking for online shopping products.

Collaborative filtering

The other major form of recommendation is *collaborative filtering*, in which data about the behavior of several users with similar interests is analyzed and used to predict recommendations for these users. The main advantage of this technique is that the system does not rely on the values for the feature variables of its items, and consequently such a system does not need to know about the characteristics of the items that are provided by it. The features of the items are in fact determined dynamically using the users rating for these items and the behavior of the system users. We will examine more about the advantage in the latter part of this section.

An essential part of the model used by collaborative filtering depends on the behavior of its users. To build this part of the model, we can use the following methods to determine the user's rating for the items in the model in an explicit manner:

- Asking the users to rate the items on a specific scale

- Asking users to mark items as favorites

- Presenting a small number of items to users and asking them to order them according to how much they like or dislike these items

- Asking users to create a list of items or the kinds of items that they like.

Alternatively, this information could also be gathered from a user's activity in an implicit fashion. Examples of this method of modeling the behavior of a system's users with a given set of items or products are as follows:

- Observing the items that a user views

- Analyzing the number of times a particular user views

- Analyzing the user's social network and discovering users with similar interests

For example, consider a recommendation system for an online shopping example that we discussed in the previous section. We we can use collaborative filtering to dynamically determine the feature values of the products available and predict the products that the user will be interested in. The sample data for such a system that uses collaborative filtering can be visualized by using the following table:

Products	Users				Product Features			
	User 1	User 2	$\cdots$	User U	x_1	x_2	$\cdots$	x_N
Product 1	5	3	$\cdots$	?	?	?	$\cdots$	?
Product 2	?	4	$\cdots$	5	?	?	$\cdots$	?
$\vdots$	$\vdots$	$\vdots$	$\ddots$	$\vdots$	$\vdots$	$\vdots$	$\ddots$	$\vdots$
Product n	4	2	$\cdots$	2	?	?	$\cdots$	?
	User Behavior Models							
	β_1	β_1	$\cdots$	β_U				

In the data shown in the preceding table, the features of the products are unknown. The only available data is the ratings of the users and the behavior models of the users.

The optimization problem for collaborative filtering and a product's user can be expressed as follows:

$$\underset{X_i}{\arg\min}\left[\sum_{i:r(i,u)=1}\left(\left(\beta_u\right)^T X_i - Y_{u,i}\right)^2 + \frac{\lambda}{2}\sum_{j=1}^{N} X_{i,j}^{\,2}\right]$$

where $X_{i,j}$ is the jth value in the vector X_i

The preceding equation is seen to be the converse of the optimization problem that we defined for content-based filtering. Instead of estimating the parameter's vector β_u, collaborative filtering seeks to determine the values of the features of a product X_i. Similarly, we can define the optimization problem for multiple users as follows:

$$\underset{X_1, X_2, \dots X_N}{\arg\min}\left[\sum_{i=1}^{n}\sum_{i:r(i,u)=1}\left(\left(\beta_u\right)^T X_i - Y_{u,i}\right)^2 + \frac{\lambda}{2}\sum_{i=1}^{n}\sum_{j=1}^{N} X_{i,j}^{\,2}\right]$$

Using collaborative filtering, we can estimate the features of the products X_1, $X_2, \dots X_N$, and then use these feature values to improve the behavior model of the users $\beta_1, \beta_2, \dots \beta_U$. The improved user behavior models can then be used to again produce better feature values of the items. This process is then repeated until the feature values and behavior models converge to some appropriate values.

> Note that in this process, the algorithm never needed to know the initial feature values of its items, and it only needed to initially estimate the behavior model of the user to provide the user with useful recommendations.

Collaborative filtering can also be combined with content-based filtering in some special cases. Such approaches are called **hybrid methods** of recommendation. There are several ways in which we can combine or hybridize the two models of recommendation, and they are listed as follows:

- Results from the two models can be combined numerically in a weighted manner
- Either one of these two models can be chosen appropriately at a given time
- Show users a combined result of recommendations from the two models

Using the Slope One algorithm

We will now study the Slope One algorithm for collaborative filtering. Also, we will demonstrate how we can implement it concisely in Clojure.

The Slope One algorithm is one of the simplest forms of *item-based collaborative filtering*, which is essentially a collaborative filtering technique in which the users explicitly rate each item they like (for more information, refer to *Slope One Predictors for Online Rating-Based Collaborative Filtering*). Generally, item-based collaborative filtering techniques will use the user's ratings and past behavior of users to estimate a simple regression model for each user. Thus, we estimate a function $f_u(x) = ax + b$ for all users u in the system.

Slope One algorithm uses a simpler predictor $f_u(x) = x + b$ to model the regression pattern of a user's behavior, and is thus less computationally expensive. The parameter b can be estimated by calculating the differences in user ratings between two items. Since the definition of the Slope One algorithm is simple, it can be implemented easily and efficiently. Interestingly, this algorithm is less susceptible to overfitting than other collaborative filtering techniques.

Consider a simple recommendation system with two items and two users. We can visualize this sample data with the following table:

Items	Users	
	User 1	User 2
Item A	2	3
Item B	4	?

In the data shown in the preceding table, the difference in the ratings of **Item A** and **Item B** can be found by using the ratings provided by **User 1**. This difference is found to be $4 - 2 = 2$. Thus, we can add this difference to the rating of **Item A** by **User 2** to predict his/her rating of **Item B**, which is equal to $3 + 2 = 5$.

Let's extend the preceding example to three items and three users. The table for this data can be visualized as follows:

Items	Users		
	User 1	User 2	User 3
Item A	5	3	?
Item B	3	4	2
Item C	2	?	5

In this example, the average difference in ratings between **Item A** and **Item B** for **User 2** (-1) and **User 1** (+2) is $(-1+2)/2 = 0.5$. Hence, on average, **Item A** is rated better than **Item B** by 0.5. Similarly, the average rating difference between **Item A** and **Item C** is 3. We can predict the rating of **User 3** for **Item A** using his/her rating for **Item B** and the average difference of ratings for **Item A** and **Item B**. This value comes out to $2 + 0.5 = 2.5$.

We will now describe a concise implementation the Slope One algorithm in Clojure. First off, we need to define our sample data. This can be done using a nested map, as shown in the following code:

```
(def ? nil)
(def data
  {"User 1" {"Item A" 5 "Item B" 3 "Item C" 2 "Item D" ?}
   "User 2" {"Item A" 3 "Item B" 4 "Item C" ? "Item D" 4}
   "User 3" {"Item A" ? "Item B" 2 "Item C" 5 "Item D" 3}
   "User 4" {"Item A" 4 "Item B" ? "Item C" 3 "Item D" ?}})
```

In the preceding code shown, we bind the value `nil` to the `?` symbol, and use it to define a nested map `data`, in which each key represents a user and its value represents a map of the user's ratings with the item names as the keys. We will define some of the following utility methods to help us manipulate the nested map represented by `data`:

```
(defn flatten-to-vec [coll]
  (reduce #(apply conj %1 %2)
          []
          coll))
```

The `flatten-to-vec` function defined in the preceding code simply converts a map to a flat vector using the `reduce` and `conj` functions. We can also define `flatten-to-vec`, by using a functional composition of the standard `vec`, `flatten`, and `seq` functions, as `(def flatten-to-vec (comp vec flatten seq))`. Since we are dealing with maps, we can define some of the following functions to map any function to the values of these maps:

```
(defn map-vals [f m]
  (persistent!
    (reduce (fn [m [k v]]
              (assoc! m k (f k v)))
            (transient m) m)))

(defn map-nested-vals [f m]
  (map-vals
    (fn [k1 inner-map]
      (map-vals
        (fn [k2 val] (f [k1 k2] val)) inner-map)) m))
```

The `map-vals` function defined in the preceding code can be used to mutate the values of a given map. This function uses the `assoc!` function to replace the value stored by a given key in the map, and it uses the `reduce` function to compose and apply the `assoc!` function to all the key-value pairs in the map. In Clojure, most collections, including maps, are persistent and immutable. Note the use of the `transient` function to convert a persistent and immutable map into a mutable one and the use of the `persistent!` function that converts a transient mutable collection to a persistent one. By isolating mutation, the performance of this function is improved while retaining the guarantee of immutability for the code that uses this function. The `map-nested-vals` function defined in the preceding code simply applies the `map-vals` function to the second level values in a nested map.

We can examine the behavior of the `map-vals` and `map-nested-vals` functions in the REPL as follows:

```
user> (map-vals #(inc %2) {:foo 1 :bar 2})
{:foo 2, :bar 3}

user> (map-nested-vals (fn [keys v] (inc v)) {:foo {:bar 2}})
{:foo {:bar 3}}
```

As shown the preceding REPL output, the `inc` function is applied to the values of maps `{:foo 1 :bar 2}` and `{:foo {:bar 3}}`. We now define a function to produce a trained model from the sample data by using the Slope One algorithm, as follows:

```
(defn train [data]
  (let [diff-map      (for [[user preferences] data]
                        (for [[i u-i] preferences
                              [j u-j] preferences
                              :when (and (not= i j)
                                         u-i u-j)]
                          [[i j] (- u-i u-j)]]))
        diff-vec      (flatten-to-vec diff-map)
        update-fn     (fn [[freqs-so-far diffs-so-far]
                           [item-pair diff]]
                        [(update-in freqs-so-far
                                    item-pair (fnil inc 0))
                         (update-in diffs-so-far
                                    item-pair (fnil + 0) diff)])
        [freqs
         total-diffs] (reduce update-fn
                              [{} {}] diff-vec)
        differences   (map-nested-vals
                        (fn [item-pair diff]
                          (/ diff (get-in freqs item-pair)))
                        total-diffs)]
    {:freqs freqs
     :differences differences}))
```

The train function defined in the preceding code first finds the differences between the ratings of all the items in the model using the `for` macro, and then it adds the frequencies of ratings of the items and the differences in their ratings using the `update-fn` closure.

The main difference between a function and a macro is that a macro doesn't evaluate its parameters while being executed. Also, macros are resolved and expanded at compile time and functions are called at runtime.

The `update-fn` function uses the `update-in` function to replace the value of a key in a map. Note the use of the `fnil` function, which essentially returns a function that checks for the value `nil` and replaces it with the second argument. This is used to treat the values represented by the `?` symbol that has the value `nil` in the nested map data. Lastly, the `train` function applies the `map-nested-vals` and `get-in` functions to the map of rating differences returned in the previous step. Finally, it returns a map with the keys `:freqs` and `:differences`, which contain maps that represent the frequencies of items and differences in ratings with respect to other items in the model respectively. We can now use this trained model to predict the ratings of the given items by various users. To do this, we will implement a function in the following code that uses the value returned by the `train` function defined in the preceding code:

```
(defn predict [{:keys [differences freqs]
                :as model}
               preferences
               item]
  (let [get-rating-fn (fn [[num-acc denom-acc]
                          [i rating]]
                        (let [freqs-ji (get-in freqs [item i])]
                          [(+ num-acc
                              (* (+ (get-in differences [item i])
                                    rating)
                                 freqs-ji))
                           (+ denom-acc freqs-ji)]))]
    (->> preferences
         (filter #(not= (first %) item))
         (reduce get-rating-fn [0 0])
         (apply /))))
```

The `predict` function defined in the preceding code uses the `get-in` function to retrieve the sum of frequencies and differences of each item in the maps returned by the `train` function. This function then averages these rating differences by using a composition of the `reduce` and `/` (division) functions. The behavior of the `predict` function can be examined in the REPL, as shown in the following code:

```
user> (def trained-model (train data))
#'user/trained-model
user> (predict trained-model {"Item A" 2} "Item B")
3/2
```

As shown in the preceding REPL output, the `predict` function used the value returned by the `train` function to predict the rating of `Item B` by a user who has given `Item A` a rating of 2. The `predict` function estimates the rating of `Item B` as 3/2. We can now implement a function in the following code that wraps around the `predict` function to find the ratings of all items in our model:

```
(defn mapmap
  ([vf s]
     (mapmap identity vf s))
  ([kf vf s]
     (zipmap (map kf s)
             (map vf s))))

(defn known-items [model]
  (-> model :differences keys))

(defn predictions
  ([model preferences]
     (predictions
       model
       preferences
       (filter #(not (contains? preferences %))
               (known-items model))))
  ([model preferences items]
     (mapmap (partial predict model preferences)
             items)))
```

The `mapmap` function defined in the preceding code simply applied two functions to a given sequence and returns a map with keys that are created using the first function `kf` and with a value generated by the second function `vf`. If only a single function is passed to the `mapmap` function, it uses the `identity` function to generate keys in the map returned by it. The `known-items` function defined in the preceding code will determine all items in a model using the keys function on the map represented by the `:differences` key in the value returned by the `train` function. Finally, the `predictions` function uses the value returned by the `train` and `known-items` functions to determine all items in the model and then predict all unrated items for a particular user. The function also takes an optional third argument, which is a vector of the item names whose ratings are to be predicted, in order to return the predictions of all items with names present in the vector `items`.

Now, we can examine the behavior of the preceding function in the REPL, as follows:

```
user> (known-items trained-model)
("Item D" "Item C" "Item B" "Item A")
```

As shown in the preceding output, the `known-items` function returns the names of all items in the model. We can now try out the predictions function, as follows:

```
user> (predictions trained-model {"Item A" 2} ["Item C" "Item D"])
{"Item D" 3, "Item C" 0}
user> (predictions trained-model {"Item A" 2})
{"Item B" 3/2, "Item C" 0, "Item D" 3}
```

Note that when we skip the last optional parameter of the `predictions` function, the map returned by this function will contain all items that are not previously rated by a particular user. This can be asserted in the REPL by using the `keys` function, as follows:

```
user> (keys  (predictions trained-model {"Item A" 2}))
("Item B" "Item C" "Item D")
```

To conclude, we have demonstrated how we can implement the Slope One algorithm using nested maps and standard Clojure functions.

Summary

In this chapter, we discussed anomaly detection and recommendation. We also implemented a simple anomaly detector and recommendation engine. The topics covered in this chapter can be summarized as follows:

- We explored anomaly detection and how we can implement an anomaly detector using the PDF in Clojure.

- We studied recommendation systems that use both content-based and collaborative filtering techniques. We also studied the various optimization problems in these techniques.

- We also studied the Slope One algorithm, which is a form of collaborative filtering, and also described a concise implementation of this algorithm.

In the following chapter, we will discuss more applications of machine learning techniques that can be applied to large and complex data-centric applications.

9

Large-scale Machine Learning

In this chapter, we will explore a few methodologies for handling large volumes of data to train machine learning models. In the latter section of this chapter, we will also demonstrate how to use cloud-based services for machine learning.

Using MapReduce

A data-processing methodology that is often encountered in the context of data parallelism is **MapReduce**. This technique is inspired by the **map** and **reduce** functions from functional programming. Although these functions serve as a basis to understand the algorithm, actual implementations of MapReduce focus more on scaling and distributing the processing of data. There are currently several active implementations of MapReduce, such as Apache Hadoop and Google Bigtable.

A MapReduce engine or program is composed of a function that performs some processing over a given record in a potentially large dataset (for more information, refer to "Map-Reduce for Machine Learning on Multicore"). This function represents the Map() step of the algorithm. This function is applied to all the records in the dataset and the results are then combined. The latter step of extracting the results is termed as the Reduce() step of the algorithm. In order to scale this process over huge datasets, the input data provided to the Map() step is first partitioned and then processed on different computing nodes. These nodes may or may not be on separate machines, but the processing performed by a given node is independent from that of the other nodes in the system.

Some systems follow a different design in which the code or query is sent to nodes that contain the data, instead of the other way around. This step of partitioning the input data and then forwarding the query or data to different nodes is called the `Partition()` step of the algorithm. To summarize, this method of handling a large dataset is quite different from traditional methods of iterating over the entire data as fast as possible.

MapReduce scales better than other methods because the partitions of the input data can be processed independently on physically different machines and then combined later. This gain in scalability is not only because the input is divided among several nodes, but because of an intrinsic reduction in complexity. An NP-hard problem cannot be solved for a large problem space, but can be solved if the problem space is smaller.

For problems with an algorithmic complexity of $O(n)$ or $O(n \log n)$, partitioning the problem space will actually increase the time needed to solve the given problem. However, if the algorithmic complexity is $O(n^k)$, where $k > 1$, partitioning the problem space will reduce the time needed to solve the problem. In case of NP-hard problems, $k \gg 1$. Thus, MapReduce decreases the time needed to solve NP-hard problems by partitioning the problem space (for more information, refer to *Evaluating MapReduce for Multi-core and Multiprocessor Systems*).

The MapReduce algorithm can be illustrated using the following diagram:

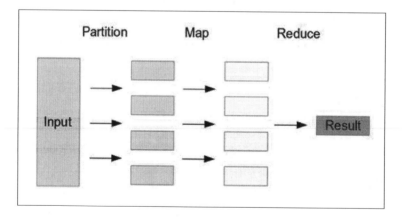

In the previous diagram, the input data is first partitioned, and each partition is independently processed in the `Map()` step. Finally, the results are combined in the `Reduce()` step.

We can concisely define the MapReduce algorithm in Clojure pseudo-code, as shown in the following code:

```
(defn map-reduce [f partition-size coll]
  (->> coll
       (partition-all partition-size)   ; Partition
       (pmap f)                         ; Parallel Map
       (reduce concat)))                ; Reduce
```

The `map-reduce` function defined in the previous code distributes the application of the function `f` among several processors (or threads) using the standard `pmap` (abbreviation for parallel map) function. The input data, represented by the collection `coll`, is first partitioned using the `partition-all` function, and the function `f` is then applied to each partition in parallel using the `pmap` function. The results of this `Map()` step are then combined using a composition of the standard `reduce` and `concat` functions. Note that this is possible in Clojure due to the fact the each partition of data is a sequence, and the `pmap` function will thus return a sequence of partitions that can be joined or concatenated into a single sequence to produce the result of the computation.

Of course, this is only a theoretical explanation of the core of the MapReduce algorithm. Actual implementations tend to focus more on distributing the processing among several machines, rather than among several processors or threads as shown in the `map-reduce` function defined in the previous code.

Querying and storing datasets

When dealing with large datasets, it's useful to be able to query the data based on some arbitrary conditions. Also, it's more reliable to store the data in a database rather than in a flat file or as an in-memory resource. The Incanter library provides us with several useful functions to perform these operations, as we will demonstrate in the code example that will follow.

The Incanter library and the MongoDB driver used in the upcoming example can be added to a Leiningen project by adding the following dependency to the `project.clj` file:

```
[congomongo "0.4.1"]
[incanter "1.5.4"]
```

For the upcoming example, the namespace declaration should look similar to the following declaration:

```
(ns my-namespace
  (:use incanter.core
        [incanter.mongodb   :only [insert-dataset
                                   fetch-dataset]]
        [somnium.congomongo :only [mongo!]]
        [incanter.datasets  :only [get-dataset]]))
```

Also, this example requires MongoDB to be installed and running.

For this example, we will use the Iris dataset, which can be fetched using the `get-dataset` function from the `incanter.datasets` namespace. The code is as follows:

```
(def iris (get-dataset :iris))
```

As shown in the previous code, we simply bind the Iris dataset to a variable `iris`. We can perform various operations on this dataset using the `with-data` function. To view the data, we can use the `view` function along with the `with-data` function to provide a tabular representation of the dataset, as shown in the following code:

```
user> (with-data iris
        (view (conj-cols (range (nrow $data)) $data)))
```

The `$data` variable is a special binding that can be used to represent the entire dataset within the scope of the `with-data` function. In the previous code, we add an extra column to represent the row number of a record to the data using a composition of the `conj-cols`, `nrows`, and `range` functions. The data is then displayed in a spreadsheet-like table using the `view` function. The previous code produces the following table that represents the dataset:

:col-0	:Sepal.Length	:Sepal.Width	:Petal.Length	:Petal.Width	:Species
0	5.1	3.5	1.4	0.2	setosa
1	4.9	3.0	1.4	0.2	setosa
2	4.7	3.2	1.3	0.2	setosa
3	4.6	3.1	1.5	0.2	setosa
4	5.0	3.6	1.4	0.2	setosa
5	5.4	3.9	1.7	0.4	setosa
6	4.6	3.4	1.4	0.3	setosa
7	5.0	3.4	1.5	0.2	setosa
8	4.4	2.9	1.4	0.2	setosa
9	4.9	3.1	1.5	0.1	setosa
10	5.4	3.7	1.5	0.2	setosa
11	4.8	3.4	1.6	0.2	setosa
12	4.8	3.0	1.4	0.1	setosa
13	4.3	3.0	1.1	0.1	setosa
14	5.8	4.0	1.2	0.2	setosa
15	5.7	4.4	1.5	0.4	setosa
16	5.4	3.9	1.3	0.4	setosa
17	5.1	3.5	1.4	0.3	setosa
18	5.7	3.8	1.7	0.3	setosa
19	5.1	3.8	1.5	0.3	setosa
20	5.4	3.4	1.7	0.2	setosa

We can also select columns we are interested in from the original dataset using the $ function within the scope of the `with-data` function, as shown in the following code:

```
user> (with-data iris ($ [:Species :Sepal.Length]))
```

```
|  :Species | :Sepal.Length |
|-----------+---------------|
|    setosa |           5.1 |
|    setosa |           4.9 |
|    setosa |           4.7 |
       ...
| virginica |           6.5 |
| virginica |           6.2 |
| virginica |           5.9 |
```

The $ function selects the :Species and :Sepal.Length columns from the iris dataset in the code example shown previously. We can also filter the data based on a condition using the $where function, as shown in the following code:

```
user> (with-data iris ($ [:Species :Sepal.Length]
                         ($where {:Sepal.Length 7.7})))
```

```
|  :Species |  :Sepal.Length |
|-----------+----------------|
| virginica |            7.7 |
| virginica |            7.7 |
| virginica |            7.7 |
| virginica |            7.7 |
```

The previous example queries the iris dataset for records with the :Sepal.Length column equal to 7.7 using the $where function. We can also specify the lower or upper bound of the value to compare a column to using the :$gt and :$lt symbols in a map passed to $where function, as shown in the following code:

```
user> (with-data iris ($ [:Species :Sepal.Length]
                         ($where {:Sepal.Length {:$gt 7.0}})))
```

```
|  :Species |  :Sepal.Length |
|-----------+----------------|
| virginica |            7.1 |
| virginica |            7.6 |
| virginica |            7.3 |
    ...
| virginica |            7.2 |
| virginica |            7.2 |
| virginica |            7.4 |
```

The previous example checks for records that have a :Sepal.Length attribute with a value greater than 7. To check whether a column's value lies within a given range, we can specify both the :$gt and :$lt keys in the map passed to the $where function, as shown in the following code:

```
user> (with-data iris ($ [:Species :Sepal.Length]
                         ($where {:Sepal.Length
                                  {:$gt 7.0 :$lt 7.5}})))
```

```
|  :Species |:Sepal.Length |
|-----------+--------------|
| virginica |          7.1 |
| virginica |          7.3 |
```

```
| virginica   |        7.2 |
| virginica   |        7.2 |
| virginica   |        7.2 |
| virginica   |        7.4 |
```

The previous example checks for records that have a :Sepal.Length attribute within the range of 7.0 and 7.5. We can also specify a discrete set of values using the $:in key, such as in the expression {:$in #{7.2 7.3 7.5}}. The Incanter library also provides several other functions such as $join and $group-by that can be used to express more complex queries.

The Incanter library provides functions to operate with MongoDB to persist and fetch datasets. MongoDB is a nonrelational document database that allows for storage of JSON documents with dynamic schemas. To connect to a MongoDB instance, we use the mongo! function, as shown in the following code:

```
user> (mongo! :db "sampledb")
true
```

In the previous code, the database name sampledb is specified as a keyword argument with the key :db to the mongo! function. We can also specify the hostname and port of the instance to connect to using the :host and :post keyword arguments, respectively.

We can store datasets in the connected MongoDB instance using the insert-dataset function from the incanter.mongodb namespace. Unfortunately, MongoDB does not support the use of the dot character (.) as column names, and so we must change the names of the columns in the iris dataset in order to successfully store it using the insert-dataset function. Replacing the column names can be done using the col-names function, as shown in the following code:

```
user> (insert-dataset
:iris (col-names iris [:SepalLength
:SepalWidth
:PetalLength
:PetalWidth
:Species]))
```

The previous code stores the iris dataset in the MongoDB instance after replacing the dot characters in the column names.

Note that the dataset will be stored in a collection named iris in the sampledb database. Also, MongoDB will assign a hash-based ID to each record in the dataset that was stored in the database. This column can be referred to using the :_id keyword.

To fetch the dataset back from the database, we use the `fetch-dataset` function, as shown in the following code. The value returned by this function can be directly used by the `with-data` function to query and view the dataset fetched.

```
user> (with-data (fetch-dataset :iris) ($ [:Species :_id]
                                        ($where {:SepalLength
                                                {:$gt 7}}))))
```

```
|  :Species |                      :_id |
|-----------+--------------------------|
| virginica | 52ebcc1144ae6d6725965984 |
| virginica | 52ebcc1144ae6d6725965987 |
| virginica | 52ebcc1144ae6d6725965989 |
  ...
| virginica | 52ebcc1144ae6d67259659a0 |
| virginica | 52ebcc1144ae6d67259659a1 |
| virginica | 52ebcc1144ae6d67259659a5 |
```

We can also inspect the database after storing our dataset, using the `mongo` client, as shown in the following code. As we mentioned our database name is `sampledb`, we must select this database using the `use` command, as shown in the following terminal output:

```
$ mongo
MongoDB shell version: 2.4.6
connecting to: test
Server has startup warnings:
...

> use sampledb
switched to db sampledb
```

We can view all collections in the database using the `show collections` command. The queries can be executed using the `find()` function on the appropriate property in the variable `db` instance, as shown in the following code:

```
> show collections
iris
system.indexes
>
> db.iris.find({ SepalLength: 5})

{ "_id" : ObjectId("52ebcc1144ae6d6725965922"),
  "Species" : "setosa",
  "PetalWidth" : 0.2,
```

```
      "PetalLength" : 1.4,
      "SepalWidth" : 3.6,
      "SepalLength" : 5 }
  { "_id" : ObjectId("52ebcc1144ae6d6725965925"),
      "Species" : "setosa",
      "PetalWidth" : 0.2,
      "PetalLength" : 1.5,
      "SepalWidth" : 3.4,
      "SepalLength" : 5 }

  ...
```

To conclude, the Incanter library provides us with a sufficient set of tools for querying and storing datasets. Also, MongoDB can be easily used to store datasets via the Incanter library.

Machine learning in the cloud

In the modern day of web-based and cloud services, it is also possible to persist both datasets and machine learning models to online cloud storage. This is a great solution when dealing with enormous amounts of data, since cloud solutions take care of both the storage and processing of huge amounts of data.

BigML (`http://bigml.com/`) is a cloud provider for machine learning resources. BigML internally uses **Classification and Regression Trees (CARTs)**, which are a specialization of decision trees (for more information, refer to *Top-down induction of decision trees classifiers-a survey*), as a machine learning model.

BigML provides developers with a simple REST API that can be used to work with the service from any language or platform that can send HTTP requests. The service supports several file formats such as **CSV (comma-separated values)**, Excel spreadsheet, and the Weka library's ARFF format, and also supports a variety of data compression formats such as TAR and GZIP. This service also takes a white-box approach, in the sense that models can be downloaded for local use, apart from the use of the models for predictions through the online web interface.

There are bindings for BigML in several languages, and we will demonstrate a Clojure client library for BigML in this section. Like other cloud services, users and developers of BigML must first register for an account. They can then use this account and a provided API key to access BigML from a client library. A new BigML account provides a few example datasets to experiment with, including the Iris dataset that we've frequently encountered in this book.

The dashboard of a BigML account provides a simple web-based user interface for all the resources available to the account.

BigML resources include sources, datasets, models, predictions, and evaluations. We will discuss each of these resources in the upcoming code example.

The BigML Clojure library can be added to a Leiningen project by adding the following dependency to the `project.clj` file:

```
[bigml/clj-bigml "0.1.0"]
```

For the upcoming example, the namespace declaration should look similar to the following declaration:

```
(ns my-namespace
    (:require [bigml.api [core :as api]
              [source :as source]
              [dataset :as dataset]
              [model :as model]
              [prediction :as prediction]
              [evaluation :as evaluation]]))
```

Firstly, we will have to provide authentication details for the BigML service. This is done using the `make-connection` function from the `bigml.api` namespace. We must provide a username, an API key, and a flag indicating whether we are using development or production datasets to the `make-connection` function, as shown in the following code. Note that this username and API key will be shown on your BigML account page.

```
(def default-connection
  (api/make-connection
   "my-username"                          ; username
   "a3015d5fa2ee19604d8a69335a4ac66664b8b34b"  ; API key
   true))
```

To use the connection `default-connection` defined in the previous code, we must use the `with-connection` function. We can avoid repeating the use of the `with-connection` function with the `default-connection` variable by use of a simple macro, as shown in the following code:

```
(defmacro with-default-connection [& body]
  '(api/with-connection default-connection
     ~@body))
```

In effect, using `with-default-connection` is as good as using the `with-connection` function with the `default-connection` binding, thus helping us avoid repeating code.

BigML has the notion of sources to represent resources that can be converted to training data. BigML supports local files, remote files, and inline code resources as sources, and also supports multiple data types. To create a resource, we can use the `create` function from the `bigml.source` namespace, as shown in the following code:

```
(def default-source
  (with-default-connection
    (source/create [["Make"  "Model"  "Year" "Weight" "MPG"]
                    ["AMC"   "Gremlin" 1970   2648     21]
                    ["AMC"   "Matador" 1973   3672     14]
                    ["AMC"   "Gremlin" 1975   2914     20]
                    ["Honda" "Civic"   1974   2489     24]
                    ["Honda" "Civic"   1976   1795     33]]))))
```

In the previous code, we define a source using some inline data. The data is actually a set of features of various car models, such as their year of manufacture and total weight. The last feature is the mileage or MPG of the car model. By convention, BigML sources treat the last column as the output or objective variable of the machine learning model.

We must now convert the source to a BigML dataset, which is a structured and indexed representation of the raw data from a source. Each feature in the data is assigned a unique integer ID in a dataset. This dataset can then be used to train a machine learning CART model, which is simply termed as a model in BigML jargon. We can create a dataset and a model using the dataset/create and model/create functions, respectively, as shown in the following code. Also, we will have to use the api/get-final function to finalize a resource that has been sent to the BigML cloud service for processing.

```
(def default-dataset
  (with-default-connection
    (api/get-final (dataset/create default-source))))

(def default-model
  (with-default-connection
    (api/get-final (model/create default-dataset))))
```

BigML also provides an interactive visualization of a trained CART model. For our training data, the following visualization is produced:

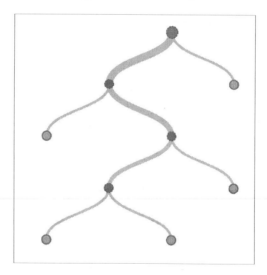

We can now use the trained model to predict the value of the output variable. Each prediction is stored in the BigML cloud service, and is shown in the **Predictions** tab of the dashboard. This is done using the create function from the bigml.prediction namespace, as shown in the following code:

```
(def default-remote-prediction
  (with-default-connection
    (prediction/create default-model [1973 3672])))
```

In the previous code, we attempt to predict the MPG (miles per gallon, a measure of mileage) of a car model by providing values for the year of manufacture and the weight of the car to the `prediction/create` function. The value returned by this function is a map, which contains a key `:prediction` among other things, that represents the predicted value of the output variable. The value of this key is another map that contains column IDs as keys and their predicted values as values in the map, as shown in the following code:

```
user> (:prediction default-remote-prediction)
{:000004 33}
```

The MPG column, which has the ID `000004`, is predicted to have a value of `33` from the trained model, as shown in the previous code. The `prediction/create` function creates an online, or remote, prediction, and sends data to the BigML service whenever it is called. Alternatively, we can download a function from the BigML service that we can use to perform predictions locally using the `prediction/predictor` function, as shown in the following code:

```
(def default-local-predictor
  (with-default-connection
    (prediction/predictor default-model)))
```

We can now use the downloaded function, `default-local-predictor`, to perform local predictions, as shown in the following REPL output:

```
user> (default-local-predictor [1983])
22.4
user> (default-local-predictor [1983] :details true)
{:prediction {:000004 22.4},
:confidence 24.37119,
:count 5, :id 0,
:objective_summary
  {:counts [[14 1] [20 1] [21 1] [24 1] [33 1]]}}
```

As shown in the previous code, the local prediction function predicts the MPG of a car manufactured in `1983` as `22.4`. We can also pass the `:details` keyword argument to the `default-local-predictor` function to provide more information about the prediction.

BigML also allows us to evaluate trained CART models. We will now train a model using the Iris dataset and then cross-validate it. The `evaluation/create` function from the BigML library will create an evaluation using a trained model and some cross-validation data. This function returns a map that contains all cross-validation information about the model.

In the previous code snippets, we used the `api/get-final` function in almost all stages of training a model. In the following code example, we will attempt to avoid repeated use of this function by using a macro. We first define a function to apply the `api/get-final` and `with-default-connection` functions to an arbitrary function that takes any number of arguments.

```
(defn final-with-default-connection [f & xs]
  (with-default-connection
    (api/get-final (apply f xs))))
```

Using the `final-with-default-connection` function defined in the previous code, we can define a macro that will map it to a list of values, as shown in the following code:

```
(defmacro get-final-> [head & body]
  (let [final-body (map list
                        (repeat 'final-with-default-connection)
                        body)]
    '(->> ~head
          ~@final-body)))
```

The `get-final->` macro defined in the previous code basically uses the `->>` threading macro to pass the value in the `head` argument through the functions in the `body` argument. Also, the previous macro interleaves application of the `final-with-default-connection` function to finalize the values returned by functions in the `body` argument. We can now use the `get-final->` macro to create a source, dataset, and model in a single expression, and then evaluate the model using the `evaluation/create` function, as shown in the following code:

```
(def iris-model
  (get-final-> "https://static.bigml.com/csv/iris.csv"
               source/create
               dataset/create
               model/create))

(def iris-evaluation
  (with-default-conection
    (api/get-final
      (evaluation/create iris-model (:dataset iris-model)))))
```

In the previous code snippet, we use a remote file that contains the Iris sample data as a source, and pass it to the `source/create`, `dataset/create`, and `model/create` functions in sequence using the `get-final->` macro we previously defined.

The formulated model is then evaluated using a composition of the `api/get-final` and `evaluation/create` functions, and the result is stored in the variable `iris-evaluation`. Note that we use the training data itself to cross-validate the model, which doesn't really achieve anything useful. In practice, however, we should use unseen data to evaluate a trained machine learning model. Obviously, as we use the training data to cross-validate the model, the accuracy of the model is found to be a 100 percent or 1, as shown in the following code:

```
user> (-> iris-evaluation :result :model :accuracy)
1
```

The BigML dashboard will also provide a visualization (as shown in the following diagram) of the model formulated from the data in the previous example. This illustration depicts the CART decision tree that was formulated from the Iris sample dataset.

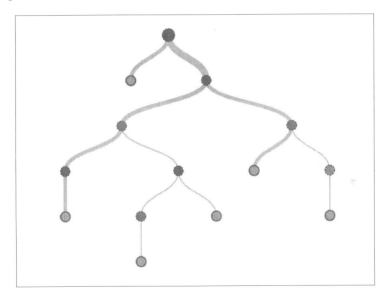

To conclude, the BigML cloud service provides us with several flexible options to estimate CARTs from large datasets in a scalable and platform-independent manner. BigML is just one of the many machine learning services available online, and the reader is encouraged to explore other cloud service providers of machine learning.

Summary

In this chapter, we explored a few useful techniques to deal with huge amounts of sample data. We also described how we can use machine learning models through online services such as BigML, as follows:

- We described MapReduce and how it is used to process large volumes of data using parallel and distributed computations

- We explored how we can query and persist datasets using the Incanter library and MongoDB

- We briefly studied the BigML cloud service provider and how we can use this service to formulate and evaluate CARTs from sample data

In conclusion, we described several techniques and tools that can be used to implement machine learning systems in this book. Clojure helps us build these systems in a simple and scalable manner by leveraging the power of the JVM and equally powerful libraries. We also studied how we can evaluate and improve machine learning systems. Programmers and architects can use these tools and techniques to model and learn from their users' data, as well as build machine learning systems that provide users with a better experience.

You can explore the academia and research in machine learning through the various citations and references that have been used in this book. New academic papers and articles on machine learning provide even more insight into the cutting-edge of machine learning, and you are encouraged to find and explore them.

References

Chapter 1

- Brin, Sergey, and Lawrence Page. *The Anatomy of a Large-Scale Hypertextual Web Search Engine*. 1998.

Chapter 2

- Anderson, Edgar. "The Species Problem in Iris". Annals of the Missouri Botanical Garden 23 (3): 457–509. 1936.

Chapter 3

- N. S., Altman. *An Introduction to Kernel and Nearest-Neighbor Nonparametric Regression*. The American Statistician. 1992.

- J. R., Quinlan. *Induction of Decision Trees, Mach. Learn.* 1, 1 (Mar. 1986). 81–106. 1986.

- J. R., Quinlan. *C4.5: Programs for Machine Learning*. 1993.

- Shannon, Claude E. "A Mathematical Theory of Communication". Bell System Technical Journal 27 (3): 379–423. 1948.

- Mansour, Y. "Pessimistic decision tree pruning based on tree size". Proc. 14th International Conference on Machine Learning. 195–201. 1997.

Chapter 4

- Bhadeshia, H. K. D. H. *Neural Networks in Materials Science.* ISIJ International 39 (10): 966–979. 1999.

- Balabina, Roman M., Ravilya Z. Safievaa, and Ekaterina I. Lomakinab. *Wavelet Neural Network (WNN) approach for calibration model building based on gasoline near infrared (NIR) spectra.* Chemometrics and Intelligent Laboratory Systems, Volume 93, Issue 1. 2008.

- Schuster, M., and K. K. Paliwal. Bidirectional recurrent neural networks. *IEEE Transactions on Signal Processing, 45: 2673–81, November 1997.*

- Igel, Christian, and Michael Hüsken. *Empirical Evaluation of the Improved Rprop Learning Algorithm.* Neurocomputing 50:105–123. 2003.

- Broomhead, D. S., and David Lowe. *Multivariable functional interpolation and adaptive networks.* Complex Systems 2: 321–355. 1988.

Chapter 5

- Fisher, R.A. *Statistical Methods for Research Workers.* Oliver and Boyd (Edinburgh). 1925.

- Graham, Paul. *A Plan for Spam* (http://www.paulgraham.com/spam.html). 2002.

- Graham, Paul. *Better Bayesian Filtering.* (http://www.paulgraham.com/better.html). 2003.

Chapter 6

- Rosasco, L., E. D. De Vito, A. Caponnetto, M. Piana, and A. Verri. "Are Loss Functions All the Same?". Neural Computation 16 (5): 1063–1076. 2004.

- Cortes, C., and V. Vapnik. "Support-vector networks". Machine Learning 20 (3): 273. 1995.

- Platt, John. *Sequential Minimal Optimization: A Fast Algorithm for Training Support Vector Machines.* CiteSeerX: 10.1.1.43.4376. 1998.

Chapter 7

- Hartigan, J. A., and M. A. Wong. "Algorithm AS 136: A K-Means Clustering Algorithm". Journal of the Royal Statistical Society, Series C 28 (1): 100–108. JSTOR 2346830. 1979.

- Sundberg, Rolf. *Maximum likelihood theory and applications for distributions generated when observing a function of an exponential family variable*. Dissertation. Institute for Mathematical Statistics. Stockholm University. 1971.

- Bacao, Fernando, Victor Lobo, and Marco Painho. *Self-organizing Maps as Substitutes for K-Means Clustering*. CS 2005, LNCS 3516, 476–483. 2005.

- Jolliffe, I.T. *Principal Component Analysis, Series: Springer Series in Statistics.* 2nd ed., Springer, NY, 2002. 2002.

Chapter 8

- Hodge, V. J., and J. Austin. "A Survey of Outlier Detection Methodologies". Artificial Intelligence Review 22 (2): 85. 2004.

- Montaner, M, B Lopez, and J. L. de la Rosa. "A Taxonomy of Recommender Agents on the Internet". Artificial Intelligence Review 19 (4): 285–330. 2003.

- Lemire, Daniel, and Anna Maclachlan. *Slope One Predictors for Online Rating-Based Collaborative Filtering*. In SIAM Data Mining (SDM'05). Newport Beach. California. 2005.

Chapter 9

- Chu, Cheng-Tao, Sang Kyun Kim, Yi-An Lin, YuanYuan Yu, Gary Bradski, Andrew Ng, and Kunle Olukotun. "Map-Reduce for Machine Learning on Multicore". NIPS 2006.

- Ranger, C., R. Raghuraman, A. Penmetsa, G. Bradski, and C. Kozyrakis. *Evaluating MapReduce for Multi-core and Multiprocessor Systems*. IEEE 13th International Symposium on High Performance Computer Architecture. 13. 2007.

- Rokachand, L., O. Maimon. *Top-down induction of decision trees classifiers-a survey*. IEEE Transactions on Systems, Man, and Cybernetics. Part C 35 (4): 476–48. 2005.

Index

C

D

data
  clustering, clj-ml library used 206-209
datasets
  querying 251-257
  storing 251-257
dataset-set-class function 155
decision boundary
  about 74
  working 75
decision tree learning 93
decision trees
  using 93-98
default-options variable 127
dendogram 210
density-based approach
  PDF, using 232
  used, for anomaly detection 231
density-detector function 234
density function 234
determinant
  calculating, Sarrus rule used 31
  defining 30
  singular matrix 30
determinant (REPL)
  calculating, det function used 32
det function
  used, for calculating determinant 32
dimensionality reduction
  about 222
  PCA 222
  working 222-226
divisive clustering 209

E

Elman neural network
  about 131
  context layer 132
  structure 132
  training 133
EM clusterer
  creating, make-clusterer function used 218
  parameter MLE, determining 216
  training 218
  using 216

EM clusterer steps
  expectation step 217
  maximization step 217
Enclog Clojure library
  about 101
  URL 128
Encog library
  URL 128
error matrix. *See* confusion matrix
evaluation/create function 262, 263
every? function 22
evidence-category-with-attrs function 84
evidence-of-salmon function 82, 83
evidence-of-sea-bass function 82, 83
Expectation-Maximization algorithm. *See*
    EM clusterer
explanatory variables 67
extend-type function 214
extract-features function 163, 169
extract-tokens-from-headers function 162
extract-tokens function 162
extract-words function 187, 188

F

farthest neighbor clustering 211
feature map
  connection weights 135
feature selection 146, 147
final-with-default-connection function 262
fisher function 164
Fisher method 158
fish-template vector 154
flatten-to-vec function 244
Forgy method 197
forward-propagate-all-activations function
    117, 121
forward-propagate function 126
forward-propagate-layer function 118
frequencies function 204

G

Gaussian distribution. *See* normal
    distribution
Gaussian kernel function 190
generalization 41
get-dataset function 55

spam score 158
SPECT Heart dataset
  URL 192
SPECT images 192
square-mat function 16
square matrix 15
SSE
  about 47
  formally defining 47
statistical methods 231
step, gradient descent algorithm 52, 53
string kernel function 191
sum-of-evidences parameter 84
sum of squared errors of prediction. *See* SSE
sum-of-squares function 212
supervised learning 41
Support Vector Machines. *See* SVMs
SVD
  about 223
  covariance matrix, determining 223
SVMs
  about 173
  alternative forms 182, 183
  used, for performing linear classification
    184-188
symmetry breaking 111
synapse 104

T

take-while-unstable function 201
test-classifier! function 166
Tichonov regularization 35
Tikhnov regularization
  about 64
  describing 64, 65
train-and-cv-classifier function 168
train-and-run-som function 137
train-ann function 115, 127
train-bayes-classifier function 90
train-clusterer function 218
train-DT-classifier function 96
trainer function 129, 136
train-from-corpus! function 166
train function 129, 188

training data 41
train-K1-classifier function 92
train-network function 130, 133
train-som function 137
train-svm function 186, 188
train-UDT-classifier function 97
transpose of matrix
  about 28
  obtaining, ways 29
true? function 22

U

underfit model 140
underfitting 140
unsupervised learning
  about 41, 101
  competitive learning 101
update-feature! function 160
update-features! function 162
update-fn function 246
update-in function 246

V

vec-distance function 203
vector of vectors
  matrix, creating from 10
vectorz-clj
  URL 11

W

Weka library
  URL 87
winning neuron 134
with-connection function 259
with-data function 253, 256

X

xy-plot function 38, 57

Thank you for buying
Clojure for Machine Learning

About Packt Publishing

Packt, pronounced 'packed', published its first book "*Mastering phpMyAdmin for Effective MySQL Management*" in April 2004 and subsequently continued to specialize in publishing highly focused books on specific technologies and solutions.

Our books and publications share the experiences of your fellow IT professionals in adapting and customizing today's systems, applications, and frameworks. Our solution based books give you the knowledge and power to customize the software and technologies you're using to get the job done. Packt books are more specific and less general than the IT books you have seen in the past. Our unique business model allows us to bring you more focused information, giving you more of what you need to know, and less of what you don't.

Packt is a modern, yet unique publishing company, which focuses on producing quality, cutting-edge books for communities of developers, administrators, and newbies alike. For more information, please visit our website: www.packtpub.com.

About Packt Open Source

In 2010, Packt launched two new brands, Packt Open Source and Packt Enterprise, in order to continue its focus on specialization. This book is part of the Packt Open Source brand, home to books published on software built around Open Source licences, and offering information to anybody from advanced developers to budding web designers. The Open Source brand also runs Packt's Open Source Royalty Scheme, by which Packt gives a royalty to each Open Source project about whose software a book is sold.

Writing for Packt

We welcome all inquiries from people who are interested in authoring. Book proposals should be sent to author@packtpub.com. If your book idea is still at an early stage and you would like to discuss it first before writing a formal book proposal, contact us; one of our commissioning editors will get in touch with you.

We're not just looking for published authors; if you have strong technical skills but no writing experience, our experienced editors can help you develop a writing career, or simply get some additional reward for your expertise.

Clojure High Performance Programming

ISBN: 978-1-78216-560-6   Paperback: 152 pages

Understand performance aspects and write high performance code with Clojure

1. See how the hardware and the JVM impact performance.

2. Learn which Java features to use with Clojure, and how.

3. Deep dive into Clojure's concurrency and state primitives.

4. Discover how to design Clojure programs for performance.

Clojure for Domain-specific Languages

ISBN: 978-1-78216-650-4   Paperback: 268 pages

Learn how to use Clojure language with examples and develop domain-specific languages on the go

1. Explore DSL concepts from existing Clojure DSLs and libraries.

2. Bring Clojure into your Java applications as Clojure can be hosted on a Java platform.

3. A tutorial-based guide to develop custom domain-specific languages.

Please check **www.PacktPub.com** for information on our titles

Machine Learning with R

ISBN: 978-1-78216-214-8   Paperback: 396 pages

Learn how to use R to apply powerful machine learning methods and gain an insight into real-world applications

1. Harness the power of R for statistical computing and data science.

2. Use R to apply common machine learning algorithms with real-world applications.

3. Prepare, examine, and visualize data for analysis.

Clojure Data Analysis Cookbook

ISBN: 978-1-78216-264-3   Paperback: 342 pages

Over 110 recipes to help you dive into the world of practical data analysis using Clojure

1. Get a handle on the torrent of data the modern Internet has created.

2. Recipes for every stage from collection to analysis.

3. A practical approach to analyzing data to help you make informed decisions.

Please check **www.PacktPub.com** for information on our titles

Made in the USA
Middletown, DE
25 May 2015